SOCIAL CHANGE AND SOCIAL RESEARCH

(An Indian Perspective)

SOCIAL CHANGE AND SOCIAL RESEARCH

(An Indian Perspective)

R. S. MANN

CONCEPT PUBLISHING COMPANY, NEW DELHI-110015

ISBN 81-7022-200-1

First Published 1988
Second Reprint 1994

Rann Singh Mann (1936-)

Published and Printed by
Ashok Kumar Mittal
Concept Publishing Company
A/15-16, Commercial Block, Mohan Garden
NEW DELHI 110059 (INDIA)

PREFACE

In the interest of their socio-cultural and techno-economic existence and perpetuation, the humans could not afford to be static. Challenges from within and outside, including the immediate social and physical environment, have always enthused human societies to be dynamic. The nature and extent of dynamics in inter-human and human-nonhuman relations have not always, and everywhere, been uniform. But the element of change could not be ruled out at any stage of human existence and history. It could be less or more, slow or fast, gradual or abrupt at one time than the other. The urge to change is partly in-built and partly forced.

In general the human societies and their social structures have, in certain spheres and at a particular point of time, the tendency to maintain status-quo within the frames of parochialism and ethnocentrism. And these inhibit radical shift unless it is forced upon for various reasons. However, the small, sporadic and gradual changes go unnoticed. Such occurrences present instance of adjustment rather than shift, keeping the society unperturbed in the face of change elements. And most of these elements serve one purpose or the other. In due course they get established in the social network. Thus, the permanent continuity, in definite form, of network of social relations is, by and large, never the rule.

At the same time the humans have never existed without some kind of social order. It's nature, form and dimensions have, however, varied depending upon the stages of human history and cultural evolution. Many factors, endogenous as well as exogenous, contributed to particular social- cultural formations which varied in time and space. Whatever would have been the heterogeneity and plurality in social structures, all could, and at all stages, be characterized by two uniform perspectives. One of these is represented by the thought-of-order or the patterns for living and the other by the lived-in-order or the patterns of living. These two perspectives of a social order though are separate, conceptually speaking, they have very intimate relationship. The surface reflexes or overt behaviour and relationship are generally the outcome of underlying principles of implicit ideals. The empirical reality is an expression of state of mind or mentalism, and it is in the latter that the principles of social matrix are inherent. But what people ideologically or philosophically conceive, regarding their ways of life and cultural heritage, may not all the time and in every sense be reflected in day-to-day life. All social organisations, that way, would be marked by certain gaps and disparities. This may sometimes be because of the in-built contradictions.

Under the situation, explained in the preceding paragraph, the relevance of social change anal,sis assumes importance at three levels, namely; (1) at the ideological level, (2) at the level of social reality, and (3) in the context of dialectic between reality and abstruse. The explanation of dynamics in the social system, therefore, does not assume more convincing and effective form unless it maps these parameters independently and in interconnectedness. Even if we explain change in a specialised aspect, its wider implications and ramifications need be explored to import social scientism in it.

Another aspect of social change is its 'haphazard' nature on the one hand and 'intended' or 'purposed' nature on the other. The former is usually caused by the unplanned alien sources and forces. The latter is intentionally generated from within, as also from outside to meet particular ends and challenges posed to the community. The directed or planned change has assumed an alarming form over the last few decades in the global society. More pertinent it is in case of developing societies of the Third World. It is in their case that the massive programmes of planned change in societies have been framed and implemented. The underlying idea is to develop these underdeveloped societies within certain specific aims and objectives.

However, the creation of induced change is the underlying common aim. And it is designed to make effective at the 'process' as well as 'state' levels. Since fifties, a massive programme of rural development has been initiated to bring about desired change among Indian rural communities, including the tribes. Various programmes, projects and schemes, within the overall purview of Five Year Plans, were started to provide impetus to development and change in village India.This accelerated the process of change and consequently social dynamics. In certain communities, and in certain areas and spheres the planned change has been more effective than others. But in other spheres and areas the change efforts failed to achieve the intended purpose. The response remained partial in yet other aspects. Plurality and heterogeneity of village India, with its diverse social-cultural systems and sub-systems, have had their own say in the matter. In addition the eco-system variations also asserted in some of the concerned spheres.

The Indian rural communities have been characterized with complex social systems and sub-systems. The linguistic, ethnic, racial, religious, social and cultural diversities have always enthused and perpetuated their respective kind. The diversity of cultural elements is still kept up and retained. This does not, however, rule out the existence of unity and certain common ways and principles holding communities together. With such a complex social framework of rural India, the various elements of purposed change, over the years, have reacted in certain definite ways and could develop definite equation with the ongoing ingredients of Indian rural social structure. These can be explained through compatibility, incompatibility, acceptance, rejection, opposition, indifference, success, failure etc. The social scientists, their social science knowledge and social research, also claimed for their usefulness in the creation and gearing up of change. But what has been their real contribution, in the context of helping induction of planned change in village India, has not been, at macro-level, explained. Is it only at conceptual level that they asserted or they really practically helped bringing about change by identifying areas of strength and weakness inherent in Indian rural social systems. How far their social researches have gone in attaining what was expected of them, in the larger interest of social change, is yet another question. What needs to be done on behalf of the social scientists in terms of social research and guidance to channelise and enthuse change in village India is yet another arena open to debate. To elaborate these arguments, the ·text of this book,barring the first two chapters, runs along the following set of question:

1. What is the kind of relationship a social or cultural element has with society/community in general, and the tribal and the non-tribal communities of rural India in particular.
2. How this element is, or can be conceived vis-a-vis proposed social change dimension.
3. What has, in reality, happened and where has the stress been laid.
4. What remained ill-attended or ignored, and which should otherwise have been attended.
5. What has been the position of social research on this count and what kind of material were generated.
6. What could not be devoted to in the arena of social research concerning the particular aspect.
7. What social researches are further needed which can help generate intended change in rural India.

It is through these arguments that the author has tried to explore new fields for research and thereby generate new ideas to promote change and development among Indian village communities. The objective, as made clear in the first chapter, is not to highlight and narrate the changes which have taken place in rural India. Rather, the focus is on analysis of directed social change vis-a-vis Indian rural social structure, and on the position of social scientists and their researches in the context of change.

Before the presentation of author's insight and views in the above framework, it was thought necessary to provide an overview of social change as conceived at theoretical plane. As such the concept, theories, mechanism, types and conditions of change were elaborately analysed in chapter two. The explanations help grasp cognitive mapping of social change. The last chapter throws light on the implications and future projections of change in the context of Indian rural situation.

Shillong

R. S. Mann

CONTENTS

ONE

INTRODUCTION

During the past few decades there has been a rapid and consistent growth of conditions far more congenial for paving way to change. As an added dimension appeared the creation of intended efforts for social and economic transformation of societies. This holds comparatively more true for developing nations of the world. The part involvement of developed nations in the ventures of development of the underdeveloped ones also encouraged change. Thus, in addition to built-in desire for change in societies, and the resources thereof, the borrowed resource, man and material, have played, and are still playing an important role in bringing about change. In the global context the implications of social change are well delineated and prominently marked. And such conditions led to a greater involvement of social scientists in studying and understanding social change. The trend took a faster lead in both, the academic as well as the practical aspects of social change, attaching thereby a mounting importance to the study of social change. The currently prevailing conditions around pose for a more fertile and richer field to social researchers and analysts focusing on social change. They are even confronted with challenge while asked for, as technical experts, to gear up and create change. This specially is a demand of the programmes of directed, induced or planned change. What emerges, as part of social change, out of non-directed efforts too is well within the scope of social researchers. And the occurrence of directed and the non-directed change goes simultaneously, more so in the Third World Countries where conditions for such a rise have been more favourable. Situations of this kind, put together, uphold that the study and analysis of social change are, now, of greater importance than ever before.

Another dimension, adding to the vastness of study of social change purview, is the fact that social change processes have now a wider coverage than what they have been having in the past. This is because of the added processes, as also the added scope and target. Since hardly any area of societal ways has, by now, remained untouched by the social change processes, the role of social scientists, studying social change, has correspondingly increased. While analysing, explaining and understanding social change, the necessary tools and technology need to be further sharpened keeping stock of 'holistic' perspective of a society. Study of social change on these lines have, no doubt, been taken up but scantily. And the growing situations demand for more active involvement of social scientists to understand and channelise change and its implications. Certainly more concern is now shown to change but it seems to lack a concerted attack in terms of individual, social and material factors that precede change, and which can help transform people's ways if diagnosed, assessed and made use of in proper perspective. It is now all the more important for social scientists, as part of general macro commitment to socio-economic transformation of societies, to get deep, in terms of their research and insight, into such ventures. In the background of various elements/features, marking individuals, communities, eco-system, technology and the social structure in rural India, the status and implications of social change, more so the planned one, have been analysed. Simultaneously discussed is the position of social research in respect of various elements and their relation to ongoing and changing perspectives.

Within the trends of social change, discussed above, vis-a-vis the involvement and responsibility of social scientists, their line of action, concerning academic and practical fronts, has gradually undergone a shift. This is for better and in tune with the growing requirements of social and economic formations. By and large the social scientists no longer bother for discussions and speculations regarding stages in the evolution of society. Unlike the nineteenth century social thinkers the social scientists now excessively devote to the study of social change concerning definite and concrete situations. The trend is for more of empiricism, which is probably taken more rewarding, than being bogged down in the ocean of abstractions and abstruse. Mental exercises have their own worth, but their relation to concrete, and hence ultimately to the interests of masses, are of paramount importance, more so under the conditions of fast change.

Empirical reality, attempted from micro to macro or vice versa perspectives can help conceive better of what is going on. In the world of academic and intellectual pursuits, the thinking, ideology and philosophy have their own place and are not to be underrated. But then the adequate correlation, between ideal and actual, matters more importantly in certain special fields of study, including one of social change. High ideals of social science interpretations in vacuum, without citing concrete situations, are no longer appreciated in the context of creation of change. It is indeed true that macro sociology stressed on the issue of changing or developing a society from the time of Saint Simon, Auguste Comte, Herbert Spencer, Karl Marx and Emile Durkheim. But then its pace and scope have, all along, been of a lesser degree. It is only during the last few decades that the need for more massive and concerted efforts, within the dimensions of sociological research on social change has fast arisen. And it is also true that not much has been achieved on this count. Much more remains to be done.

Not that the change in human society and its quality of life is, at the moment, at its apex. The changes keep on occurring normally with the assumption that every time they are more and comprehensive than the past. Otherwise there is reported change in all human societies all the time. It is universally agreed upon by the students of society that unstability characterizes the conditions of human life. And when the conditions are unstable they provide opening for change. Degree of change, thus, would depend upon the magnitude of shake the conditions of human life receive under particular circumstances. And, therefore, while presenting change account, one has to have a closer examination of such circumstances. In other words the horizon of social change, and its study thereof, has expanded specially in the light of complexity of atmosphere for social change. When unstability marks human life, thereby paving way to change, there are reflections, of newer kind, on human behaviour. People opt for new ways of behaviour. In this context Spicer (1952:18) has rightly stated that "people everywhere constantly change their ways, and that no generation seems to behave precisely like a former generation." Such an aspect of behavioural change is more, among others, important for those who study social change. While getting at it, one is to specially bother to search for the state of disequilibrium marking societies. This is to be done keeping in view Green's observation, according to whom "social change occurs because all societies are in a constant state of disequilibrium" (1960:595). It is the latter which makes people anxious to change thereby suggesting for abandoning of the old and taking up of the new. In this regard Dube (1956:29) points out "how the rural Hindu expresses verbal idealization of traditional pattern of village life, but that in spite of this ideal of traditional guides, there is in fact a strong expectancy of change." It may further be mentioned that the causation of state of disequilibrium in society can be attributed to endogenous as well as the exogenous factors. Change is, thus, the result of some movement from within and some movement from without. Some social thinkers have, however, gone to the extent of feeling that seeds of modernity are hidden in the traditional social systems. To Max Weber, for instance, traditional societies had within them the seeds of modernity. Likewise, for Nisbet "most of the structural-functionalists as well as the social system theorists speak of the sources of change within the social structure" (1972:13).

In the study and review of social change, another important aspect is about the social change format. There have always been dialogues on the dimensions of such a format. Since the change is not necessarily governed by any single factor, and since the ways of life or life-designs themselves are so varied, change is revealed as partial, even, uneven, large etc. But usually the radical shift in total system from one form to altogether a different one is unheard of. In this regard Cohen (1973:176) rightly observed that ""no social" system ever changes in toto. Even the most radical changes-revolutions - are never changes in all features of a social structure. Change is always uneven and partial." However, it does not suggest that the change analysts ignore the holistic perspective even if they are studying a specific area of change. If not in toto,atleast some repercussions of such a change are likely to be reflected in the other relevant spheres. Some of such repercussions are visible apparently, while others need to be explored with more intensive efforts. Since such instances of change assume varied forms, it sounds, most of the time, difficult to generalize problem of social change. And MacIver (1959) has rightly shown that different aspects of society change in different forms, and this is why it is so difficult to generalize about the problem of social change unless we specify the actual aspect under study. Any instance of social change is the resultant of a specific and probably unique conjuncture of a considerable diversity of conditions. This explains the complexity of social change. Hence the interpretation of social change is a task beset by great difficulties. For instance, if we explain a crime or religious movement, we will have to see many reasons, material, social, biological etc. Thus, the various factors combine to produce social change. Even in the primitive societies, practising hunting and fishing, the economy is related to many factors of social life and invested with cultural significance. They are surrounded with tradition, legend, tribal lore. And for variation in rate of change, Ogburn's observation is quite valied. For Ogburn (1962:1270) "Various parts of modern culture are not changing at the same rate, some parts are changing much more rapidly than other, and that since there is a correlation and interdependence of parts, a rapid change in one part of our culture requires readjustment through other changes in the various correlated parts of culture. When one part of culture changes first, through some discovery or invention, and occasions changes in some part of culture dependent upon it, there frequently is a delay in the changes occasioned in the dependent part of culture. When the material conditions change, changes are occasioned in the adaptive culture. But these changes in the adaptive culture do not synchronize exactly with the change in the material culture. There is a lag which may last for varying lengths of time, sometimes indeed, for many years."

Comments on change and social change are wide and numerous. These specially pertain to the ways change is viewed about. When does a change occur or when do we call particular incident as change are some of the issues discussed in various perspectives. Same holds true for the dimensions of social change. In general, to sociologists, the term social change refers to alterations in the non-material culture, that is, social behaviour, institutions, value system etc. Such changes are believed to often follow other innovations including the technological ones. Economic,social, political factors etc., generate alterations and hence change. And active processes at work may include acculturation, diffusion, assimilation, transculturation etc. In the field of perception of social change the views expressed by

Zaltman, Kurt Lewin, Schein, Cohen and Srinivas are, among others, worth mention. According to Zaltman (1973:23), Lewin (1951) spoke of change "as involving three steps: unfreezing, moving, and freezing of group standards." Zaltman further stresses that Schein (1969) has elaborated on these stages, 'using the terms unfreezing, changing, and refreezing. Unfreezing refers, essentially, to the processes involved in overcoming resistances to change, that is, in counteracting those personal and social factors that help to stabilize existing behaviours and beliefs. Changing refers more specially to the processes whereby new behaviour is induced, that is, whereby the individual is led to adopt new patterns of action, belief and attitude. Refreezing refers to the ways in which these new patterns become integrated into cognitive and social structures and thus, to a degree, stabilized'. The relative importance of social change, that is change in relation to persistence has been discussed by Cohen. Unless the social persistence is disrupted the change hardly emerges. And with this goes the argument that study of change is incomplete without the study of nature and degree of disruption of social persistence. For Cohen (1968:44) "Social change is only conceivable in relation to persistence. What one studies is change in social structures and systems; which is another way of saying that the study of social change is the study of the disruption of social persistence, and the study of social persistence is the study of processes which inhibit or fail to produce change." Srinivas has rather been more precise and pin-pointing. Avoiding unfreezing, refreezing, disruption of social persistence etc; he straightway comes to dynamics as the crux of social change phenomenon. Srinivas (1977:24) argues that "in all cases the actual process of social change is one of dynamics, the several factors acting and reacting upon each other, so that, in the final result, it would be difficult to assign shares or to distinguish independent from the dependent variables." The complexity of social change, therefore, cannot be denied. And it has been discussed, in this text, in terms of various elements/ features of individual, community and social structure vis-a-vis planned change. Trends of social research and new areas of exploration have also been delineated.

TWO

SOCIAL CHANGE

Concept

The vastness of social change is indisputable, and the same is well supported by the theorists and thinkers as well as by the proponents of practical sociology/social anthropology. Even at the level of its conceptual framework, the arena of social change involves divergence of views. Social scientists have conceived the definitional perspective of social change through a number of dimensions. The same holds true for the conceptual interpretation of social change-versus-culture change purview. The multiplicity of views and expressions are well housed in the literature available on the subject.

A review of the existing versions points to the fact that the issue is ladden with concensus as well as controversies. Some theorists repeat, though in a different language, the same ideas as to what is meant by social change. Others speak on a different plane. Looking to the important place and urgency of social change study in social science research, there does not seem to be a compromise on the issue of what constitutes social change. The social scientists, in general, seem to have used the term as per their convenience. And it has quietly been accepted. In the oceanic situation of ideas the deviations could also afford to get a coverage, without any finger being raised from any corner. The situation seems to persist as it is, more because of lack of channelisation of ideas.

Within the necessity of social change studies have also been included the mapping of man's interaction not only with man but also with nature as well as supernature. Thus, the eco-system and super-organic world vis-a-vis society form an integral parameter while studying social change. In other words the changes in them, or the attitude thereof and the shift in man's interaction with them too form part of social change. Such complexities of social change net-work prove more revealing, if systematically explored, providing thereby better insight and coverage of this special field of social enquiry. In this perspective, Edari has laid a special stress while conceiving social change. Edari (1976:2) explains that "when we talk of social change, we meant, at the very minimum, two things: (i) the change in the constitution of social entities over time, and (ii) the change in the relations among entities over time. But for adequate accounting for social change also requires the examination of the relationships between man and nature, as well as man and supernature." Likewise, for Maclver (1959) too 'social change is a process responsive to many types of change, to changes in the man-made conditions of living, to changes in the attitudes and beliefs of man, and to changes that go back beyond human control, to the biological and physical nature of things'. But then to many others social change remained essentially confined to social system alone. Rogers and many others bifurcated this social system, from the point of social change, into its 'structure' and 'functioning' parts. And while defining the social change purview both of these parts have adequately been taken care of. According to Rogers (1962:3) "social change is the process by which alteration occurs in the structure and function of a social system." It is further made clear by Rogers (1969) that the structure of a social system is provided by the various individual and group statuses of which it is composed. The functioning element within this structure of status is a role, or the actual behaviour of the individual in a given status. Change is seen as a process, not as a state. Because of its process nature, social change is without beginning or end, continuous and flowing through time. At the heart of all social change is an innovation, defined as an idea, practice or object perceived as new by an individual'.

The above frame of reference of social change, though extensively quoted, is not free of objections, if analysed minutely. For instance, when an innovation is at the heart of social change, why should it remain only as a process, and not treated as a state too. In fact social change is to be treated as an inclusive category covering process and state. To treat social change only as process, and not as state, does not at all go in the traditions of social change studies which have been so illuminating in terms of process as well as state. Simultaneously get highlighted abstraction and reality. Social change minus objectivity does not sound convincing, nor the titles available keep confined only to its subjective framework.

If we map our reading over the vast mosaic of social change conceptions, we find that the balance is heavier in favour of those who dealt social change as process. In addition to Rogers, Boskoff (1957:263-65) states that "social change refers to the intelligible process in which we can discover significant alteration in the structure and functioning of determinate social systems. The implications of this definition can be explored by focusing attention on the key terms: social system, structure, function and significant alteration. (Each social system, from the simplest to the most complex, exhibits certain regularities in relations of its members with one another. Taken together, these uniformities constitute the structure of a social relation, a social role, social group, or society. The function of a social system refers to the contributions of that system to (I) the basic and acquired needs of its members and (2) larger social systems in which it may be realistically included as a subsystem)." Taking stock of social development, social evolution, social progress and social dynamics, Boskoff further widens the scope of social change, treating these terms "that involve special interpretation or evaluation or extended processes of social change. All have reference to the direction of successive changes and all seem to imply some judgement about the desirability or inevitability of an imputed direction in change. Social movement comprehends (as used by Hobhouse and others) some over-all movement toward greater efficiency and complexity-but with the recognition of concomitant problems. Social evolution, on the other hand, classifies long-term social changes into a series of graded stages or phases, each of which is assumed to possess greater complexity, greater social opportunities, and greater ethical qualities than its predecessor. In social progress, in place of more or less constructed stages, there appears the notion of a continuous development toward some supposedly realizable objective such as happiness, brotherhood, or rationality - an inevitable accumulation of wished - for social changes. Social dynamics or kinetics, like social change, is a culturally neutral concept. Of course Comte identified social dynamics with social progress, but in the last few decades social dynamics has come to signify an enduring quality of social phenomena: namely, the inherent possibility of alteration in social affairs. Social change rests on the potentialities supplied by social dynamics as these are acted upon discernible causes or agencies of change. In reality we infer social dynamics from comparative studies of specific social changes. In general, studies of social movements and social planning have emphasised four aspects of social change. First, they inevitably focus on conditions of strain and maladjustment. Second, there is often an attempt to determine the social characteristics of leaders and active participants. Third, the crucial question of power and force is explicitly confronted as a reality (good or bad) in matters of social change. Fourth, the widespread concern for understanding the success or failure of specific movements has produced many hypotheses basic to the comprehension of change" (1957:266,280).

Among other strong adherents to 'process' concept of social change are Kuppuswamy and Spencer. To Kuppuswamy (1972:9) "social change may be defined as the process in which is discernible significant alteration in the structure and functioning of a particular social system. The term 'change' itself is wholly neutral. It only implies that there is some difference through time in the object to which it is applied. When we speak of social change we simply assert that there is some change in social behaviour and in the social structure." However, the latter part of Kuppuswamy's definition brings one close to the interpretation of social change as a 'state', though the former treats it as process more forcefully. In his 'Principles of Sociology', Spencer interpreted social change as processes of growing complexity in structure. He postulated a grand and irreversible evolutionary process in which "incoherent homogeneity" is replaced by " coherent heterogeneity" and political integration. Auguste Comte, Max Weber and George Simmel construed social change as accompanied by processes of increasing rationality and rationalization. For Alfred Weber change involves three complementary dimensions; the social, the cultural and the civilizational. And out of these the 'social process' refers to the more formal development of organizational systems (the state, the nation etc.). Like Kuppuswamy, Loubser also combines 'process' and 'state' as part of social change while stating that "social change is a change of social structure, a self evident definition considering that structure denotes constant elements of social system and change implies that these constant elements are no longer constant. The definition of social change can be easily drawn from the definition of social structure: social change is a process through which the distribution of actors and possessions change as the institutionalised norms change. Because this definition has two pillars, that is, 'distribution of actors' and 'distribution of possessions', I can divide it into two parts. 'Possession' in this context means a wide range of things. It includes four kinds of items, that is, material facilities (e.g. means of production), non-material facilities (e.g.power), material rewards (e.g.income), and non-material rewards (e.g.prestige)" (1976:687,692). But Sorokin again highlighted on 'process' treating social change as the set of processes by which one type of super system is replaced by another. Among those who focused more on 'state', than 'process', aspect of social change concept, a mention may be made of Moore, Vasudeva, Freedman, Lundberg, Ginsberg, Nisbet, Oommen etc. They, it appears, have bothered more for concrete or apparent outcome than abstruse which is realised through conceiving social change as a process. The concrete or empirical constitute the major ingredient of social change, though the conceptual understanding of social change is not ruled out. For the social analysts, referred above, more weightage is given to implications. According to Moore (1968:366), "social change is the significant alternation of social structures, that is, of patterns of social action and interaction, including consequences and manifestations of such structures embodied in norms (rules of conduct); values, cultural products and symbols." Likewise, for Vasudeva (1976:1-3) " social change is an on going feature of cultural reality. Change is a primary social fact." The vastness of Vasudeva has been narrowed down by Freedman when he chiefly limited himself to behaviour change as social change. Thus, for Freedman social change is any non-repetitive alteration in the established modes of behaviour in a given group or society. However, Lundberg joins Freedman by widening the scope making use of the terminology of social phenomena than mere behaviour. And accordingly, for Lundberg (1954:670) " social change represents any observable difference in any social phenomena, over a period of time." Supporting Lundberg, Ginsberg felt that the field of social change is very wide. And he further advocated that by social change he understood a change in social structure, e.g. the size of a society, the composition or balance of its parts or the types of its organisation. For him, the term social change must also include changes in attitudes or beliefs, in so far as they sustain institutions and change with them. Similarly to Nisbet change is a succession of differences in time in a persisting identity. Observation of difference, or differences is the beginning of all awareness of change. Change, for Nisbet, is inseparable from the dimension of time. The perspective of fact/manifestation is again given importance, in the study of social change, by Oommen. Change is to be recorded as factual alteration whether it pertains to one element or number of them. Oommen comments, "Assuming that social phenomena - no matter how they are defined constitute a system, the concept of social change may mean either a change of the total system, or a change in one or more of the sub-system. In a purely empirical sense, however, change would mean change in one or more of the facts represented by social phenomena" (1977:102).

Among others who have given a detailed account of social change elements, a special mention may be made of Mukherjee. While delineating the categories of these elements, his special focus, again, remains on empirical manifestation than on abstract or process. His frame of reference is a clear indication of the fact that the study and analysis of social change,on the surface perspective, is more important than what is beneath the surface. The practical implications in the lived-in-order seem to take a strong edge over the thought-of-order. In other words the illumination of social change as a state is brighter than its being a process. And in this context, Mukherjee's criticism of Lundberg (1954) and Rogers (1969) holds quite valid. He rightly explained that process does not necessarily denote change in operation. And their conception of social change does not, thus, fit in the descriptive and explanatory research. For Mukherjee (1979:30), "prima facie, the frame of reference of social change may be given by the following sequential premises: (1) An alteration observed in society refers to a societal arrangement which may be economic, technological, demographic, political, cultural, psychological, and so on in character; (2) An alternation in a societal arrangement will alter a corresponding behaviour pattern of the people, and this will be expressed by the emergence of a new social category or revision of the previously operating social category, with or without the disappearance of the corresponding category existing previously;

(3) An altered behaviour pattern will have repercussion on other behaviour patterns, so that the set of altered behaviour patterns (which may be economic, political, cultural, ideological and so on in character), will produce a set of revised and/or newly emerged social categories, with or without the disappearance of the corresponding categories existing previously; (4) The set of social categories produced as above will represent symbiotically one or more newly emerged or revised social groups which will record alterations in the social structure and thus register social change unless such alterations, along with the coexistence of the previously operating social group, are transitory or sui generis to the system or variation under reference; (5) The newly emerged or revised social groups may not only record sustained and effective alterations within the social structure but also lead to the alteration of the social structure by unequivocal replacement of the corresponding social groups operating previously. The process of sequential alterations will thus bring a course of social change to its culmination by engineering social transformation." Mukherjee continues saying that "the definitions of social change by Lundberg at al (1954) and by Rogers (1969) are complementary and valid. But they are inadequate because any difference in process does not necessarily denote change in operation and so, in the words of Boskoff (1964) in the general context of view on social change, they are too general, and therefore too simplified in their attention to the complex variables of social behaviour. In respect of descriptive and explanatory research, on the one hand, the two definitions are ambiguous" (1977:43).

An innovation and social change are dealt separately at theoretical level. But they are otherwise thickly interwoven. And Rogers (1969) rightly said that at the heart of all social change is an innovation. But since innovation can be an idea, practice or object taken as new by an individual, it does propose to treat change as process and as state, especially when innovation is widely accepted. In this regard La Piere's observation is valid. For La Piere (1965:107), "An innovation is an idea for accomplishing some recognised social end in a new way or for a means of accomplishing some new social end. The idea or pattern of ideas may become manifest as a new kind of tool or mechanical device, as a new process or technical procedure, as a new material or substance, as a place or terrain previously unknown to man, as a new mode of human action, or as a new concept or belief." But then within the requirement of social change, an innovation is to be adopted to the extent that it affects social as well as the personality structure. Under these circumstances it is rightly said that the innovation by itself does not lead to social change. And it is proposed that to make an innovation socially effective it must be followed up by propaganda and demonstration.

Shifting the focus from 'social' to 'cultural', some social thinkers have conceived their ideas, concerning social change, in a rather wider perspective. At times it appears, from the arguments around, that cultural and social change are intermingling and over-lapping. But then certain other statements point to their difference and polarity. Some still others treat one category as large housing the other. However, while making an overview of the whole situation, it strikes that the two, that is the social and cultural change, are highly interconnected, though thinly differentiated, atleast at practical level. Although, when such occasions arose, the controversy, if at all it is to be taken seriously, has been one of focus of terminology, the ingredients, specially the factual ones, remaining almost common. At theoretical plane ideas and value system, however, do speak of culture as abstract but the social system/structure they propose for come to their manifestation. Though the debate on social change versus culture change has all along, since the inception of these concepts, been there, more so at the level of thought than reality, it needs to be resolved to give a clear direction to the social science students and researchers. Unless the clarity is provided for, it sounds more confusing when titles under social change do provide explanation and narration on culture change and vice versa.

In the words of MacIver and Page (1953:511) "Culture and civilization embody themselves in products which persist and exercise an influence by their continued presence, while the society in which they arose, lives on only as a changing equilibrium of present relationships. Social change is therefore a distinct thing from cultural or civilizational change, entering in a different way into the time process ... our direct concern as sociologists is with social relationships. It is the change in these which alone we shall regard as social change ... A social structure is a nexus of present relationships." Likewise the treatment of social change and culture change, as distinct, is supported by Woods. For Woods, culture as patterns of behaviour is different from culture as patterns for behaviour. "In the former case culture refers to the 'way of life' and in the latter to the 'design' for that way of life. In this way culture change consists of modifications in the rules and the behavioural correlaltes they prescribe" (1975:XII). Kingsley Davis supports that culture change is a category of change broader than social change, including changes in technology, philosophy, belief systems, systems of expressive symbols or art, and systems of values. Further, the difference of focus between culture change and social change is well highlighted by Moore. According to Moore "Social change is the significant alteration of social structures (that is, of patterns of social action and interaction), including consequences and manifestations of such structures embodied in norms (rules of conduct), values and cultural products and symbols ... The broad definition also comprises both what is commonly identified as social change, with a primarily behavioural focus, and cultural change, with a primarily symbolic or meaningful focus" (1967:3-4). Sociological interest lies mainly within social change is again highlighted by KIngsley Davis. For Davis social change refers only to alterations which occur in social organisation - that is, the structure and functions of society. And thus social change is a part of broader category called 'cultural change'. However, he further emphasises that no part of culture is totally unrelated to the social order, but it remains true that the changes may occur in these branches without noticeably affecting the social system. Sociologically, therefore, we are interested in cultural change only to the extent that it arises from or has an effect on social organization. And Davis is clear in his statement that we are not interested in it for itself apart from social change.

That no part of culture is totally unrelated to the social order, and that there is the relationship between the two are also supported by Barnett and Maclver and Page. Barnett enters into this debate through his concept of innovation. He brings in the dimension of mental organization and the overt and tangible expression. According to Barnett (1953:7) "Innovation is the basis of all culture change. And he defines an innovation as ... any thought, behavior, or thing that is new, qualitatively different from existing forms ... every innovation is an idea or a constellation of ideas; but some innovations by their nature must remain mental organization only, whereas others may be given overt and tangible expression". Likewise

MacIver and Page (1953) have stated that the rejection of the deterministic principle prepares us to look on culture as a dynamic of social change. Everyone acknowledges that there is an intimate connection between our beliefs and our institutions, our valuations and our social relationships. Certainly all cultural change involves social change, for, as we have seen, the social and the cultural are closely interwoven. Further in regard to the concomitance of cultural and social change it can be said that social systems are directly or indirectly the creation of cultural values, directly in the organisation of culture itself and indirectly in the organization of utility.

Within the framework of issues, raised above, concerning social versus culture change, their fundamental difference, on the one hand, and interconnectedness on the other, some further reactions have come to the surface. An increasing concern has, rather, been about the substance of research, and not the social-cultural dichotomy or interconnectedness. More prominently reported is the necessity of understanding society as a changing equilibrium, irrespective of the area focussed. In this context, a comparatively more important observation is of Mukherjee who talks of substance more stressingly than the process. While commenting on the issue whether cultural change should be included within the purview of social change (Moore 1967) or they are to be be clearly distinguished (MacIver and Page, 1953), Mukherjee observed, "when we consider change as the end product, the remark of MacIver and Page is obviously of substantial value; namely, social structural change enters in a different way into the time process because the culture and civilization embody themselves in products which persist and exercise an influence by their continued presence, while the society in which they arose lives only as a changing equilibrium of present relationships. Since, however, descriptive or explanatory research will reconstruct the case of change which has happened, whether it is called cultural, social, political or any other form of social change is a matter of nomenclature, and not of the substance of research " (1977:44).

Within what the social theorists and thinkers have proposed, in terms of ideas concerning social change, the demand of reality aspect of change shows, at times, a significant variation. The whole exercise and the views thereof do ask for further clarity of purpose. Things are not as simple as the writers on social change have conceived. But at the same time the field of social change is so vast that almost all the arguments find some place, for their inclusion, within the purview of this aspect of sociological interest. But then the difference of opinion and the conflict of arguments characterize, at least at ideas level, the arena of social change. What does it cover and what not, and how does it go with cultural change are, among others, some of the issues which do, on number of occasions, prove misleading to those who explain the practical perspective of social change in a society.

The placement of fronts, explored and explained, becomes a difficult task in terms of its delineation as social or cultural. Writings overlap to the extent that the readers get perplexed if they are already familiar with the course of development of ideas regarding social-cultural change. Some dichotomy, in this sense, continues to mark the social scene. Lack of clarity at conceptual level adversely reflects on practical approach, and consequently on data, its quality and interpretation. And as such any social analyst needs to bother for both, the nomenclatural purview as well as the substance of research. More so it is desired when social scientists claim that they are extremely useful in the creation of change to bring about intended socio-economic transformation in a group of people. And if the ideological directions lack, the implementation part may not come upto expectation, causing thereby some setback to the claim of social scientist's role in the context of causation of change.

Theories

The conceptual framework of social change, already discussed, is so elaborate that to bring it under the fabric of one theory is a difficult task. The dimensions and elements of social change cannot, indeed, be dealt within the purview of a single theory. And those who have tried to do so have certainly not gone beyond inadequacy, thereby not explaining all essential aspects of social change. As such their claim of applicability of the single-factor theory to explain social change got forefeited. So much so that even some of the grand-range theorists have not been able to prove what they intended to. This applies to both, the Marxian as well as the non-Marxian explanations. Diverting the focus a bit, Bennis and Benne have rightly said that "no viable theory of social change has, unfortunately, been established. Indeed it is a curious fact about present theories that they are strangely silent on matters of directing and implementing change. What I (Bennis) - and I include the newer theories of neo-conflict (Coser, 1956; Dahrendorf, 1961), neo-functionalism (Boskoff, 1969), and neo-evolutionary theories-mean is that they tend to explain the dynamic interaction of a system without providing one clue to the identification of strategic leverages for alteration. They are suitable for observers of social change, not for practitioners. They are theories of change and not of changing" (1969:64). In addition to multiplicity of social change aspects, the areas of time and space were specially inducted by Talcott Parsons and Mukherjee while hinting at the inadequacy of social change explanations. For Parsons (1951), 'A general theory of the processes of change of social systems is not possible in the present stage of knowledge'. What Parsons meant, according to Loubser and associates, by this statement was that the construction of a general theory of social change is extremely difficult because it must be based upon comprehensive scientific knowledge over both time and space, and knowledge of this scale has not been assembled; he did not mean that his theory and methodology, were inapplicable for explaining change. Likewise, Mukkherjee (1979:20) stated, "In trying to explain all social changes in all known societies for all historical periods, theorists have inevitably set forth over-extended and mutually competitive principles of change". Further important are Cohen's views in respect of single-factor theory of social change. And his comments are in tune with Parsons and Bennis and Benne. Tracing the situation from XVIII century, Cohen (1968:178,197,203) has stated that "Social theorists who have sought the mechanisms of social change, have tried on the whole to explain all or most forms of change in terms of a single factor. These theories can be divided into two groups: those explaining change in terms of indigenous factors or processes, and those emphasising exogenous factors. The former have dominated most sociological thinking. The best known explanations of social change in terms of a single or dominant factor are (1) the technological theory, (2) the economic theory, (3) the conflict theory, (4) the malintegration theory, (5) the adaptation theory, (6) the ideational theory and (7) the cultural interaction theory". And with all this, Cohen argues that "the idea that sociology can provide a single theory of social change is a myth. Social systems provide many sources of change" (1968:203). [Cohen, 1968, has, in brief, explained the contents of these single factor theories. According to technological theory any technological change which is great enough will produce some other social change as a consequence. For example new techniques of manufacture are bound to affect social relations in the relevant industry. The economic theory of change or the Marxist's theory rests on the fundamental assumption that changes in the economic 'infra-structure' of society are the prime movers of social change. This infra-structure consists of the 'forces' and 'relation' of production; the 'super-structure' consists of those features of the social system, such as the judicial, political and religious institutions, which serve to maintain the'infrastructure' and which are moulded by it. Marx does not assert that the 'super-structural elements are completley renewed with the changes in infra-structure, nor does he suggest that all societies at the same stage of economic development possess identical super-structure features. It could be argued by Marxists that the real changes in social structure only occur after economic development. To conflict theory of change, Cohen continues with Marx's theory stating that in the latter the economic change only occurs and produces other changes through the mechanism of intensified conflict between social groups and between different parts of the social system. Recently social theorists have suggested that conflict, in its broadest sense, must be the cause of social change. The reasoning behind this is that if there is consensus in society, and if the various sectors are integrated, there is little pressure for change; therefore, the change must be due to conflict between group and/or between different parts of the social and cultural system. Social conflict exists where the goals of one group are pursued in such a way as to ensure that the goals of another group cannot be realised. The malintegration theory explains change in terms of incompatibilities between different parts of social system. The assumption is that if actions in one sphere inhibit those in another then, one or other must change. Malintegration occurs because of the imperfect socialization of man. The gist of ideational theory of change is that no material or any social factors can produce change unless there is also a change in ideas within society, and possibly, ideas about society or nature. The extent to which ideas can be thought of as exerting an influence on the course of social change depends partly on the level of ideas which is being considered and also on the nature of the social system concerned. The culture interaction theory states that when the members of two cultures interact there is a tendency for cultural change to occur or for an acculturation of cultural change to occur. The increase in the number of cultural items available to each leads to the possibility of new combinations of these items.

Further, reviewing the framework of social change and its constituents, two aspects, among many others, have invited special attention. One of these is the social structure and the other, the individual. As a matter of fact social change cannot be conceived without taking stock of social structure, on the one hand, and individual on the other. Even at practical front the change in either of these perspectives is dealt as social change. The arguments, broadly speaking, have all along been on the lines that the individuals give rise to social structure, and the social structure governs or regulates the life of the individual. Correspondingly, even within the purview of theory of social change, the two elements, that is, of the individual and the social structure, have been increasingly highlighted. This area of theoretical interest has specially been dealt by Zaltman and Firth. According to Zaltman (1973:9) "There are two types of theory of social change: those placing their roots in the social structure - the macro level of life-as the starting point for change, and those placing their roots in the individual-the micro level of life-as the starting point for change. In fact, individuals are affected by social structures and institutions, and social structures and institutions are influenced by the values, beliefs and actions of individuals; the individual and social structure are interacting in the change process". Firth also discussed this issue, though with relative importance. Firth stated that, "a theoretical framework for the analysis of social change must be concerned largely with what happens to social structures. But be truly dynamic it must allow for individual action" (1952 : 83).

The man-social structure interaction, as discussed within the above framework of Zaltman does provide a strong foundation to the relationship of man to his social heritage or internal environment. In other words it finds place for antideterministic expressions concerning social change. But for some there has been a strong bias for deterministic explanations of social change. This deterministic-antideterministic dilemma is better dealt, among others, by MacIver and Page. Deterministic theories of society and social change, for MacIver and Page (1953), mean' any doctrines that regard human behaviour and changes in human behaviour as primarily to be explained by environmental, external or material conditions. No one would deny that these factors are an important part of the explanation of behaviour. Materialistic conception or economic production or stage of technological development determines the mode of production and the relationships and institutions that constitute the economic system. This set of relationship is, in turn, the chief determinant of the whole social order'. However, pure determinism is not approved by MacIver and Page. They connect the external environment with the internal one, composed of belief and other systems. MacIver and Page (1953) made it clear that 'purely deterministic explanation is surely to misunderstand the extreme complexity of relationship between life and environment; and specially the incessant and intricate interaction between man and his social heritage, that inner environment which is constructed not merely by his arts and his techniques but also by his beliefs, his desires, his fears and his aspirations. It is here that antideterminists join issue with determinists'. At this juncture it is important to add that in the event of later theories of society, the overt and covert, explicit and implicit, reality and abstract, cognitive and empirical, have well been put together, for their study, if society and culture are to be explored and understood in their total and true perspective. The approaches and methodologies inherent in cultural ecology, French structuralism, improved version of British structure-functionalism and American cultural materialism do propose for combination of external and internal environments to get at the realm of social-cultural milieu of a society and the change thereof. Taking stock of development of such anthropological ideas, the determinists and antideterminists have no viable alternative but to merge in respect of their thinking concerning social change theories. Obstinacy for either view, in isolation, will not be rewarding if one is to bother for holistic perspective of society and change. However, some social situations may be comparatively more favourable, for their explanation, to deterministic ways; others may be so for antideterministic ones. And certain studies have already made this argument valid.

Theories of social change and their classification form the other important aspects in the matter under reference. Some are considered as the grand-range theories whereas others are rated at slightly a lower range. Whatever it be the theoretical perceptions concerning social change are many, providing alternative explanations though no one is accepted, in totality and for all the societies, as the sole repository of theoretical ideas about social change. At the same time no conceptual explanation, in this sense, is outrightly unacceptable because all have relevance at certain levels and in certain social situations. That one theoretical explanation is preferred over the other is, however, a matter of convenience and suitability in studying social change perspective of a society. Arguments and counter-arguments do suggest for a brief review of ideological explanations put forth by various thinkers, rated at different planes. Among other eminent thinkers, the Grand Theories of social change were specially developed by Auguste Comte (1798-1857), Herbert Spencer (1820-1903), and Karl Marx (1818-1883). At broader level, the theories of social change can be classified under 'linear' and 'cyclical' ones. Those who subscribe to the linear theory of social change assume that there is a significant cumulative change in human social history. Among the linear theorists the more prominent and significant are Auguste Comte, Herbert Spencer, Karl Marx and L.T. Hobhouse. More prominent thinkers among the cyclical theorists are A. Toynbee, Oswald Spengler and P. Sorokin. In cyclical theory, for Pareto, "Social change is brought about by the struggle between groups for political power, and there are alternating periods of harsh rule by a vigorous and newly triumphant elite, and of mild, humanitarian rule by a declining elite" (Bottomore, 1971 : 291-295). Thus the stress of Vilfredo Pareto is on the circulation of elites.

In the context of social change, Auguste Comte, the French social thinker, stressed upon intellectual dimension. And he argued that social change is the outcome of intellectual development. Keeping intellectual growth at the forefront, Comte argued that the intellectual progress causes moral development thereby setting in change in social institutions. He did not end up here, and even spoke about the creation of change. In this context one of the explanations given was that the society would become dynamic if knowledge (specially through education) were imparted more equitably in society. This knowledge, as part of intellectual growth, does not refer to some sudden attainment but is acquired through stages. And with this end in view Comte formulated his popular law of the three stages of intellectual development. "It is a progress from the theological (connected to god and religious belief) mode of thought through metaphysical (speculative philosophical; abstract reasoning or talk) mode of thought to the positive mode of thought represented by modern science" (Kuppuswamy, 1972 : 4-6). The major ingredient of intellectual development as a prerequisite for social change, is, at times, questioned about its being original thinking of Comte. Some are of the opinion that the idea derives from Saint-Simon. The outcome of social change cannot be seen in isolation of mental calibre. Once the later develops, the change is bound to be geared up. In other words Comte's assumption does talk of ideological perspective. The idea-system needs to be reoriented if changes are planned for and directed. And education is the best medium for the purpose. Such sociological insights regarding the dynamics in societies or masses formed, probably, the earliest thinking. Subsequently, though with dim speed, grew other kind of thinking. Auguste Comte remained, although, an ardent supporter, as a philosopher, of linear growth, well fitted into the format of his three stages of intellectual development. Comte, in this sense, floated more into the philosophical arena than involving himself into any serious kind of empiricism. And without the later the force and momentum of his arguments assumed a bit brittle form.

Charles Darwin's theory of evolution inspired thinkers to conceive thoughts about social evolution. And Herbert Spencer, the British thinker, took a lead. Spencer was more empirical, specially in comparison to Comte, and provided support to his theory of social evolution through empirical data. Though influenced by Charles Darwin, he conceived his theory of social change more comprehensively. The underlying assumption in Spencer's social evolution was that there is a 'cosmic progress, in all societies, from undifferentiated homogeneity to differentiated heterogeneity. In other words he proposed for a universal movement from 'an indefinite unstable homogeneity' to a 'definite stable heterogeneity'. One of the very strong arguments, inherent in the idea of cosmic progress, given by Spencer, is that the progress of societies is an ongoing and continuous process. It goes on whether people will it or not. The non-uniformity of progress in societies is, however, attributed to certain factors which may operate more actively in one social situation than the other. Regarding the underlying ramifications of social evolution, as argued out by Spencer, Kuppuswamy (1972; 4-6) has rightly explained that "in discussing the actual course of social evolution, Spencer regarded increasing differentiation of functions within the society and the increasing size of the societies as important factors." And this is what was probably reflected in 'differentiated heterogeneity' marking functions and human groups. And the variations do propose for progress or evolution. Keeping some reservations at the forefront, Bottomore stated that, "Spencer's analysis of social change ultimately depended upon a theory (long since rejected) of cosmic evolution, according to which there is a universal movement from an indefinite unstable homogeneity to a definite stable heterogeneity" (1971 : 291-295). It may be mentioned that the classic social evolutionism invited many unfavourable reactions and as such the idea was thrown into the dark for a couple of decades, giving some new explanations for societal understanding and the dynamics thereof. However, in the second quarter of the current century, 'neoevolutionism' was stressingly proposed. V. Gordon Child and Leslie A. White were labelled as the pioneer neo-evolutionists. Bringing in culture environment/ecology relationship, White suggested that culture/society evolve and progress as per the 'energy' harnessed by their members. More the energy harnessed per capita, more would be the evolution or progress. Under this phenomenon there has been almost a universal evolution. Why certain societies could not evolve at par with others is again explained in terms of the less energy harnessed. Marshall Sahlins and Elman Service also contributed in terms of certain areas of neo-evolution.

Among the other linear theorists, a frequent mention is made of L.T. Hobhouse (1864-1929), a British thinker. The theoretical framework propounded by Hobhouse has a close relevance to some other linear theorists, notably Comte, followed by Spencer. Karl Marx, however, did not come close to Hobhouse. But there is a strong intimacy with Comte's explanations regarding social change theory. Within his conceptual framework of social change, Hobhouse brings in mind-social development analogy. As such, according to him, the development of mind brings about social development. More like Comte, the development of moral ideas, as stressed upon by Hobhouse, is part of mental development. And these, in turn, give way to the rise of rational ethic. The transformation of social institutions, within the format of progress, is encouraged by the sequence of mental development to development of moral ideas to development of ideal of a rational ethic. Therefore, social change at institutional level is essentially the creation of mind, trickling down through various phases to its manifestation purview. In other words the governing factor for change/progress is the mind. Another more convincing part of Hobhouse's effort was reflected through his greater rigour in the use of historical and anthropological data in support of his theory of social change, though he did bank upon Comte and Spencer in terms of theoretical ideas specially concerning the place of development of human mind in causing change, and in adopting the notion of social evolution as a process involving thereby skill, complexity and internal differentiation. As per Kuppuswamy (1972), Hobhouse 'worked out five stages in the intellectual history of mankind, beginning with the preliterate societies and ending with the development of modern scientific thought from the sixteenth and seventeenth centuries'. Another important part of Hobhouse's theory of social change lies in his argument that his social development does not pertain to the development of societies as a whole, as could be thought of by some other linear theorist. The social change theory of Hobhouse did refer to change in major institutions or activities. In other words his social development referred to specific spheres of social activities and institutions. His perspective was not one of totality, but of partial treatment though of major importance. Once the social items and events of more importance are involved in the process of change, they do encourage progressive transformation of society. One may not necessarily agree with Hobhouse regarding the sequence of elements of his strategy (from mental development to development of moral ideas to growth of rational ethics and finally to progressive transformation). But one would certainly appreciate the point that for social progress of development, the mental development is a very strong prerequisite. The development of mind does ensure an ongoing or evolutionary or progressive change. And without that the change or transformation may merely be of temporary nature, providing more room for reverses.

Karl Marx, the German Philosopher, thinker, sociologist, economist and political thinker, as he is differently designated, has propounded altogether a separate theory of social change. Ideologically Marx sounds in contrast to Comte, Spencer and Hobhouse, except in that he also joins their stream as a linear theorist. Somehow, the Marxian perspective of social change continues to be comparatively more popular, though it, in any way, does not denounce the thinking of other philosophers already dealt in the context of social change. The means to achieve social change and transformation, in the arguments of Karl Marx, appeal as revolutionary and more suggest for a radical shift in the system. Though basically coined, and also applied to, for industrial societies, Marxism has, of late, found feet even in agrarian societies specially which have been represented by the distinct classes of 'haves' and 'have-nots'. That way the ideology has travelled from industrial Europe to the farming communities of Asia. However, it does not rule out the effective existence of non-Marxist's ideology and approaches in causing socio-economic transformation, and elimination of disparities, in many parts of Asia, and for that matter in Africa and elsewhere. In comparision to other social change theory, Marxian one is believed to provide quick returns, as the means proposed in others appear to be somewhat delaying, more so for societies of underdeveloped and developing countries. But even with this kind of inherent efficiency the Marxian thinking is not appreciated by many who specially speak for peaceful and smooth transformation of societies.

Broadly speaking, the philosophy of Karl Marx, regarding social change, remains occupied with four major elements, that is, technology, economic base, social classes and the conflict. The explanations focus round the network of these elements, with definite steps and sequence. Out of these four elements, the two are taken as still more significant in the relevance of social life. These are the technology, including the production of goods and services, and the social classes. It may be worth to mention here that the techno-economic version of Karl Marx, concerning theory of social change involves "forces of production, relations of production, means of production, basis and superstructure, modes of production and socio-economic formation" (Edari, 1976 : 29). The two more prominent elements of Marxian theory have also been indirectly hinted at by Zaltman who explains that "Marxism took over its theory of imminent development in a conception of dialectical materialism. This was a form of progress theory in which the mechanism of social development was located in economically based class conflict" (1972 : 19). Regarding techno-economic part of Marxist's theory, and their relation to class formats, Kuppuswamy (1972) rightly stated that for Marx, there is a 'correspondence between a particular stage of development of the productive forces and the system of class relations stabilised and maintained by the dominant class. Marx asserted that the development of the productive forces changes the relations among the classes'. At the same time, Marx assuemd that the major technological changes are bound to produce some other social change, including social relations, as a consequence. Another simultaneous assumption in Marxists' theory was that the major changes in the economic 'infra-structure' of a society are the prime movers of social change. This infra-structure, for Cohen (1968 : 178), "consists of the forces and relations of productions; the super-structure consists of those features of the social system, such as the judicial, political and religious institutions, which serve to maintain the infra-structure and which are moulded by it. Marx does not assert that the super-structural elements are completely renewed with the changes in infra-structure, nor does he suggest that all societies at the same stage of economic development possess identical super-structure features".

Another major thrust of Marx remained on the argument that substantial changes in social structure occur only after the economic development. But how does it go about is again an issue of attention. Keeping Marxian ideology in view, Bottomore (1971) provides with the nature of means stating thereby that 'the continuing development of productive forces changes the relations between classes, and the conditions of their conflict, and in due course the hitherto dominated class is able to overthrow the existing mode of production and system of social relationships and to establish a new social order'. The changes in relations among classes, as caused by the development of the productive forces, lead to inevitable social conflict giving way to new social order. Marx further asserted that every society goes through these stages and finally attains the state of classless human society. Comparatively more detailed account of the exercises involved in arriving at a new social order, within Marxian framework, is provided by La Piere. In the Marxian theory, Lapiere (1965) said, it will be recalled, 'the depressed and progressively exploited masses of a society eventually generate an awareness of the collective nature of their plight and, aroused by an especially atrocious example of the ruthlessness of their masters, rise in wrath against them. By destroying the persons of those in positions of traditional leadership, the masses destroy the traditional power system itself; and out of the resulting chaos there then emerge new leaders, children of the masses, dedicated to the establishment of a just, equalitarian social order'.

Among the means to attain a new social order, through Marxist philosophy, quite a prominent position is occupied by the element of conflict. Generation of conflict is helpful in causing change. Analysing Marxian theory, Cohen(1968) has rightly said that 'economic change only occurs and produces other changes through the mechanism of intensified conflict between social groups and between different parts of the social system. Recently social theorists have suggested that conflict, in its broadest sense, must be the cause of social change. The reasoning behind this is that if there is a consensus in society, and if the various sectors are integrated, there is little pressure for change; therefore, the change must be due to conflict between groups and/or between different parts of the social and cultural system. Social conflict exists where the goals of one group are pursued in such a way as to ensure that the goals of another group cannot be realised'. Such explanations support that the use of conflict to achieve social change is unquestioned. The stages and implications of conflict have also been delineated. Stressing on this issue Zaltman(1972) said, 'conflict theory of social change is an outgrowth of Machiavellia politics and marxian dialectics'. This perspective is cogently stated by Saul Alinsky : 'change means movement, movement means friction, friction means heat, and heat means controversy'. The friction and controversy is the essence of conflict. Conflict can be manifested in many different ways. It can be nonviolent (voting majority, strike), quasi-nonviolent(threats) and violent (riots, revolution) (Cameron, 1964).

Karl Marx's theory of social change never had an absolutely smooth sailing. It has been having as many admirers as the critics. And the social scientists from both these groups carried forward their respective difference of opinion. Against Marxist ideology for the creation of a just social order, there are a few objections. One of those is that Marx provided only a single factor theory of social change. It is not all the time and everywhere acceptable that an instance of change is only the outcome of one factor. There may be more than one cause. The Marxian approach does not, however, approve of it. Secondly, the Marxist conception of social classes is over simplified. In fact the classes, at times, are not that easily observable nor categorised, in true perspective, with easy and simple approach. Instance of definite classes with marked polarity is indeed a difficult task for assessment. Thirdly, the Marxists almost make predictions about the social and economic developments (say, for instance, the elimination of middle class between capitalists and proletariat), which have not for Zaltman (1972) and many others, in fact come to pass. Within such arguments there are opinions from various corners authenticating that Marxism failed to establish a general theory of social change. But at the same time such an argument does not deny that economic conflicts pave way for many social changes. This, however, is not always the cause of change.

Among the cyclical theorists of social change, Toynbee's assumption is that the societies and their social structures grow, then get arrested over a period of time and then start decaying. And thus his cyclical character is expressed in the conception of the growth, arrest and decay of civilization. But even with all this, Arnold Toyanbee remains more optimistic than Spengler, another cyclical theorist, in his assertion that each succeeding civilization is a little higher in stature than the preceding one. The growth part of societies is explained, within Toynbee's framework, in the context of challenge and response. Any society would grow in the event of a challenge. While responding to the challenge the society builds it up. And Toynbee held environment responsible for most of the challenge, especially at the initial stage. Then the further encounters of challenge are social rather than environmental or geographicall. And therefore Toynbee took stock of both type of challenge, that is, internal and external. Another extension of Toynbee's argument is that such challenges are not necessarily controlled by the society; the society can overcome or succumb to them. The nature and magnitude of the challenge, as also the level of existence of the society do count in the matter. And such a state of affairs poses for cyclical explanation of social change. Toynbee observed that the course of history itself is cyclical. The major underlying concepts of Toynbee's theory of social change are, thus, challenge and response, the features which keep on occurring thereby providing protection to Toyanbee's assertion that each succeeding civilization is somewhat higher than the preceding one. Passimism of Oswald spengler is reflected in his argument that civilization reaches its peak and then declines and decays. The peak stage of a society's rise, Spengler calls culture and the falling phase as civilization. The reflection of Spengler's argument is met with in his analysis of modern western civilization stating thereby that it had come to the peak and that its future was for its downfall and decay. 'The Decline of the West', a classic work of Spengler supported the assumptions. Further, in consolidating support to his cyclical theory of social change, Spengler did analyse eight civilizations. In each of these high order civilization Spengler tried to prove the organismic existence of each with birth and adolescence, maturity and decline, followed by decay and disintegration.

In addition to Toynbee and Spengler, another thinker who proposed for a cyclical theory of social change was Vilfredo Pareto. However the underlying idea of Pareto's social change theory is different from other cyclical theorists. Theory about the circulation of elites is the baby of Pareto. Among different groups of people there is always the struggle for political power. And it is such a struggle which causes social change.. The force behind the struggle is provided by the elites and their circulation. The cyclical perspective is supported by the argument that 'there are alternating periods of harsh rule by a vigorous and newly triumphant elite and a mild humane rule by the declining elite'. Putting together the elements of elite, struggle and political power, as represented in Pareto's theory, it may broadly be said that social change is brought about by the struggle between groups for political power. Pareto's factorial differentiation from other ideas, already discussed in the context of linear and cyclical theories of social change, is the induction of lust for political power, and consequently authority. Since human beings are not devoid of aspiration like power and authority, the theory does have a close relevance to social change. But the question again arises whether the struggle for political power is the sole factor in bringing about change. And it is at this front that one would have reservations.

Another social thinker whose writings and pronouncements have some cyclical features is P. Sorokin. In the history of societies, as per Sorokin's version', three types of cultures, that is 'ideational',idealist', and 'sensate' have been succeeding each other in cycles. He talks of swings, irregularities and fluctuations of the course of history between ideational and sensate. This has been made abundantly clear in Sorokin's writings on 'Social Culture and Dynamics', a voluminous study. Ideational culture, to Sorokin, speaks of its being abstruse and abstract, where manifestations like art, religion, ethics and literature are appealing only to the mind or spirit. In other words it is more of a symbolic phenomenon. Within the framework of sensate culture these expressions and manifestations, referred above, appeal to the senses. And then they satisfy many desires, including the sensual ones. The mixed cultures, which are neither purely ideational nor purely sensate, are termed by Sorokin as idealistic. This mixed culture was coined by Sorokin on the plea that no society is absolutely sensate or absolutely ideational because "excess of 'sensatism' makes the pendulum swing and leads the culture towards the ideational pole. According to Sorokin, the medieval period of Western history is a supreme example of ideational culture, and the modern twentieth century Western civilization, on the contrary, is in an over-ripe sensate phase. Thus, in his opinion, history exhibits not cycles but fluctuations, because of the principle of limits by which no culture moves to the extreme. There is a swing in the other direction. This swing, Sorokin asserts, is due to an immanent self-direction. This is the principle of change" (Kuppuswamy, 1972; 8-9). According to Edari, Pitirim Sorokin (1937) examines three types of theories regarding social change: "The first of these is the externalistic type which looks for causes of change outside the social phenomenon under consideration. The second type of theory of socio-cultural change is that of immanent change. This type of theory holds that social phenomena change due to their own internal forces and properties. The third type of theory is the intermediary or integrated type. This attempts to take into account both internal and external factors" (1976:22).

Mechanism

Numerous dimensions mark the mechanism of change. The latter is a very intricate phenomenon exhibited by a wide range of ideas involving divergence, consensus and non-conformity. For understanding, evaluation and generation of change, one finds directives inherent in the framework of mechanism. Origin of views, regarding the mechanism of change, bears a long history. Many thinkers in sociology and social anthropology have, time and again, expressed themselves in the context of social/cultural change. Since the human societies are said to never have been static, the social philosophers, analysts and thinkers continued to devote to the field of social dynamics. And as the pace of change has been uneven, so the ideas. The focus kept on shifting as per the grasp and inclination of the individual thinker. The later need for rapid change, more so in case of underdeveloped countries, necessitated for more broad-based and hillarious ideas. The philosophy and genesis of mechanism of change chiefly devote to, and stress upon processes and stages which involve numerous elements.

Regarding processes of change, there is dichotomy of views. One school of social change analysts is single explanation-based, that is, they seek explanation of change, in terms of process, in one factor. The other school of thought is multiple explanation-based, where experts seek for more than one factor. More notable among those subscribing to single process theory can be included Auguste Comte (with intellectual base), Karl Mannheim (with educational base), Max Weber (with cultural, more religious and ethics base), Karl Marx (with economic contradiction base), Emile Durkheim and Znaniecki (with value crisis base), Robert Redfield (with tradition base), Mahatma Gandhi (individual reformation and non-violence based) and Gray (moral development based). Those seeking for multiple explanations stressed that specific change has specific cause. And this demands for multiple cause and processes. For instance, Harris spoke for power, economy and dominance causations for change.

Likewise, the view diversity characterizes stages in change. Katz (1972) outlines seven stages in change to mark the processes of change or development. On the other hand, Loomis (1957) mentions only four stages. Rogers, among others, gives a different format of elements of change process. The systematic placement of event, to mark the process of change, speaks of the scientific strategy for initiating and gearing up change. And since such a necessity is of late origin, the verdicts of social scientists are also nascent. On the other hond the analysis of unintended change, and the processes thereof, bear a long history.

Among some of the important processes of change are mentioned modernization, Westernization, Sanskritization, socialization etc. Whether at family, community, or still wider level, the socialization mainly supports internalization of native culture. It does not, by and large, presuppose culture contact. As such socialization can be intended as well as unintended. As member of a group one observes and acquires a large number of traits. Modernization, Westernization and even Sanskritization presuppose the situation of culture contact. This generates acculturation process, chiefly one way involving flow of culture traits from dominant to the weak group. In such cases the dominant populations are taken as reference groups by others who try to borrow things, material and non-material, from them. The culture contact creates favourable situation for borrowing and lending, depending upon the convenience of the groups involved. Diffusion of traits may ultimately culminate into assimilation. In the process of Westernization the people identify the superiority of western culture traits and try to acquire them. In modernization they look for the, so called, modern ways of life, which may not all the time be western alone. The stress, here, is on 'modern' rather than 'western', though the two are thickly interconnected. In Sanskritization the weaker sections, with roots in non-Sanskritic traditions, try to acquire Sanskritic traits represented by higher echelons of caste society, especially Indian. And since the people of such twice-born category have had more privilege of borrowing certain traits of modernity, the same may also be desired, in terms of acquisition, by the weaker sections representing castes of the middle and lower segments, plus the tribals. In other words the efforts of latter category of people to elevate their position is through those reference individuals and groups who have been closer to modernity and western ways. The direct access to the latter is, however, not totally ruled out, though the focus remains on indirect borrowing. The arena of modernization is large and as such there can be numerous responses, direct or indirect to the same. According to Woods (1975 : 65), modernization has been defined as "a process whereby individuals change from a traditional to a more complex, technologically advanced and rapidly changing life-style".

Creation of change or occurance of change have roots in a large number of elements forming components of diverse processes of change. And this is more important to understand because there lies the philosophy of change. On this score have emerged a variety of explanations. The rise of retreatists (Merton, 1961), for instance, enthuses change. The retreatism too has its roots in certain other requirements. One of these, to Edari, is social displacement. "Withdrawal of status respect describes a situation in which a group of elites or lesser elites lose the respect they once enjoyed. These socially displaced persons react with anger and frustration, and after some lapse of time (generations) their descendants come to reject culturally prescribed goals and means as a reaction against their progenitor's predicament" (1976 : 42). And, therefore, to be retreatists, the requirement of elitism and resentment to the old are also there. In other words to be retreatist involves a complicated process. A typical kind of attitude, within the framework of elitism, is first to be generated which ultimately brings one to the state of withdrawal from the past, thereby paving way to behavioural change. In this regard Zaltman (1973 : 20) rightly said that "attitude change must precede behavioural or institutional change". The elitists do imbibe an attitudinal change. And the rise of elitists is fast promoted through the intelllectual propagandists belonging to the new order. For Auguste Comte the intellectual development remains the source of change. Human material, through intellectual development and its institutionalization can unfold and reshape archaic forms of institutional structures regulating human behaviour and social relationship.

A closely connected field to what has been said above concerns education. Some social analysts have hypothesised that education provides the major force of change, and in its absence the process of change may remain not only slow but even imbibes scope for reversion to the old forms. In the strategy of change the education, therefore, is considered as a very crucial variable. And unless the educational system is reformed and restructured, the change may not take place to the intended extent. While suggesting for change, in a fundamental way, in the education system Karl Mannheim argued that this forms an important basis of social process influencing men and women. For him the reformulation of educational system is a prerequisite to promote change that sustains for quite some time.

In another explanation, concerning the process of social change, the focus remains on interpersonal relations. In other words the individual finds more prominent place. Nature of individual action and interaction with other human beings determines the level of interpersonal relations. And to bring about change some shake in the sphere of interpersonal relations is desired. Though sounding of small nature the field of interpersonal relations has wider implications. It is not only limited between two individuals but extends to groups and the organizations which uphold the groupings. Such a structure from organization to individual has root in cultural parameters, cognitive as well as substantive. So, the assessment of interpersonal relations is not only limited to inter-human interaction and behaviour, but also extends to what governs the same. And it is the readjustment in this total paradigm that helps guide and direct the change that is proposed for a group of people. With such a background in view Zaltman took interpersonal relations. "as one of the most important influences in adopting or rejecting change. And interpersonal change process could be treated from four points of view : culture, organization, group and individual" (1972 : 4).

Leadership and change are again said to be intimately connected. It is the leaders who are, by many, held responsible for both the continuity of the past traditions as well as the change. The traditional leaders stick to fixity unless they are motivated and made agree to the new. The formal or non-traditional leaders are, by and large, pro-change unless they are otherwise interested, for personal gains, in continuity. The rise of new leadership is attributed to two kinds of phenomena - one agreed upon through common consensus and suggested from outside, and the other through some charismatic person born within the group or recognised so from outside. The latter is believed to have certain qualities which people start appreciating. His verdicts and pronouncements are respected and carried forward by the people without more of reservations. Inculcation of change through such a person is said to be easier as this medium is usually not questioned by the people. Charismatic leaders are not created by any human agency. They are born with certain qualities to which the contemporary human society, that they represent, gives recognition. Such persons lead people as per their directive. And if they are motivated for change, there would be no hindrance to the same. They can help suggest new social alternative leading to new patterns. Charisma is said to be a more powerful tool in bringing about change. This is so because the followers of a charismatic person take him as extra-ordinary in his present insight and future intuition. Max weber, the noted sociologist and thinker, stressingly conceived the rise of new social arrangements through a charismatic leader. At times the charisma is also explained as religion-based, that is, it seeks support from religious values. But it is hardly said to be economy based. Max Weber specially highlighted religion and the culture grown there upon. His assertion remained that the rise of modern capitalism is due to Protestant Reformation, more so the calvinism. Keeping change phenomenon as culture based, Max Weber emphasised that religion-based ethics of a community and its economic structure have very intimate and direct relationship. Keeping Max Weber's explanations in mind, Kuppuswamy (1972 : 78) rightly said that, "while Karl Marx looked upon the economic factor as the most important factor to bring about social change, the German Sociologist Max Weber emphasised that the economic phenomena themselves rest upon culture, particularly religion".

The place of ethics and values, as part of culture, in the social change arena could be stressed upon time and again. And in many quarters it continues to be so. The value, as an important process of change, is recognised on the basis of certain convincing explanations. Since the value system upholds a social system, it is the change in the same that is bound to generate patterns of social change. On the other hand if values persist intact, the development of new patterns does not find scope. And even if it does, there is not much of room for its extension. It dies, of its own, in due course. Values are the underlying support to the infrastructure marking a society. And the participants of that society are, by and large, aware of the intricacies and implications of such a background. They also understand the magnitude of social group pressure in the event of any shake in value complex. The values are, otherwise, hard to change, since they form the core of any culture. But if some change or readjustment in the same is made feasible, there would correspondingly be reported an instance of social change. The values are hidden whereas the overt behaviour is obvious. But the two are inseparable except at conceptual level. The mental framework of a particular kind is the generation of values, consciously or unconsciously held high. Thus, to reshape values is rather difficult as it involves cognitive perspective. But once such an implicit venture is achieved, the change at explicit level would not be difficult. Let us admit that it is the value-based ideas and ideology which have upper hand over activities, since the latter are the corresponding outcome of the former. Instances of deviancy are, however, not always ruled out, though they may pose as stray case. Under such circumstances the stress, for quite some time, has been on valuc system vis-a vis change. In this context while analysing Emile Durkheim's sociology and philosophy, Pocock rightly said that as per Durkheim, "Values are designed to transform social phenomena in some way. Values that lead to change develop in periods of collective ferment (crisis) and are employed by groups or communities to promote major socio-cultural development" (1953 : 90). Likewise, value conflict, as opposed to economic or class conflict, was strongly proposed by Znaniecki. For Znaniecki, social change seeks support from conflict between important values. And such conflicts, for him, are given. Znaniecki theorised that, "persons who recognise practical incompatibilities between values tend to alter their attitudes and behaviour in attempts to reorganize the system of relationship in which they normally participate. Reorganization, which is motivated by the objective of eliminating (or reducing) value conflicts entails substituting different structures" (1934 : 297-301). Thus, the process of social change is enthused by value conflicts. But in the creation of an intended change, the conflict of values may not always be a prerequisite. Change can also be promoted through readjustment and redefining of values in the light of new requirements. And such an attempt need not necessarily go to the level of value conflict or contradiction. Thus, the ideological re-education in the interest of readjustment in new requirements is important. This may amount to moral and ethical revaluation and development. For Gray (1971) and Schram (1974) the 'Chinese planners have found it ncccssary to supplement material incentives with moral incentives. Moral incentives form a part along with the material incentives of the overall strategy of motivating the people to contribute to the national goals of higher output and economic growth. Moral incentives (self-sacrifice, hardwork, asceticism and initiative), as per Mao, follow from his faith in the hidden potential of the common man. Faced with the reality of China's backwardness and poverty, and the need to mobilise resources for economic development, Mao seeks a solution in the revolutionary enthusiasm of the people to draw out their latent resources. Once his hidden potential is opened up through ideological re-education great material feats are possible. Thus, the underlying principles are believed to be more fruitful. And the stress remains on individual reformation which ultimately culminates into social one. Change in ideas is the chief assumption in creating and gearing up social change. Such a culture base of social change has also been suggested by many others. According to Harris (1980 : 201), "Sources of change must be located in the production of values, and the processes whereby subscription to those values is maintained". Likewise, cultural framework of social change is suggested by Narbadeshwar Prasad (1970) while theorising for systematicity inherent in the phenomena. Likewise Louis Dumont (1964) talks of cognitive transformation while conceiving social change. A more elaborate picture of views put forth by Prasad and Dumont has been well analysed by Yogendra Singh (1980). "Prasad categorises the factors of social change into external or objective and internal or subjective levels. Objective levels are : material and behavioural. The subjective level consists of values, motives, needs, perception and belief. Each can influence the process of change in terms of its quality, quantity and function. Changes may begin at either of the two levels but their success depends upon the mode of fit between the two levels of categories and their interaction. Dumont conceives of the Indian social system not as a system of social relationship but as system of ideational and value configurations or patterns. Social change study, according to Dumont, should be focused on analysing the 'reaction of Indian minds to the revelation of Western Culture'. According to Dumont "this reaction would lie in the cognitive transformation from the principle of hierarchy to equality. Essentially, change consists in the adaptive or transformative processes within the traditional Indian cognitive system. Thus, cultural change is the precursor for individuality and of the social change" (1980 : 132, 136). While conceiving change Mahatma Gandhi also stressed on the value system, and hence on cultural basis, Unnithan (1979 : 123, 224) has said, "For healthy change Gandhi stressed on the re-establishment of old values based on non-violent and just means. Hindu religious scriptures and philosophic doctrines provided him with a system of values. The fundamental Gandhian means for bringing about social change rests on the reformation of the individual. Gandhi wanted improvement of the individual internally, morally and spiritually. If all individuals practised self-control, a control over all senses, followed the principles of truth and non-violence in their daily dealings and tried to incorporate these principles in their thoughts and attitudes, society would gradually gravitate towards the ideal he cherished".

Specially focusing on caste society of India, Srinivas (1966) put forth the concept of Sanskritization, a process meant to analyse social change. According to Srinivas (1966 : 67-9), Sanskritization is the process by which a low caste or tribe or other group takes over the customs, ritual, beliefs, ideology and style of life of a high, and in particular, a twice-born (dwija) caste. The Sanskritization of a group has usually the effect of improving its position in the local caste hierarchy. It normally pre-supposes either an improvement in the economic or political position of the group concerned or a higher group self-consciousness resulting from its contact with a source of the Great Tradition of Hinduism such as pilgrim centre or monastery or proselytizing sect". The members of socially low groups take the people of twice born category as their reference individuals or groups. And so is taken their way of life. Since the superior position of the reference groups is traditionally accepted. the rest take it as their privilege to copy them in various possible ways of life. The underlying idea holding such attempts concerns their desire to socially elevate their position once the borrowing is attained. And this is the force behind change generation. The new ritual attainment, possible through cultural borrowings from higher caste people, is satisfying to the people at mental level. Their new state of mind certifies, to them, of a higher status. How far this is agreed upon by the groups from whom ritual ingredients are borrowed is a different question. They may or may not recognise the element of superiority of the lower groups traditionally so defined. And this may be the reason why Srinivas (1966) makes it amply clear that Sanskritization helps one to identify the cultural or positional and not the structural forms of social changes.

Since the process of Sanskritization is one way, it poses an element of differentiation from socialization. In Sanskritization the socially higher groups do not ask the members of socially lower group to internalize their life-styles. But the latter do it of their own. On the other hand, socialization, according to Varadachar (1977:372) "is a life-long developmental process and does not cease in its importance after childhood. The learning of any new social role, requiring as it does the understanding and internalization of values, attitudes and behaviour characteristic of given religious, political, occupational, economic, caste groups reflects the process of socialization at work". It amounts to acquisition through learning. Socialization is a universal phenomenon but Sanskritization, as conceived by Srinivas, is a feature of stratified societies, specially the one of India, representing centuries old established order of Great Tradition. Westernization,as a process of change is again, as conceptualised by Srinivas, marked by limitation that it results through contact with the west, specially the Great Britain. The change, including institutional innovations, born of contact with Westerners are explained and analysed through Westernization. For Srinivas, secularization, another process of change, "is a counterpart of the process of Westernization specially as it emerged after Indian Independence as a national ideology. This ideology calls for a spirit of religious and cultural tolerance and coexistence amongst the religious group" (Yogendra Singh 1980-101).

As part of Sanskritization Srinivas did refer to the borrowing of customs, beliefs and ideology, But then these elements do give rise to certain traditions that perpetuate till people think of other alternatives as part of internal desire or external pressure. A sharp focus on the analysis of tradition, to explain social change, was given by Mckim Marriott, Milton Singer and Robert Redfield. For understanding of social change, specially for societies bearing long civilizational history, Redfield (1955) conceptualised tradition as a frame of analysis. Since such societies are marked by many levels of social structure, the social change can be explained with reference to the same. While unraveling the complexity of social organization of traditions, Redfield coined the concepts of Little Tradition, (represented by folk or the unlettered peasants) and Great Tradition (represented by the elites or the reflective few). These two together symbolize a world-view which holds the unity of a civilization. But at the same time the elements of these two traditions (Little and Great) are marked by mobility, sometimes caused from within (through orthogenetic or primary process generated by the participants of a tradition themselves) and other times from outside (through heterogenetic process generated as a result of external contact). Conceiving civilization and its growth, Redfield hypothesized that it starts with primary process and undergoes transformations through heterogenetic process. And this is how one can understand the dynamics of social change. Traditions are open to change, and there is most of the time interaction and reaction amongst the elements of Little and Great Traditions. While studying

Indian society, Mckim Marriott (1955) and Milton Singer (1959) further elaborated such modes of interaction through the process of parochialization (referring to the downward percolation of Great Tradition to the extent that its original form is lost and it becomes organic part of Little Tradition) and universalization (referring to the upward circulation of the elements, that is, customs, rites, deities etc., of Little Tradition to the extent that they are identified with the legitimate form of Great Tradition).

In addition to a large number of elements and parameters, already highlighted, there are certain others which carry tremendous significance in the mechanism of social change. Economy, including technology, is one such parameter. By some, the technology and its level, have increasingly been brought to the surface. The non-economic dimensions, ideological and sociological, have been relegated to a secondary position. Once the economic perspective is identified with reasonable accuracy, the other areas are taken care of as far as the interest of social change, its analysis and induction are concerned. La piere (1965:255) has stated that, "it has now come to be commonly assumed that technology is the base upon which the remainder of society - the ideological and organizational component-rests. Ogburn, like many thinkers before him, held that the normal pattern of social change is first innovation in technology, then disparity between the newly innovated technique and pre-existing ideological and organizational elements, which leads eventually to adaptive changes in these latter aspects of society". Normally the economically sound category of people, capturing major means and modes of production, also enjoy the privileges of power and dominance. Usually, they are socially dominant in terms of hierarchy/placement and other considerations. And as such they are more powerful. Such position of power and dominance are displayed on various occasions characterizing the way of life of particular groups. At the same time the powerful one, in a formation, are the deciding factor for acceptance or rejection of change. Those belonging to powerful groups represented, many a time, by stratification, have an upper hand in decision-making. With such a bearing Harris rightly said, "Any study of the process of social change requires the analysis of the structure of dominance within a social situation, or formation. This is so for three reasons. First, the unequal distribution of resources is a vital factor in the maintenance of a given mode of assembly, and failure to maintain that mode of assembly is a precondition of a transition from the formation characterised by that mode of assembly. Secondly, the development and spread of new practices and forms of practice within a formation (which is a precondition of transition to a different formation) is dependent on the manner in which dominant groups exercise their power. Thirdly, the differential power of social groups within a population as evidenced by the degree of their monopoly of economic, political and ideological resources, the pattern of struggles between them and the different degree to which they can determine outcome signify the structure of the individual formation upon whose existence the hierarchy of domination depends" (1980:218). Parameters of power, dominance and economy found prominent place even with the social change theorists of nineteenth century. The process of change, which many of them suggested, involved an element of clash and conflict between powerful and powerless, dominant and subordinate and capitalist and downtrodden. Pointing to some nineteenth century social theories, La Piere (1965:477) stressed that they "involved the the idea that all change is and can be accomplished only through conflict, through a head-on violent clash between those who represent the new and those who have a vested interest in the old between downtrodden workers and their capitalistic exploiters, a submerged ethnic minority and the dominant majority, a progressive society and one that is decadent. By conflicts, Karl Marx and other nineteenth century theorists meant a violent, physical clash of people who have unalterably opposed irreconcilable interests, values, sentiments and loyalties".

Within the complexity of change mechanism, the details of which have already been provided, it is again of interest to understand as to when an innovation assumes acceptance. Irrespective of its being an idea, technique or object, an innovation does pass through a number of stages prior to its adoption by an individual or a group of people. Such stages have systematically been defined. And it is further suggested that they are to be respected in the interest of better induction of change. Since the creation of change, in the interest of humanity, is of utmost importance, many views poured in to outline smooth creation of change. The social scientists, in this arena, showed an increased concern while elaborating definite strategy for the purpose. It started with the necessity of awareness of innovation and the accompanying infrastructure. This is to be followed by the interest to be generated through the merits of an innovation. It brings forth evaluation where one, at mental level, weighs the merits of an innovation. Once convinced of such merits, there is the need for trial. To start with, this is done on a small scale. If it is found satisfactory, one decides to adopt. Else, the proposed venture is discarded or put to a fresh trial. In other words the change agents are also desired to see that the stage systematism is well maintained. Any haphazard attempt is not liable to bear intended fruits. The requisites of adoption of an innovation are well laid down by Katz and his colleagues in their paradigm of diffusion of an idea. The complete process of diffusion, for Katz (1972), is defined as the (1) acceptance, (2) over time, (3) of some specific item - an idea or practice, (4) by individuals, groups or other adopting units, linked to (5) specific channels of communication, (6) to a social structure, and (7) to a given system of values, or culture. Diffusion process is the spread of a new idea from its source of invention or creation to its ultimate users or adopters. Thus, diffusion entails the communication or dissemination of an idea, and culminates in its adoption by individuals'. While explaining the important processes involved in social change, Loomis has mentioned of certain other additional requisites. For Loomis (1957;17) the social change processes include: "(1) Communication - By communication is meant the process by which information, decisions and directives pass through a social system, and the ways in which knowledge, opinions and attitudes are formed or modified; (2) Decision making - This is the process whereby alternative courses of action available are reduced; (3) Bounday maintenance - This is the proccss whereby the system retains its identity and interaction pattern, that is, retains its equilibrium involving both integration and solidarity; (4) Social-Cultural linkage - This is the process whereby the elements of atleast two systems come to be articulated so that in some ways they function as a unit. Thus social-cultural linkage usually requires that the value orientation and the social structure of the change agent system and the target system are brought together in atleast temporary closure. Socio-Cultural linkage involves the following three processes - initiation, legitimation and execution".

Types and Conditions

Quite in tune with the theories of change are its types and conditions. Types or nature of change have been identified in various contexts. And for each the variable/s are well delineated. Conceptualization of types are, therefore, duly recognised and accepted in the disciplines of sociology and anthropology. Such typologies are mostly based on human intentions and efforts, quality and quantity of change, time period, idea of progress, indigenous and alien causation etc. Concepts concerning types have, thus, been evolved over the course of years by the social analysts and thinkers keeping in view the background and content of change. Comparatively more widely documented are the planned and non-directed change. The promulgation of the former, and the associated focus thereof, are of nascent origin. Non-directed change is a phenomenon as old as the societies themselves. Occurrance of such change has always, and in all societies, been there though usually at snail's pace. Rapid change caught momentum with the induction of massive programmes of induced change. Imbibing of change/innovations remained, most of the time, subject to the degree of contact with others, in addition to rather sporadic instances of invention originating from within the system. And since the parameters of historicity, and spatial distribution and contact have often been divergent, in diverse situations, the incidence of change too varied. In addition to factors from within and beyond, the surrounding non-human environments have had their own contribution. Impinging forces of nature, and the human reactions and responses thereto have been the other underlying factors for change explanation. Within such a complexity surrounding the arena of change, a variety of explanations have emerged. And the social scientists have, more so of late, tried to give them definite shape at the level of conceptualization.

To startwith would be analysed the explanations concerning planned or directed change, a philosophy as well as programme so popular among the nations of the Third World. The socio-economic transformation of the inhabitants of underdeveloped countries has, all over, been the slogan for many decades. Huge infrastructures came into being to gear up change. And these got originated out of a scientific strategy evolved for the purpose. Within the social science framework, the planned or directed change could be conceived in a number of ways. According to Woods (1975:37), "Directed change is the active and purposeful intervention of individuals or groups into the technological, sociological and ideological practices of another people." In other words this involves an underlying intention to cause change. So long as the intended element is missing, any dynamics gets closer to unplanned change. Most of the definitions, in one form or the other, keep up the intended aim while delineating theoretical framework of planned change. For Zaltman, Philip, Kotler and Kaufman the planned social change, "refers to deliberate efforts by change agents to affect a change in a target system of individuals. In different contexts the concept of planned social change has been referred to as social planning, planned change, social communication engineering, social marketing and change management" (1972:2). The element of scientific knowledge, as an essential ingredient of strategy of planned change, was stressed upon by Bennis and Benne. "Planned change is a conscious, deliberate and collaborative effort to improve the operation of a human system,whether it be self-system, social system, or cultural system, through the utilization of scientific knowledge. Planned change, for them, can be viewed as a linkage between theory and practice, between knowledge and action. It plays this role by converting variables from the basic disciplines into strategic instrumentation and programme" (Bennis and Benne, 1969:4,65). Thus, the human intention to improve upon a situation is not only a typical philosophy and genesis-based, but also suggests for practice and action within the desired framework. As such,one involved in the task of planned change has not only to bother for inherent theory but also the connected practice.

The unplanned change hardly carries any philosophy with it. And the events happening beyond the framework of planned change are taken as unplanned ones. Such happenings are taken as the outcome from natural forces. However, the understanding of unplanned change, and the connected processes thereof, are said to be important prerequisite to promote intended change. The argument is that the unplanned change makes one understand of the basic mechanism regulating structural and functional change in society, which one decides to change being an organ of planned change machinery. Further, about immanent and enacted change, Sorokin and Naegele have given a little more elaborate explanation. According to Sorokin (1962:1311), "The first implication of the principle of immanent change may be formulated as follows: As long as it exists and functions, any socio-cultural system incessantly generates consequences which are not the results of the external factors to the system, but the consequences of the existence of the system and of its activities. As such, they must be imputed to it regardless of whether they are good or bad, desirable or not, intended or not by the system. One of the specific forms of this immanent generation of consequences is an incessant change of the system itself, due to its existence and activity. For Naegele, "social change bears a complex relation to the purposes of men. Among other, Sumrer has reminded us of the difference between coercive and enacted change. In truth, the changes characterizing the institutional arrangements by which we live, result both from intention, and from the convergence of unintended consequences of the daily or extra-ordinary acts or dispositions of specific individuals, acting on their own or as members of corporate structures. In formulating historical materialism, Marx also focused on the notion of intent as insufficient for understanding the course of history. He thus pointed to the study of the unintended consequences of purposive social action." Further reflections on immanent and enacted change have come from Rogers and Shoemaker(1971). Depending on the nature of original impetus to change, the resulting social change, to Rogers and Shoemaker, may be called immanent social change (when such change results from voluntary behaviour) or contact social change (when such change results from some organised effort). In other words the factors underlying immanent and enacted change are orthogenetic and heterogenetic (Yogendra Singh, 1973) respectively.The contact situation poses for more situational variation. And when that is so the individuals try to adapt or adjust, depicting thereby some change in their behaviour. In native social systems the situation variations are rather limited, and the same holds correspondingly true for human behaviour. External factors for change, originating from purposed or non-purposed contact, provide wider platform to alternative mode of behaviour. Resorting to such alternatives may, however, vary depending upon the nature and background of a social system. Keeping in view such ideological parameter Heisler distinguished historical or processive change from the behavioral one. Heisler (1981:119) stated that, "It is useful to distinguish the historical or processive changes of and among parts of social systems from the behaviour which follows participation in different situations. The latter can be known as situational changes. The behaviour of individuals must be explained directly in terms of the pressures exerted on them by the situation in which they are located and not by alterations among the variables which operate in wider societal systems."

Within the framework of enacted or planned change, there is more probability of situational change. And since the newly-created situations, then, are perpetually taken care of by the specific infrastructure, its maintenance and desired improvement assume ongoing form. Changes under such circumstances are proposed, planned and brought about under three-pronged attack from above, below and from a combination and compromise of both. And pampering of any of them is strongly connected to the political system marking a population. Considerations of this nature led Gans to devise categories of top-down and bottom-up changes. "In top-down change, as favoured by power elites, the elites initiate change, the poor are audience, and the people of lower class sit by quietly, even sullenly, often without listening. Bottom-up change usually involves a greater degree of conflict, in that restricting change poses a threat to authority. Bottom-up change is more likely to be successful at time of perceived crisis in a system. Also it is more likely to be successful when a social movement is headed by a charismatic leader." (Gans 1962:2). Again, within the variables of opposition and disequilibrium. Godfrey (1959) makes mention of primary and secondary change. The change that arises on account of change in external environment or cultural forces of society, Godfrey calls primary change. And the change that arises from pressure of disequilibrium, is called secondary change. Primary change has parity with development or social modification as it involves no opposition.

In terms of types of change, some more views can be put forth in terms of quantity and quality parameters. More prominent of such types were conceptualised in the framework of 'partial', 'minor, 'fundamental', 'systemic' changes etc. These are well defined categories and one needs to be careful in interpretation of data while delineating such areas. Significance of each over the other is of no less value. According to Cohen (1968:176), "The social reform and the extension, or even creation, of social services, might be called partial change in a system which is based on inequality and private ownership of property. On the other hand a change to worker's control of industry might be considered a change in the system as such. No social system ever changes in toto. Even the most radical changes-revolutions are never changes in all features of a social structure." Minor and fundamental changes have also been defined by Cohen according to whom, "There is a reasonable and realistic sense in which one might distinguish minor changes from fundamental changes in a social system. One might do this by isolating a number of core or strategic features of a system and then defining of a major change as one in which such features themselves change " (1973:176). Minor and partial changes have been taken in the sense of readjustment by Radcliffe Brown. And change of system is treated by him as change of type. The inherent meanings, however, converge. "It is necessary, writes Radcliffe Brown, to distinguish two types of change; we call the first kind 'readjustment'. Fundamentally it is a readjustment of the equilibrium of a social structure. The second I would prefer to call 'change of type.' However slight the latter may be, it is a change such that when there is sufficient of it, the society passes from one type of social structure to another" (Nisbet, 1972:15).

The sociologists and social anthropologists are, by and large, of the view that minor or partial changes do not ask for alteration in the fundamental principles of a social system; but the change of type or system does so. And for such explanations the minor or partial changes are 'organizational' in character, and remain far short of assuming structural character. A more elaborate analysis, concerning these aspects, has been given by Raymond Firth. While commenting on aspects of social change, Firth (1959:340-41) writes, "Another aspect of social change is social movement. This is an alteration not in principle but in detail, where the position of individuals or groups in the social system have altered but the character of the system as such is not affected (e.g.succession to Chieftainship). In structural change one is concerned with alterations not only in the personnel of social units and in the position of these units vis-a-vis one another, but with the nature of units themselves. One is concerned not with the different persons who have come to fill social roles, but with the disappearance of former roles and the emergence of new ones. Yet the replacement of some persons by others and an alteration in the size and position 0f social units may lead to further alteration in the nature of these roles and units. Without forcing the distinction too strongly, one can, for ordinary purposes, conceive of some changes as being primarily structural in character and others as being primarily organizational. Yet, the relations between these may be intimate. Organizational changes are changes in ways of doing things, which themselves continue to be done, and in the extent and range of particular complexes of social relationships, which remain formally unaltered. The further distinction is useful, although in the last resort structure and organization are rather two aspects of the same reality than two different things. Organization is structure in action, its actual working out in practice, in space and time. Oganizational change does seem to involve some change in the quality of social relationships involved, and so in their structure."

Change of system or type has, again, been elaborated by Beattie while bringing in the concept of radical change. This is isolated as an arena different from the changes that are provided for. But though the terminology used by Beattie is new, the contents do not differ much from the organizational and structural change frames of Raymond Firth defined earlier. For Beattie (1964:244), "Anthropologists have distinguished two kinds of social conflicts, and so between two finds of social change. First, there are those conflicts and changes which are provided for in the existing social structure (one dies, other occupies). The second kind of change is more radical. It is change in the character of social system itself: some of its constituent institutions are altered, so that they no longer mesh with other coexisting institutions as they used to do. This is structural or radical change; and the conflicts to which it gives rise are not resoluble in terms of existing value of the socicty."

From the stock of ongoing changes in Indian society, one can derive that they refer to organizational or positional types of change. Vital instances of structural change are missing. While evaluating the process of Sanskritization in Indian context, Srinivas (1962) supports that nature of change is positional and not structural, as such changes have not led to basic alteration of the system. Adaptive changes are many around. The studies on social change in India too have not taken stock of structural perspective. Milton Singer has stated that "we may characterize the recent discussion among social anthropologists and sociologists of the Indian family as moving from morphology to social physiology .but not quite yet arrived at structural changes" (1968:426). However, Yogendra Singh is somewhat optimistic on the issue while stating that though the analyses of social change in India has predominantly been culturological, there is no total neglect of structural aspects. In this connection it may be pointed out that though the instance of sporadic attempt for structural analysis is available, it needs much rigorous exercise to prove sharper in terms of sociological insight. It's validity and exhaustiveness continue to be questionable by many. Otherwise, structural analysis and structural change have assumed alarming importance in the theoretical literature.

Types and Conditions

Societies are in the sway of change. But what conditions have been outlined to view an event as change is a very pertinent question. Yet another important purview is formed of the prerequisites and requisties which enthuse change or gear up change phenomena. The sociological and social anthropological literature provide many explanations on these points, though at times debatable and controversial. Conditions for creation of change and occurrence of change, for instance, may not always be in conformity. A large number of scholars have put forth their views keeping up sociological, ideological and technological bases of change. And such a complex has been represented by social scientists belonging to different academic disciplines. The universality of some of the arguments is not acceptable because of the heterogeneity of human society. Anyhow the discussion on the broad framework of conditions of change is not only rewarding but an eye opener for those engaged in the ventures of social change and its analysis.

The acceptance of an occurrence as change has to be supported by certain conditions. For Woods (1975:11) , "Actual culture change does not occur until the new response is learned and accepted by sufficient number of people so that it becomes characteristic of the people." In other words an incident is not to be considered as change unless it assumes a massive character and it gets going as part of the system. And when it sounds as a characteristic of the native population, it appears as if it has lost its alien character. The acceptance of innovation has not only to be wide but also a characteristic of the people. Sporadic instance of adoption remains, as per Woods, short of acquiring the character of culture change, Another important requisite of change, and which has not been highlighted in the above argument of Woods, concern the unfolding of traditionally ongoing patterns. For instance, Zaltman states that, "A crucial step in the induction of change involves the unfreezing of existing patterns - the overcoming of resistances-so that the person will be open to the adoption of new patterns" (1973:27). Therefore the adoption of new patterns, and the elimination of all resistance thereof, certify that the change has taken place. So long as the resistance to new stands there remains a fear of reversal to the old even if some adoption has already occurred. When the expression of resistance is ruled out, the acceptance and persistence of adopted patterns is not challenged until some still new forms are proposed for the client system. Further, a large scale or massive change (as propounded by Woods and Zaltman) explanation do not go well, in terms of focus, with certain theorists who speak of the individual. To Max Weber and Everett Hagen the directed social change "depends on individual change. Change is predicated upon change in the personalities or beliefs of individuals. The change of society, as a whole, then is seen as the aggregate of the individual change-first an internal activation of individuals, and then a freedom from social constraint which allows them to take full advantage of opportunity" (Zaltman, 1973:67). The theorists, stressing upon the individuals, also demand for change in belief system. Unless the latter is done the change may be discontinued not only at individual level but also at the level of community. Belief, as a mental phenomenon, is said to govern overt actions and manifestations. Continuity of the old belief system ensures persistence of traditionality, and hence resistance to the new. Learning or adoption of new response is subject to change or modification in belief system, first of the individual and subsequently of the community. Yet another requisite of change, social or cultural, involves the attitude system. Development of new or alternative attitude is to be accomplished if an occurrance is treated as change or part of change. Formation of specific attitude is again connected to value system. So, its change requires shift or alteration of the same. Isolated attitudinal change may not support the broader requirement of change as the new attitude formation, in that case, remains shaky.

Change, social or cultural, therefore not only concerns the development of the new but is equally concerned with the revision of what was going on, as state of mind, in the situation prior to new response. In the absence of latter, and in the event of mere addition of new, the occurrances are not treated as change. This is so because such a rise may collapse any time reverting back to the position of status quo. And it is very much within this context that Naegele put forth his version of social change. He does talk of two domains - the new and the old. According to Naegele (1972:20), "Social change occurs on two levels: ;it involves inner shifts within any one domain that, combined with the others, constitutes a given society; and it involves shifts among the domains, with particular regard to their relative dominance."

Another dimension that makes one treat an eventuality a social change concerns the level of its integration in society. This comes closer to what Woods (1973) stated in his explanation. An alteration can assume the form of a significant social change not merely when it is accepted by the majority but also when it is properly integrated in the society. And it is only then that the alteration finds scope to endure. Otherwise it remains a transitory change which is not included in the framework of significant social change. In order that a change gets integrated into the larger system, it is again desired that it takes the institutionalised form. So long as the change remains outside the orbit of institutionalised norms there is every possibility of its fading away. And if that happens no one feels disturbed, nor the system gets affected. Further, when the change needs to replace already existing institutionalised norms, the same is to be resorted to. In other words the reorganisation of norms is another condition of change. Those who argue on this count feel that the change remains superfluous so long as the norms holding it do not find a suitable place in the target audience. Once the norm-complex provides impetus, the long term existence of change event is protected.

The behaviourist theorists of social change give priority to behaviour/relationship pattern. An addition or deletion is to be treated as change when there is some shift or modification in the basic relationship pattern. Unless that is done the comprehension of change may remain a misnomer. In this connection Firth asserted that, "structural change occurs when the alteration of procedure at last goes so far that the basic relationships between the members of society are modified" (1959 : 42). It may be mentioned that the norms and procedures are inter-connected and the relationship is an outward expression of the same. But then they may not, all the time, keep parity. And hence the procedures need a focus; the norms alone remain short of serving the purpose. In addition to norms and procedures, already hinted at, the institution is another underlying factor determining the causation of change. Unless the institution, holding a typical behaviour/relationship gets a jolt, including its revision, the change should not be said to have taken place. It is said to be the institutions that govern the overt actions. The institutional framework has wider dimensions and implications mapping thereby variety of behaviour. This specially applies to care institutions which mark every society. In this regard Lockwood (1964) suggested that a society can be viewed as having changed from one type to another if the core or dominant institutional order changes. The dominant or core institutional order may vary from one type of society to another, and the identification of such institutional orders would seem to be first and foremost a way of defining what is meant by saying that a society has changed. Since a core or dominant institution reacts to many others, a balance is to be maintained. In the absence of adjustment between various institutions the change is not acceptable in complete. Srinivas (1977) designs for more elaborate condition of change. He combines institutions, procedures or categories, norms and values. And since these areas are inseparable, his explanation appears to be more logical. According to Srinivas (1977 : 21), "social change arises only when the quantum, comprehensiveness and time-span of change are such as to induce or result in significant alterations in the social structure, the relations between categories, the institutions, norms, symbols and values associated with the older order." In other words the philosophical and psychological parameters, in addition to sociological ones, have an important place in the determination of social change. It's rather milder side that concerns the outward expressions, say practices and modes. Explanations of the latter kind have been highlighted by Harris. For Harris (1980 : 214-15), "the establishment of a new formation will require the transformation of the forms of primary practices so that they fit the new mode of assembly, a process which must be gradual, since many practices will have to continue without interruption if life is to continue. For a transition to be thorough-going it will be necessary to establish a new mode of assembly and new forms of practice."

Therefore to be sure that change has occurred, many conditions need to be fulfilled. And their range is from state of mind to the level of a practice. The implicit as well as explicit frameworks are identified. It is not merely the values and norms, which are important, but also that which is significantly obvious. The consolidation and sustenance of the latter seek support from the former, and unless that is taken care of, the occurrance of change remains a ritual, and not much of a reality acceptable to social science community. It may, however, go well with others.

To bring about change, or to make a change acceptable, there are certain conditions highlighted by the social change theorists and experts. These may not be applicable all the time and in all social situations. But their review and understanding are helpful to all those engaged in the task of causing change and in change analysis. To Arensberg and Niehoff(1965), a change will be easily acceptable when it supports the established social order. In other words the designing of change has to take stock of the existing social/cultural order. If that is ignored the element of support may not be taken care of. Since the social-cultural order is a very vast arena, some writers became more specific in their stress. For Edari (1976 : 18), "to understand how a socio-cultural system changes over time, it is necessary to isolate the system's respective culture mentality. [The configuration of elements making up the internal subjective domain is referred to by Sorokin (1937) as a "Culture mentality", or "mentality of Culture." He claims that a cultural system has two aspects : (a) the internal subjective world of "inner experiences", consisting of elements such as ideas, feelings, values and meanings and (b) the external aspects of the cultural "objects, events and processes" which represents the realization or objectification of the internal aspect]." Likewise, to Katz (1960), it is unthinkable to study diffusion without some knowledge of the social structures in which potential adopters are located. The impetus of social change, for Zaltman(1973) may have its origins inside the social system or from outside the social system. Very close to Edari's argument is one given by Kuppuswamy. Taking place of change, in view of Kuppuswamy, is connected to value system which is an integral part of mentalism. According to Kuppuswamy (19 72:20), "Any change in social structure or in social institution will take place when there is a change in social values." In terms of values and their placement in a social system, there are differing views concerning social change. Unlike Kuppuswamy and Edari the stress of Nisbet (1972) remains on the external forces while conceptualizing major changes, though such an external is again connected to the internal structure provided by value structure. On the other hand Teggart supports Nisbet while keeping his explanation of analysing major social change to conflict within the value system. In the writings of Nisbet it appears that the place of external in change causation is more important, internal arena of values gets a jolt from outside only. Nisbet (1972 : 29) stated, "I would not claim that great changes can never take place as the consequences of 'internal' forces within a social system or structure. I say only that taking the major changes of human history in the aggregate, very few of them can be understood save in terms of the impacts of external events that either create a crisis or are themselves occasioned in part by already existing crisis. Crisis is the result of conflict of values, of perception and of idea systems. Crisis is, however, the common result when a way of behaviour long taken for granted by the participants comes for the first time into sharp and perceived conflict with some other way of behaviour, and with the values embodied in that other way of behaviour." Teggart points out that, "when conflicts of values and ideas systems are sufficiently intense, when the crisis precipitated are sufficiently attention arresting, extraordinary changes are the result." Because of values and ideas forming base of continuity and change, some social theorists talk of change being uneven and partial (Cohen, 1968). It is said that the change in ideological or value frameworks does not, in toto, correspond to change in institutions supported by such frameworks. Often the institutions change but some of the values, in one form or the other, persist. These, at times, sound dysfunctional and mere cultural survivals. Beattie's assertion is that, "the changes do not proceed evenly on all fronts; often values and expectations long outlive the institutions to which they were appropriate. When this happens, old ideas about government and administration coexist, sometimes very uncomfortably, with the modern and very different ones. It is easier to make formal alterations in social and political institutions than it is to change people's ideas and values" (1964 : 244).

There are still others who seek favourable conditions, in the creation of change, in a particular section of the community. Such category of people is believed to be of early adopters, and it is they who pave way for changes in case of others too. Such explanations are based on the plea that this group of people is the repository of value and idea system. And it is on their strength that others carry them forward. In other words their dominance is unquestionable. And once they go in for something new, the others look to them for borrowing. Such a selected lot is said to exit in all the communities. Over the years, such people and their descendants become the reference group for others who otherwise form majority. Because of such a background the diffusion of innovation, among others, gets easier. These reference individuals, though in minority, behave as important centre of diffusion. But if they retaliate adversely to outside intended efforts of change, things may go the other way round. The possibility of such incidents is, however, less as such minority is keen to get recognition of outsiders by cooperating with them. They, thus, would backout only when their interest is hurt. Keeping such a background in view, Toynbee stated that "growth of civilization is due to the constant response of the creative minority, who must ever respond to new challenges as the old ones are surmounted" (Edari 1976 : 16). Likewise, Zaltman (1973) supported that a change will be accepted when it is congruent with the opinions and feelings not of the marginal but of the minority who control the society. And no population is free of such minority. Such a control may refer to social, political and economic spheres.

To some, materialism, including technology, plays an important role in the context of change. For them, value system and perception come in the second category. Even the occurrance of change, to such theorists, is measured in terms of material attainments which sound tangibles. As the ideas and values are not substantive expressions, they hardly reflect growth or development. Such material strategists again seek their base within the community, though they do not rule out the aspect of adjustment with external environment in whose adjustment their technology is devised and improved. Amongst the evolutionists, Morgan regarded technology as the key factor in social evolution. Even among the neo-evolutionists, notably Leslie White, the general assertion is that culture progresses as per its material adjustment to new requirements and challenges posed by the ecology. Within one parameter of material strategy vis-a-vis social change, Zaltman argues that, "prosperity permits change; poverty restricts the resources available for imaginative improvements; but when the situation is desperate, and collapse is imminent there may be a moment of readiness for any radical change" (1973:129). Thus, the rest of change assumes an economic form. In support of the former argument of Zaltman, La Piere (1965: 247) has stated that, "affluence can, perhaps, best be characterised as a pre-requisite to social change; for only those individuals who are free from immediate want are able to devote themselves to innovative endeavor (i.e., they must be socially subsidized in order to engage in currently unfruitful activity), and only those people who can afford to postpone current consumption in prospect of higher subsequent return are in a position to develop and adopt innovations." Change is connected to purpose. Unless the latter crop up, the human being remains idle and stereotype. To meet some newly-intended purpose, the individual and society try to usher in change, irrespective of its being represented as planned or non-directed. And such a purpose is, most of the time, economy or material based. The effort to attain a purpose seeks strength from will that an individual or group of people develops. Considering the effectivity of will and purpose Green has gone to the extent of stressing that, "social change is never independent of human will and purpose, but certain combinations of will and purpose often usher in changes that were unplanned and unwanted" (1960 : 595). The limit of environment and technology, as part of materialism, is also highlighted in social change. Such material phenomena have their own role in deciding about change, its nature and degree. In this context Beals and Hoijer (1959 : 661) said that, "changes develop slowly through the fact that each individual and generation cannot perfectly reproduce the behaviours of their parents, hence modifications and secondary developments constantly arise, although these may be within certain limits imposed by the environment and technology." The change, therefore, has two ramifications; one concerning human environment and the other non-human. But both are inseparable in the sense that change in one reflects on the other. What forms of reflection it assumes is, however, specific situation bound. In this context Maclver (1953) emphasized that every change in man's relation to his environment meant some change in his relation to his fellows. Combining social and material environment, Harris argued that the source of change lies in the relation between the concepts/tools constitutive of a practice and the consciousness which reflects the experience which is a by-product of engaging in that practice under specific conditions, changes in which arise from the activity of practioners" (1980:189).

Invention and diffusion are the two important processes of change. Evolutionary changes originate from within, except that some sudden external condition does provide impetus to the mooting of an idea or activity. Sources of diffusion are planned as well as non-directed. Intended efforts of change are a recent phenomenon among all the developing societies. Unplanned changes have been reported from the time when societies came into contact with the so called exotic people. The development of culture contact paved way to change irrespective of its being useful or harmful to the group representing subordination. The societies, exposed to alien conditions, are, thus, in the grip of two processes of change-purposed and non-purposed. But the understanding, analyses and cause of one cannot be grasped unless there is some comprehension of the other. One cannot keep the two in water-tight compartments. This is because the implication of one in the other, by and large, is reported. So much so that Zaltman (1973 : 3) has gone to the extent of telling that, "knowledge about unplanned change is of course essential to our understanding of planned change and in a special way the reverse is true in that planned change, implicitly atleast, represents a test of theories of unplanned change." Those who intend to cause change as part of guided or planned programme of change, thus, need to be in the know of structural and organisationalcomponents of unplanned change, if the same are viably reported in a community. It is then that they can plan for and give way to their superiority in the eyes of members of the recipient group. While focusing on this aspect, Zaltman (1972) pointed out that people are likely to accept a proposed change when it is introduced by people whom they consider important and competent and who have adequately consulted them or their respected leaders. And that people are likely to accept a proposed change when it appears to have advantages which can be intelligibly demonstrated in the present or which are anticipated in the future. By differentiating unplanned changes, and by keeping stock of the system's continuity, one can plan for or propose something which can come to such an expectation of the people. One should not, however, assume that change necessarily emanates from the other. It may happen but not essentially. In any case the understanding of existing changes is useful in the interest of induction of an intended change, though one may not agree with

Max Weber, in his study of rise of capitalism, that changes simply emanate from structures or from prior changes. On the other hand Nisbet (1972) seems to be reasonable when he states that changes do not breed changes; ;every change arises from a milieu. Even to Durkheim the causal bond does not exist in a series of changes. "The antecedent state does not produce the subsequent one; the relation between them is exclusively chronological" (Nisbet 1972:38). Another close argument is given by Nimkoff (1965) when he said that a factor which itself undergoes little change cannot be the cause of change in other parts of society.

Further, for understanding social change two levels of relations, that is of human action and societal form, must be established. This has been specially emphasized by Harris (1980) who chiefly concerned himself with the sociological perspective. In other words the stress remains on action, relation and network of actions. Within such a parameter of change framework, it is desired that there should be constant adaptation to human action and societal form, more so in case of human action where higher frequency of flexibility is normally anticipated. The societal forms are usually slow to change. And they require for wider adaptability. In other words the adaptability is taken as a necessary condition providing impetus to change. And that is the reason why many social scientists (Edari, Sumner etc.) argue that change is governed by the principle of enhancement of adaptive capacity. Further, the adaptability is considered more difficult in social culture than the material one. This happens because the core features of a culture are excessively hidden in social sphere than the technological one. As such the tradition of material objects and technology is generally not resisted. On the other hand the behavioural pattern does expect a resistance, and so requiring more adaptability. At the same time the adaptation capacity of younger persons is more than those who are bogged down deep into the framework of traditionality. The latter, by virtue of their being thickly involved in older order, take more time to adjust and adapt to the new pattern. This holds true at individual as well as societal levels.

Since societies are exposed to forces of change, the clash in adjustment between old and new also poses for conflict and discontentment among the people. This can happen at the individual and societal levels. Such trends are also enthused by certain built-in contradictions in social systems. And for such a background a section of social scientists have expressed, and continue to do so, that social change is built-in because of disharmony, inconsistency, tension and conflict in social system. Analysing further deep, Loubser (1976:687-692) has stated that, "when one structure is not sufficiently effective for the maintenance of the system, there will be tension and difficulties within the system. The latter will be solved only when a modified structure is organised, that is, when a new equilibrium is achieved. If the process of equilibration is prevented by some sort of structural rigidity, tensions and difficulties within the system will be further intensified. As such the intensification will be changed by nothing but the change of the structure." In other words the conflict seems to be a necessary condition for paving way to change. The subsequent intention of overcoming conflict introduces change at the perceptional and substantive levels, whatever the case be. But such an acceptance of change is usually subject to the condition that it is not in conflict with traditional beliefs and values which are held high satisfactorily. Within the above explanations, to be more precise, the rise of conflict is one condition, and its control or overcoming is another to meet the requirement of change. Some of such conflicts and subsequent effort for change are built-in, and others get favourable response from outside. Therefore, the change strategists have to bother for both to imbibe strong fillip to their intended efforts.

THREE

INDIVIDUAL VERSUS CHANGE

Though the individual, society and culture are closely linked, and many a times sounding difficult for separation, the three have conceptually been dealt separately. It is the individuals who constitute society, and it is the totality of societal ways which broadly constitute social structure and culture. The frame of ideology, propounded by a society, then, becomes operative on the individual plane. However, the ideological requirements may not be centpercent met in all the cases. But certainly the broader dimensions of behaviour, and also its control, are well laid down, and the same remain in the knowledge of the people. And these have considerable scope of prevailing upon the individuals and their behaviour and relationship. The culture and social structure purviews are the most powerful shapers of the destiny of an individual. It is in the broader interest of the latter to do so. He or she can not ordinarily afford to run away from the system. But is it essential that an individual is always guided by, and prevailed upon, by the norms and requirements of culture and society? At times it may not be so. Certain individuals do deviate from the culturally prescribed norms of behaviour. It is not always that they want to condemn or discard the system. But such a recourse is self-interest oriented, which the society otherwise does not permit to go in for. Further, the occasional non-adherence to certain norms of society, by particular individual/s can be linked to individual intensions. The self-interest has a strong relationship with the intensions of an individual. Unless the latter overpower a person, the self-interest, and subsequently the creation of courage to behave as anti-traditional, may not appear that forceful. Therefore, what kind of behaviour is to be cultivated, and when has a deep correlation with the intensions of a person. Such a psychological background of what is to be resorted to, and what not, is more of an individual phenomenon, and goes along the line of individual personality traits. The creation of particular kind of intensions at mental plane would accordingly reflect on the outward nature of behaviour and relationship. Such intricacies of the field of intensions are more or less universal of humans. No individual, irrespective of his or her socio-biological affiliation to a primitive or non-primitive group, is devoid of the pressure of intensions. However, it may somewhat vary as per the nature of sphere and scope of the ways of living of the group. Some difference in this aspect of individual may be observed in case of comparatively more closed societies than the open ones. But the universal prevalence of intensions is impossible to be ruled out. And the Indian tribal and the non-tribal rural populations are, for that matter, no exception to such a rule. Intensions being individual phenomenon, no human group can be seen in isolation of the same. The positive and negative perspectives of intensions determine the degree to which an individual subscribes to, or deviates from the laid down procedures prescribed within a societal frame. Though the pressure of traditional norms is superb, but the individual intensions are of no less potential. And the same is proved when the individual takes lead in his or her acts culminating somewhere beyond the arena of widely recognized culture-specific traditions and ways. The same may hold true in respect of the proposed innovations from outside. Inner or in-born intensions, or those caused by motivation from outside, are, in all probabilities, strong enough to make one prepared to get into even the unknown acts and activities. In normal course the possibility of rise of such a trend is weak. Hence, social change from within or outside have an intimate relation with the intensions of individuals. But causing change in intensions appears to be rather challenging.

A glance into the processes and trends of change and development in village India reveals that the least discovered and attended remains the field of intensions. As a matter of fact the later could, among a few other psychological areas, hardly be bothered, and cared for. It appears that the necessity of providing place to this element, in the context of social change sphere, was not realized. The thrust of planners and the agents of change remained somewhere else, especially on items apparently and outwardly posing as of bulky shape, say on the supply of improved seed, fertilizers, implements etc. The inside of minds of recipient group remained almost unpenetrated. Whether the new idea, tool or technology showed acceptable or unacceptable reaction could better be confirmed through the reading of mind. Observation of the latter, then, provide better tools to reformulate mental make-up. And the reformulation of this kind remains nothing short of guaranteeing the diffusion of intended innovations. The area of intensions, as an essential part of mental make-up, has, thus, a great say in the introduction of new ideas and technology. And non-tackling of this front goes against the very interest of social change and development.

No less inattentive, than the planners and change agents, have been the social scientists in respect of studying intensions. A stock of the researches conducted by the latter, in the context of social change in rural India, makes it abundantly clear that the research on intensions vis-a-vis social change have immensely lacked. That way the sociologists, social anthropologists, and even the social psychologists have not been proportionate in their research weightage. The researchers, focusing on the barriers and stimulants, where intensions occupy a prominent place, of change, too, have lacked in their due consideration of intensions. In fact, it is this part of research on social change that there should have been an adequate coverage of role of intensions in promoting or hindering social change. It appears that the coverage of the field of intensions is insufficient for lack of research tools to get over such an aspect hidden in mind. Simultaneously, a large number of social analysts do not seem to be properly oriented to reearch technology, in whatever form it has existed. In comparison to other areas, research on intensions needs special techniques and efforts. This is because the material of this sort is to be dug out from deep inside. Mere observations or questioning do not really help to throw open the reality of intensions as applied to specific programme. This specially holds true for a population as that of rural India where illiteracy and ignorance continue to have sway over favourable factors to admit studies on the delicate topic like the one of intensions. Otherwise, the area of intensions is extremely important because it is one among others which houses the root cause of change factors. We need to fast gear up research efforts in the field of intensions. However, a prerequisite to this seems the improvement in research tools and techniques for such an exercise, followed by a proper orientation of concerned researchers. Once the level of intensions is scientifically grasped, it would be easier to channelise and equip the agents of change in the light of defined objective.Easier, then, will be the making of adjustment with people's requirements and expectations in the light of old and new.

In close collusion with intensions are certain other fields prevailing upon an individual. But at the same time a few of them are difficult to be seen in isolation of intension. In such other areas of individual concern, the individual psychology again plays an important role. Though these traits seem to be of individual concern, they have, like the intensions, a great relevance with the community and its requirements on the one hand and the arena of social change and development on the other. Such traits, to be discussed in the lines that follow, apparently sound too mild and minor but have, otherwise, a strong hold on the individual and his behaviour. Such traits which are partly in-born and partly cultivated by the individual direct him or her to the acceptance or rejection of innovations. At the same time these are like the personal possessions which an individual does not easily afford to partwith. However, the emergence of certain situations can, at times, give them a shake, and if necessary may transplant some new ones replacing the old. And then the elements like ambition and determination also influence them from time to time, leading thereby to their substantialization or decrease. But irrespective of form, these continue to be part and parcel of the life of every human being. Among others, these traits, like the intensions, are the 'will' and 'purpose'. As already stated, no human being is free of them. And when this is so, the change, too, cannot be taken as independent of such traits. Instead, the human will and purpose considerably exert on the decision-making of a person for or against a new thing, idea or object. At the same time the personal will and purpose are inter-linked to the communty's socio-physical environments. Many a times the latter have their influence on the shaping of former. This is also true that the commonness or nearness of will and purpose makes the individuals unite, cooperate and think on similar lines, ultimately giving way to community reaction. Such a reciprocal reaction of community and the will and purpose of the individuals thereof can be said to have a significant indication whether an element of change is feasible in the community's living. It also holds true for the other way round trend, that is, the non-feasibility. Environment, too, plays an important role in the emergence of a specific nature of purpose, and subsequently of will. This, at times, happens inspite of will and purpose being individual phenomena. However, the environments may not have that significant a place.

Those responsible for actually bringing about change have, somehow, not given the desired attention to the importance of will and purpose in the context of purposed change and planned development. Matters concerning broader dimensions of the community, rather than those concerning individual, were kept at the forefront. Even the list of priority could hardly provide place to elements like will and purpose, treating them as minor. Even the policies and approaches, as enunciated and used by those shouldering the task of causing change and development remained short of recognizing and respecting such individual psychological traits. They acted above them, without reacting to the root level forces attributing to status-quo patterns. It seems obvious that the policies, programmes as well as their carriers were perpetually dominated by the assumption that individual psychology is not that important in the issue of social change. Or, it may be that they could not afford to wait to search for hidden psychological traits, the step which may have delayed what the, so called, experts impatiently took up to elevate the socio-economic condition of rural masses. Set aside was the factor of patience. It was done in favour of haste to carry ideas, tools, technology and other provisions to rural population, assuming that they are badly needed, and that their acceptance, and the subsequent transformation of society, are definite. Such a feeling failed to focus on the existing constraints, and even on those that could arise in the process of change. Least cared for, in this sphere, were, probably, the elements of will and purpose. Continued massive material provision, which remained the target almost all through, was also the reason ignoring psychology of person in the event of change.

The concentration of social researchers, too, chiefly has been governed by the existing or ongoing policies, programmes and approaches. What actually happened in the purview of social change has widely been traversed by the concerned social researchers in rural India. The areas covered start from planning to the implementation stages, as also the results, in terms of impact, of various kinds of programmes including agriculture, health, education, cooperation, animal husbandry, industries, communication etc. The research scope, therefore, confined to, and continues to do so, to the aspects highlighted by the planners, policy-makers and implementors. The least researched areas are those not taken note of by the agents of change, say the one connected to the field of will and purpose. By and large, the social research findings, in respect of social change, do not provide coverage and place to such elements. Otherwise, for academic sociologists, social anthropologists or psychologists, such ventures are of prime importance and value. And of the secondary concern is to find out how much percent of the people adopted an innovation. It may not be difficult even for a person who is untrained in social research technique, but otherwise educated, to give a stock of percentages and frequencies to explain the degree of impact of change efforts. To show how many people, say in a village, are literate and upto what standard, to show the impact of formal education, does not really require and involve a strong sociological insight. But the latter is a prerequisite when one is keen to search for explanation involving 'how' and 'why' of such occurrences or non-occurrences. And a still deeper exercise, which the social scientists are expected to make, is to get into the socio-psychological and economic elements supporting the explaining of 'why.' It is in academic hunt of this kind that the spheres like the will and purpose can be dealt with in their context to social change. Coming from this level to the level of percentages and frequencies will not only be more scientific approach, but better socio-psychologically established claim. Aids, used in the field of psychology, need to be adequately understood and put to practical use. Exploring such a hidden nexus, in the interest of assessing and guiding social change, is certainly a better and more useful contribution of social scientists than the mere exposition of elementary and fringe areas as part of their researches. At the same time the results of researches, with a deeper insight, would be more convincing and helpful to the planners, administrators and other change agents who may not, otherwise, import seriousness in the consideration of social research findings and their relevance to programmes of change. In the introduction of social change, at practical level, another requirement is to properly lay out and establish the connection of individual traits, like will and purpose, to the broader view-point of community around. Where, and in what way, they submerge, strengthening or weakening the particular ways, are to be broadly delineated and passed on for due recognition of those engaged in the gigantic task of socio-economic transformation.

In the psychological complex of any normal human being, there are certain other elements which have a bearing to the already dealt traits of purpose, will and intensions. As an intended purpose promotes specific kind of intensions, and the will behind to achieve the same, the desire for which one does not possess gives way to purpose to attain or achieve the same. And very closely connected to what one does not possess is the curiosity to know the unknown. A person's curiosity to what he or she does not know is almost an established fact. The element of curiosity and the desire to possess are the vital traits of an individual's personality. As such, no group of human beings, irrespective of their high or low state of socio-economic and technological living, is to be seen in isolation of these psychological traits when analysed in the background of change and development. But it is true that among the more primitive social isolates, the desire to possess and the man's curiosity to know are less and limited in comparison to advanced and complex societies where the social and physical climate are more conducive to encourage the same. The basic potential exists in both the population situations, but the chances of its exploitation in primitive, homogeneous and isolated population seem less. It is just the opposite in case of literate, complex and acculturated communities. The culture contact provides scope to enrich one's knowledge about things which have earlier been unknown. The same applies to the phenomenon of acquisition and possession. But how far the two materialize docs largely depend upon the motivation of native potential. The outer agencies may have a vital role to play in activating the inherent as well as the acquired potentialities. What we carry, in terms of ideas and commodities, from outside as part of the programme of social change are to be appropriately connected to man's curiosity and the allied mental faculty for its acquisition. But such a task is not that simple as it apparently sounds. The most stupendous task is to take stock of curiosity, and feeling to possess. Will it be possible to do so with the existing staff of change agents and the training they have? It may not be easily possible. Neither it may be proper to hand over such a task to change agents at field or higher level. As it requires a specialized knowledge and skill, the persons trained in psychological techniques can deliver the goods better. If somehow their direct involvement is not possible, provision, for the use, through training, of their tools and techniques sounds unavoidable in the interest of change. As an agent of change is made familiar with, say, improved agriculture practices, he can also be equipped to read for psychological leaning in respect of change which is to be brought about in the target population. Creation of aids to increase the curiosity for new, and to develop the feeling to acquire what one does not possess would certainly be backing change programme. Simultaneously, however, what is feasible, looking to the nature and capacity of individuals and the community to which they belong, and what is unwanted are not to be lost sight of. To venture for something too above the expectation is an unwise inclination. Therefore, the psychological traits, under reference, have a bearing to the existing socio- economic conditions of the people. It may go against the procedural ethics of change programme if a helicopter is taken to be used by the members of a food-gathering community. There should not be too much of dichotomy between perceptional capacity and an item of change. However, a gradual disturbance in parity is understandable, as also advisable.

A review of what was designed to be introduced in rural India indicates that there has been part parity and part imbalance between grasping capacity on the one hand and items of change on the other. Efforts to introduce things were, many a times, made even when the socio-economic and psychological carrying capacity of goal group were not approving it. But other times the two went hand in hand, creating favourable chance for change acceptance. Change got a set-back in the event of a situation of wide imbalance. The change trend gets a further fillip when one's curiosity and sense of possession receive impetus. But the provision of such an impetus has been ill-attended and weak.

When one gets into the arena of socio-psychological researches vis-a-vis change, the picture is, again not encouraging. Experiments, and subsequently researches, concerning the role, place and utility of elements like 'curiosity' and 'desire' in the context of a programme of social change badly lacked. Only a very limited account of such sporadic exercises is seen in the pages of reports or books dealing with applied psychology. At times, there is comparatively more mention, but that is more of a general account than the one of change-specific. As far as individual's position, in the change context, is concerned, keeping in view curiosity and desire, lot remains to be done. Even among the factors explaining why certain change failed to be accepted by a group of individuals, one hardly finds adequate coverage of factors like curiosity and desire. The same holds true when applied to the factors giving an account of stimulants to change. More of the research coverage, of the barriers and stimulants to change, is in terms of socio-economic perspective than the psychological one. Likewise, the place and role of physical environments or external ecology, in respect of change, are better covered through social researches. Simultaneously, the stress, in research, also remained on the weakness of human agency carrying the programme of change. This has been in addition to the research postmortem of the nature of schemes and programmes themselves. Hundreds of research works are available throwing light on man's outer sphere of involvement, including natural objects and phenomena, but it is just the opposite in case of treatment of man's internal pursuits and their assessment. The impression and reaction of many, holding high positions in bureaucracy or in political hierarchy, is that India cannot afford to spend on the luxury of research, more so of the social and especially of psychological nature. They do bother to care for tall claims, but quietly backout when the point of subscribing to socio-psychological research is brought forth. The interest in the latter is given up announcing that it is more of a luxury looking to Indian economic situation. This is done without realizing that such a research provides scope for better and early acceptance of change. On the other hand the social scientists try to fully exert on the issue. How far they are listened to is anybody's guess. It lacks compromise, though there is sufficient room for it. Whatever it be, the psychological research findings have a significant place in creating and guiding change. This is specially true for village India where elements like curiosity, desire, intension, will, purpose etc., are deeply bogged in hard-boiled traditions, more sharply imposed by religious attributes. And it is no less a difficult job to get into such a nexus in the interest of causing change. The suggestions emanating from socio psychological research findings, then, need to be put to practical use. To practical sociologists and psychologists, it may remain meaningless unless the research results are put to use. They should see that it is done; they cannot escape by the mere saying that part of the job lies somewhere else. Mere throwing the ball to somebody's court, without concern, is nothing short of being unjust to the society and its development. One has to exert.

The individual is again prevailed upon by a few more elements having root in human psychology. No human personality is devoid of such traits. The prevalence, intensity and force of these elements are largely governed and conditioned by the background of the person, including the nature of environment and other opportunities he or she lives in. How much one can afford to get away from, or to get in such traits, inseparable from personality, is again decided by a few other relevant factors in and outside the personality. Many a times the operation of a trait, independent of other/s, sounds almost an impossibility when analysed in the context of practical living styles. The individual's existence and the surrounding human and non-human climate are ultimately connected. The community, to which the person belongs, the neighbouring social formation and the environmental provisions help one determine and decide for a specific course of action, many a times backed by one or the other psychological attribute.

In determining and directing one's course of action, the sense of insecurity and risk have a vital role to play. Also, a closely connected element is that of frustration which follows when one gets suffocated under the pressure of insecurity and risk, and is, thus, not in a position to try what one ordinarily is keen to do. The reluctance, born of fear of insecurity and risk, pulls back the person leading to the state of frustration. The feeling of insecurity and risk are not independent in themselves, though they are, otherwise, in-born among the individuals. Why one feels insecured and risk-scared can be attributed to the nature of socio-economic living, cultural constraints, community pressure, fear of alien and personal inclinations. Those who are socio-economically weak, and under more cultural impositions and community pressure, are less exposed to alien world and its ways. With their low inclination, they may remain bogged down to traditional living. The elements of modernity, or the ways and things beyond what they have, may not easily be accepted by them even if they seem appealing. The people of this category essentially look for security and usually keep away from doing experiments and exercises where they smell risk. Many a times they withdraw from trying something unkn own, thinking that any insecurity or risk would personally be unbearable to them. But other times, it is the cultural and community pressure which does not allow the individuals to come out of their defined cells. And this happens even under the circumstances where the official laws, promulgated by the state, are a support to the new. Therefore, sense of insecurity and feeling of risk, as experienced by an individual, find feet not only in his or her personality or the level of his socio-economic living, but also in the community and its culture. Equally countable is the alien situation to which the individuals are exposed. But that does not undermine the importance of sense of insecurity and risk, as cultivated by an individual, while viewing at new ideas or technology as items of change. So long as the feeling of insecurity and sense of risk dominate the individuals, there is every likelihood of poor response to innovations. Diffusion of change is, thus, likely to be hampered. On the other hand, the eradication of feeling of insecurity and risk would help back the causation of change. But for inclusion of security and eradication of sense of risk, one has to have a broader review of certain aspects, as mentioned earlier, connected to these elements of personality. For material change, the change agents can get over these psychological barriers through convincing demonstrations. But for non-material change the solution is to be found out from within than from outside. It is the barrier of reluctance which is to be broken in the interest of change and development.

In village India, the two massive programmes of change, after Indian independence, have been those of Community Development and Tribal Development. Time and again they assumed various forms including integrated development, rural reconstruction etc. While scaning through the approach, methodology, man-power, institutional network and other modes of working of these programmes at field level, it becomes abundantly clear that the coverage to minimize sense of insecurity and element of risk, as ingrained in an individual's mind, was of the least order. The programme implementors did manage for grant-in-aid, subsidy, free supply of certain kinds of input and other material. But was it all sufficient? No, because all this remained limited in terms of its bulk, and in terms of coverage of population. Secondly, it never remained as something regular. Likewise, it could not convince people at the state of mind, getting rid off their feeling of risk and insecurity.

More, in the latter stream, were the small and marginal farmers, and a large population of socio-economically weak, who generally continued to be reluctant for fear of risk and insecurity. It was a small section of upper strata of Indian village community who could alone be instilled with sense of security and a risk-free feeling. Rest of the community sailed as their forefathers did. The assumption that the mere creation of facilities and opportunities would make the villagers jump at them is not always correct. To judge it correctly one is to get at what is inside the mind. Feeling of insecurity and risk may not always be overtly expressed and observed. But people, with this background, do try to withdraw themselves from most of the new ideas and exercises.

The position of research on the front of insecurity and risk, in the context of change, is sufficiently clear. In the field of agriculture and other innovations, the social scientists have carried out studies at various places, and in different ethnic groups. In many a cases the elements of risk and insecurity, as expressed by the informants from the recipient population, were identified as barriers to change. But in most of such studies, the economic constraints and impositions have been dealt as the chief source housing risk and insecurity. The nature of economy, and its hardships and limitations are correlated with people's expression of risk and insecurity. The villagers get reluctant to try for something new for the fear that it may not give the intended returns. And if it happens so, their economic life would subsequently be paralysed. Most of them cannot afford to undergo loss even once, because they face extreme scarcity in terms of alternative to the same. But is it economy alone where risk and insecurity prevail? This may not always be true. In many a cases the prevailing social and cultural climate is no less responsible in encouraging the feeling of insecurity and risk. This is, infact, the front which continues to be far less explored by the social researchers. The social research ought to have also concentrated on the social and cultural factors contributing to the existence as well as persistence of feelings of insecurity and risk in an individual's life; more so when the same are analysed in the light of proposed changes, and the otherwise changing conditions. Simultaneously it does sound illogical to treat economy, social organization and other cultural traits as independent of, and isolated from one another. And adequate coverage of the feelings and expressions of insecurity and risk goes in favour of change agents who can adjust their venture accordingly. They do, however, continue to operate in their own style in the absence of such explanations. The non-availability of valid explanations, in respect of insecurity and risk, makes them work in the usual style where they often get confronted with failure. It is there that they fail to feel the pulse of people, who, many a times, do not oppose an innovation; but at the same time remain indifferent to the same. When it comes too much on their heads, they quietly backout, making excuses of various kinds, some of which do not, really, have relevance to what one cares to do. The diagnosis of such implications can be best done by social scientists and their technology. The same is far beyond the reach of change agents themselves.

Another aspect of relevance concerns the factor of constraint on intellectual morality. The latter has lot of bearing to the arena of individual vis-a-vis social-cultural change. The social-cultural progress through individuals, and the associated intellectual morality thereof, is an aspect of deep concern. The trait of intellectual morality sounds more of a subject of abstract nature. It may, ordinarily, be hard to measure the dimensions of intellectual morality, more so when levels of ways of living differ so widely as characterized by the masses of rural India. The strata of society in village India range from food-gatherers and hunters to trappers, beggars, musicians, artisans, horticulturists, shifting cultivators, herders, agriculturists, traders, priests etc. A wide social categorization is of Scheduled Tribes, Scheduled Castes, Backward Classes, upper and twice-born castes etc. It may not be true to say that the formation of such categories is intellectual morality-based. But at the same time it cannot be said that the members of such categories are free of the difference in intellectual morality. In many instances such a difference is explained through folklores, folk-tales and locally prevalent proverbs and sayings. Specific class of people are differentiated on the scope of intellectual attainment and the linked morality. So much so that these expressions, in the eyes of native inhabitants, have assumed the forms of accepted facts. It may, however, be wrong to assume that all members, of a specific caste or class, cling centpercent to a common scale vaguely defined through local beliefs and traditions. There may be some, in a group of people, who are conspicuously marked as exceptions. And the same is, in general, recognised by the members of the group, and many a times, and on certain occasions, by the people of other groups around. In terms of intellectual morality, they, thus, do not subscribe to the class or category to which they otherwise belong. But the presence of intellectual morality is universal, irrespective of its levels. The specific way of living, the socio-economic climate, other opportunities, and the mental capacity of individuals have say in intellectual stratification. The world-view of food -gatherers and food-producers does differ. And where does the intellectual morality stand needs to be judged by the environments where an individual lives in. A man who has to hunt or trap the birds and animals to survive cannot, under those environments, get at what Eienstein could. His intellectual attainment and morality level are to be assessed, and defined, in the context of environments where he is sandwitched. It is there that he strictly maintains his intellectual morality, and remains careful of the same. Every individual is careful of the retention of such a character, and avoids anything that comes in its way. Imposing constraint on intellectual morality of a person or group may be intolerable, and is sharply reacted to and it is in the course and processes of change that the threat of such constraints may take lead. The native system, on the otherhand, normally remains silent. When the pressure of constraint on intellectual morality increases, the persons, and their group, may even revolt against the new ideas and innovations. But if the constraints can wisely be taken care of, the antagonism may subside, and the change agent can get the work done comparatively easier.

Among the most ignored areas by the agents of change, including the planners and administrators, is one of intellectual morality. The details meant to provide design for the socio-economic and cultural progress and transformation of rural India, provide no room for consideration of constraints or stimulants to the trait of intellectual morality. In general, the programmes of change stress less on individual than the group, village or community. And even while stressing' on the individual, the psycho-philosophical dimensions, more so the one like intellectual morality, do hardly form areas of concern. Material culture and change in it continue to be observed as area of great concern. This was followed, as the trends continue to indicate, by the concerns in social culture. One hardly finds mention of areas of concerns having root in mental or abstract culture. It all happened, probably, because of a widely prevalent assumption, of those responsible for creating change, that the socio-economic and techno-economic perspectives alone hold the fort of the community. That means the ideological and psychological aspects of the individual and community could not invite attention of the kind necessary to back change. One has not to forget that the ideological shifts stand guarantee of sustenance and perpetuation of change elements, once they are adopted. On the other hand, the old ideas, and the contribution of psycho-ideological traits to them, does provide scope to status-quo.

In comparison to certain other socio-psychological traits, the social scientists and their researches almost failed to take note of the necessity of carrying out researches in the sphere of intellectual morality. The stock of socio-psychological and other researches, in the context of social change in village India, makes it sufficiently clear that the research concerning the level of intellectual morality did not come up. To get into the research nexus concerning constraint on intellectual morality remained still a far cry. Under the circumstances, it could not be known what place the various levels of intellectual morality will have in the broader interest of continuity as well as change of various kind in society. How is the intellectual morality kept up, in what style does it operate and how people react in the event of impact on it are some of the vital issues from research point of view. It is likely that the resistance to change, which does not easily find satisfactory explanation in other aspects of living, may be linked to the sphere of intellectual morality of individual or the group of people. And the same may not be independent of certain socio-cultural requirements of the community. Thus, the element of intellectual morality is quite a sensitive dimension concerning individual as well as the community. When the innovations impinge, threatening its conception and reality, on such morality, the individuals are bound to retaliate for rejection. The socio-psychological researches have not, largely, given account of such state of affairs. The research and evaluation organizations undertook variety of researches but not, in general, one of the above kind. Among others, one difficulty would have been to assess and measure such a field of social enquiry. In comparison to others, it is difficult to be extracted for its essentially abstract and hidden nature. It might have also been assumed by the social analysts, and others concerned with social dynamics, that such research ventures may be taken up at later stage, if it is deemed necessary. At initial stage, the realization did not develop, most likely for the reason for its sounding more a philosophical arena, where the practical requirements might not have been met. But the fact is that the researches on the constraint of intellectual morality have an important place, and are not to be lost sight of for reviewing status-quo and change implications. The development of intellectual morality goes in support of diffusion of change.

Quite close to the constraint on intellectual morality is the element of personal freedom. The latter is an aspect which is governed by a number of factors, including one of intellectual morality. The feeling of personal freedom is inherent in every human being. It may, however, not be proportionate; one may realize for it more forcefully than the other. It is also likely to vary in accordance with age-grades to which the individuals belong. Even the sex, too, seems difficult to be isolated in such a calculation. Among other factors, contributing to it, can be included the family and the other immediate environments. In addition to the in-born feeling, for freedom, in an individual's personality, the forms, modes and contents of socialization, both informal and formal, have a sufficient role to play. At times, the rise of particular kind of situation, adding to rapid awakening of individual faculties for freedom are also held responsible. Likewise, on many occasions, the growth of culture contact does create conditions favourable to realization of freedom of self. Thus, the feeling and motive for personal freedom are not only something in-built in an individual personality, but they are also linked to the community and its socio-cultural climate. What one expresses and acquires, as part of personal freedom, is a cullective exposition born of the pressure of variety of forces; some of these are of local character, and the others bear an alien touch. Simultaneously, the 'closed' or the 'open' nature of social systems seem to have a close bearing to personal freedom. In closed social isolates, the individual freedom is usually constrained by a number of impositions. But the general freedom, for certain specific traits, is, in many groups, of wide magnitude. And in this case, the people are said to have a great deal of personal freedom. But then the agencies of socio-political control are the strongest, in terms of function and effectivity, the latter curb the personal freedom to a very large extent, creating thereby an urge where one feels more for group than the self. Group interests are to be protected, bothered and respected at the cost of personal freedom. This is done in the absence of viable alternatives to fall back upon. One is for group, and the group's culture is extremely dominant in almost all walks of individual's life. The scope and means for personal freedom, thus, get curtailed. On the other hand in complex societies, far more open to alien contact and influence, an individual's scope to go in for personal freedom is more. The openness of the group's social system arranges for a good deal of permissibility. One has alternatives to go in for. Even the force and pressure of traditions considerably subside, providing room for personal freedom. At the same time there is more availability of choice. It does not, however, support the view that the societies with open systems have no constraints. There are many of them, but people can afford to by pass some of them without inviting community's criticism. In what has been said above, it appears that the individual, his personal freedom the nature of prevailing social system and the surrounding alien social climate form a vicious circle.

When the connections of the element of personal freedom are so wide, it cannot be kept aloof of the arena of social change and social dynamics. As a matter of fact the position of personal freedom in the context of change is an important one. It may not always be feasible to realize personal freedom and change simultaneously. In the interest of certain innovations, the two may not go hand-in-hand. It is likely that some curb on the personal freedom comes in alongwith a particular event of change, and without the same the introduction of change element remains almost an impossibility. But in other cases the protection of personal freedom is possible even with the induction of change element. This would depend on the nature of change and the meaning of personal freedom involved. Under such possibilities, it becomes rather essential to make a correct assessment of the concept of personal freedom, alongwith its dimensions, and of the nature and forms of change proposed to be introduced. Such an approach is most likely to demarcate the areas of compromise, as also those of incompatibility. And it is for the latter that a proper care is to be taken to get into some model of equilibrium. This, it is presumed, is to be governed by the understanding of the agents of change.

The nature, form, course and direction of change and development programmes in Indian context make it clear that the least considered has remained the element of personal freedom. Theoretically, personal freedom and individual liberty have been guaranteed to all citizens, irrespective of religion, caste, creed etc. And no one, including the state, is expected to intervene in, and encroach upon certain rights of an individual. But simultaneous to this is the strong slogan of social and economic development through the planned programmes of change. Now keeping in view the efforts for social and economic transformation of society, one will have to see whether the areas, like the one of personal freedom, are keeping tune with the exercise done by the exponent of change. Or, they go contrary to the theoretical prescriptions. In certain cases, there is scope for clash; on others there may be compromise avoiding confrontation,that is, where personal freedom and change may go together uninterrupted. But the attention to such issues has not been attracted. Although, the stress remained on the programmes and schemes of socio-economic transformation, rather than on the curtailment or non-curtailment of personal freedom thereof. Probably it hardly occurred, in the minds of those engaged in the massive task of rural reconstruction, that the element of personal freedom occupies an important place in the realm of social change.

Almost the same, as above, has been repeated in the area of social research. By and large the social scientists went, in their researches, as per the policies, programmes and schemes of the government. They have made many efforts to analyse the social system and culture of target population where the changes are being introduced. The relevance of social and cultural factors to social change has been highlighted. They have, many a times, strongly recommended, taking stock of certain social and cultural elements, that change is not independent of native population and their way of living. But even the social scientists and their researches did not focus, in tune with the requirements given in the earlier paragraphs, on the place of personal freedom vis-a-vis social change. And as such they could not really demarcate areas and population groups where personal freedom and change could be realized simultaneously, or there is no need, at all, of such a realization. The explanation holds true to research studies in tribal as well as the non-tribal areas of country side. Even the foreign scholars remained far short of doing justice in this aspect of social research. It is realized, more so under the growing clouds of change and transformation, that the element of personal freedom, and its place and role in change context, has its own importance. However, the same remains to be empirically discovered at micro as well as macro level. And it is through conducting social research that such an insight can be made. The quality and level of personal freedom, and how people conceive it, what happens when it is curbed or suppressed or ignored, what is appreciated when it is protected even in the instance of change, how best can it be adjusted with the proposed innovations, how does it pose barrier to change in general or of specific kind, what can be done to convert personal freedom into a stimulant to change, are some of the issues to be scientifically explored, analysed and resolved. It is essentially the social scientists who are capable of doing this job. Looking to the vast heterogeneity of population, one has to go in for representative pockets. Applied researches of this kind, which have not been much cared before, need to be taken up on priority basis to establish an added claim of necessity of social science in the programme of socio-economic progress and transformation.

Looking to the psychological traits which chiefly remain at mental plane of a person, it becomes unavoidable, in the interest of change, to search for something hidden. In fact it is in the latter form that the real laws, conducting outer attitude and behaviour, find feet. And the world as-a-matter-of-fact is simply an outward expression controlled and guided, consciously or unconsciously, by the laws operating upon the mental processes. Therefore, what is inside the mind of a man, and what one intends to carry out are closely connected. In other words, intended things may take shape when the mind allows for the same. That means the chances of change acceptance are bright when there is 'inner' shift of individual. In the absence of causing inner shift, the flow of new ideas, things and technology and their acceptance sound more as superfluous. In such an event, people may revert back to the original or traditional things at any moment. They simply carry out new experiments in the state of uncertainty, and out of the relationship of respect with the agents of change. But many a times they do not mean to accept them. It has practically happened in a large number of cases that the ideas or things once adopted by a person or group were subsequently dropped, not for better but for the original and traditional ones. This specially happened in caste society of village India in respect of the programmes like fishery, poultry, piggery etc. Same applies to certain other items which a group of people once adopted but gave it up at a subsequent stage. Why did it happen can be attributed, among certain other things, to the ignorance, in respect of making inner shift, of the change causing machinery. The villagers were simply persuaded outwardly. It is also true that the inner shift of an individual is linked to so many social and cultural factors whose guiding machinery originates from the laws of social system or social structure. The concise and abstract forms of laws chiefly reside inside the mind and, thus, form core of the 'inner' self. In majority of cases, it is this nexus which remains unexploited and unchannelised as per the needs and requirements of new programmes. Individuals in no society, primitive, advanced or advancing, are free of this inner self. At the same time every culture or social structure has a bearing to such nexus of individuals. And some variation in the maintenance of inner is also possible depending upon the individual capacity, and certain other conditions impinging on self. Under these circumstances the assessment of inner is itself a difficult job. One has to take account of so many things to be partly sure of one's perception, of someone's inner ideas, desires and inclinations. The understanding of inner, and the causing of inner shift would, thus, require an insight into various aspects of individual, group and its culture. But the understanding of inner self and the desired shift in the same are, otherwise, of paramount importance. Inner shift does stand guarantee for corresponding shift in man's behaviour, including the development of pro-change outlook.

The extension agencies, meant to promote change in rural masses of India, gave only an inadequate coverage in terms of their efforts to cause inner shift of individual. Adult education, social education and non-formal education aimed at causing awareness among people. They devoted to educating villagers for various items of change. The idea was to inculcate the new by making people mentally prepared for it. A massive infrastructure, to carry out this task, was built with a very wide coverage. The underlying idea was to mobilize the adult village population for purposed development. The programmes of overall development were to seek support of social educators. But what really happened to the social education or adult education programmes is well known to social analysts, and even to others who were directly or indirectly connected to it. The programme, by and large, stressed on the learning of alphabets.

Even there too, no substantial progress could be made. The Social Education Organizers, the Mukhya Sewikas and others associated with social education programme almost failed to deliver what was expected of them. The other programmes of socio-economic change were not enthused and assisted in the way the same were designed. In majority of cases the mental frame, in respect of their ways of living, of villagers persisted as before. As such the inherent purpose of social education got defeated, causing damage to other aspects of development. In fact, it was through the agencies and efforts of social education that the inner shift of the individual was to be taken care of. No other agency could do it better. What the social educators could propagate did not filter down deep into the minds of people. It only continued to touch the surface and the material thereof. Even the formal education, imparted through schools in rural areas, remained far short of serving the purpose of change and development. Most of those who got educated almost withdrew themselves from their own society. They were so alienated that the community could derive the least benefit of their new awareness and understanding. To sustain change, for better, and to promote it further the role of formally and nonformally educated ones is of paramount importance. It is to be seen that they are channelised in a way which can extend maximum impetus to change. Such a channelisation need not always be uniform for all the communities. It is the community background which will also have say in this matter.

The researchers belonging to the field of psychology, sociology and social anthropology have carried out a number of research studies, of their respective interest, in the tribal as well as caste India. In addition to special studies on social change and development, even the other works do discuss, though with comparatively less stress, of the implications of change. Even the village studies and tribal ethnographies do contain portion, at times a special chapter, dealing with change and its repercussions. Most of the research accounts on change, whether exclusively devoted to this aspect or forming a part of a text stressing somewhere else, have gone silent on the element of inner shift. There is almost silence on the place and role of inner feelings, in the arena of change, and the shifts to which these have undergone. More highlighted is the account of what has been adopted by the individuals and the community, more so in the material forms. Mentions have also been made of reactions of such adoption to the social life of the people. But what reaction has it caused to the inner feelings is either missing, or gets only an inadequate coverage, though the element otherwise is of a great significance. The explanation of change, given by the social scientists, stays only half done so long as a scientific assessment of the inner shift is not made. And individual or a group of individuals is most likely to discontinue with a change item which does not seek root in the 'inner' frame. Else, its adoption continues to be superfluous. Therefore, to explain that a change item has been finally accepted, one is to discover its place in the inner feelings, and the possible inner shift which such an element has caused. Accepting change at mind level and its outside display are almost inseparable when one speaks that a change has been accepted. Unfortunately, these are the fronts which have excessively escaped the attention of social researchers. And taking up of such areas of research is highly essential to make a scientific and correct assessment of change, as also to provide scope for rightly channelising the agents of change for better results. Ignoring of such researches will, many a time, continue to give way to misleading statements, which sound unjust expressions.

Another very vital area of concern to the individual, when he or she is connected to the sphere of social change, is one connected to enterpreneurship. The nature of entrepreneurial character can, to a large degree, determine the level of involvement of a person in the processes and end- products of change. Less of it is detrimental to the cause of change. And conversely, the more of it is conducive to encourage change. The better quality of entrepreneurship is most desired in the context of gearing up the diffusion of innovations. It does help create change of a desired order. Its absence might also lead to constant reluctance and opposition. The quality of entrepreneurship, like a few other elements associated with an individual, is both in-born as well as acquired. One has this potential as inherent; and also one can develop it depending upon the availability of opportunities connected to such a character. The relevant training and coaching can help develop this potential in the direction to make a new idea or item acceptable to the members of target population. Reviewing the attitude of a person one can be, through training and coaching, equipped to take up an enterprise. In normal course one may resist or go far more slow for the same thing. Taking up of an enterprise, at individual level, is almost directly proportionate to the entrepreneurial capacity of the person. Other factors, however, are not to be completely ruled out. By and large the entrepreneurship hints at the organizational and managerial capacity of a person for some kind of undertaking, more of a commercial type. A skilled entrepreneur will, thus be able to deliver better goods than an unskilled one. And the skill to organize and manage can be made to develop through various ways. Even in the context of change, an appropriate technology, to improve upon the skill, is not difficult to be devised as per the schemes and programmes of development. Among the other factors that are closely connected to entrepreneurship are courage and willingness. One has to be willing and courageous to be an entrepreneur. Will-power and courage are the traits which are basically in-born in an individual's personality. But this does not mean that there is no room for their improvement through external means. Various kinds of motivation, as relevant to intended areas of change, are helpful in this matter. Now it depends upon the sharpness of innovator's tools as to how far deep he can go. His effectivity is directly linked to the enriching of courage and willingness. Characters of courage and willingness mark every section of humanity. But whether the two go always together and maintain parity is somewhat doubtful. A majority of the members of tribal communities, especially those living in hills and forests, appear to be far more courageous but they do seem to lack willingness for the adoption of new. In fact the tribals in village India have lacked far behind as regards the adoption of new practice and ways. On the other hand some of the caste groups appear to be less courageous than the tribals, but they have shown more willingness for new ideas and innovations. It is true that the motivation, through contact with outsiders, has been more in case of castes than the tribes. Given an equal opportunity, the tribals also may get into the change process with a faster pace. The community impositions and constraints, in various walks of life, are also the determining factors for courage and willingness. How the individuals are burdened with such restrictions has its own reflection in the sphere of courage and willingness, and hence in the entrepreneurship. How a community provides fillip to entrepreneurial nature, and how do its rules and requirements curtail it are some of the vital issues in understanding and directing the change and development. Therefore, to take up a new enterprise and to develop the managerial and organizational skills, the community atmosphere has its own place. The same applies to the creation of willingness to adopt the new. The courage is more of individual built-in.

For the creation of change and its implications, the entrepreneurship and its constituent elements could not be properly attended to. Even the identification of entrepreneurs was not done the way it should have been. In many a cases, certain innovations were proposed which did not tally with the nature of entrepreneur's taste and inclinations. At the same time, efforts to develop the necessary courage and will mountingly lacked. Even the provision of training to develop the managerial and organisational skill of individuals continues to be inadequate. Many a times, the prerequisites, needed for an item involving entrepreneurship, are not metwith chiefly for administrative bottlenecks. In hundreds of cases, the technical devices, meant to make use of an innovation did not reach to the villagers in time. Even out of those which were made available, so many did not work for the reason of technical defects. Among the tools and implements which were made available to the people, especially to artisans, craftmen and farmers, a large number went out of order. In most of the cases, these could not be repaired for want of repairing facilities in interior areas. It specially happened in case of agriculture implements and equipments. Such a trend adversely reflected on entrepreneurship. The same was done in case of certain other proposed innovations which were not needed in certain pockets of people. People had no attraction for them. Items with imposition background did not find favour with the masses. This, however, does not mean that the innovations were not at all accepted by the people. Rather, many of them found feet, especially those which matched with the quality of entrepreneurs. But the rejection of others can be, among other factors, attributed to the lack of entrepreneurial capability. The existence of latter, among individuals, has been as per the ways prevalent in the caste, village community and society to which they belong. As the old items and ways are to be replaced by the new ones, the corresponding entrepreneurship had to be developed. The old one, for various reservations, considerably failed to carry on the new additions. Ignoring of impetus to entrepreneurship, simultaneous to the proposing of change items, is unwanted in the interest of change. Taking care of one side alone does not serve all the purpose.

As the planners and agents of change considerably ignored, at practical level, the aspect of entrepreneurship, the same trend then correspondingly reflected in the research studies. The other aspects, which were kept at the forefront by the planners, administrators and agents of change were also taken up in research priority. These were analysed as per the individual, caste, village community and the still broader social groupings. Not all the aspects have been covered but whichever were taken went the same way. Among other areas of research, to which the social scientists could not provide an adequate coverage, entrepreneurship is one. There are studies on diffusion of innovations, adoption and rejection of new practices, barriers and stimulants to change, individual and community attitude and reaction to change, handicaps in change process and schemes, drawbacks of bureaucracy in change sphere etc. But far less discussed in these studies is the position of entrepreneurs. What kind of entrepreneurs exist in rural India, what is the nature of entrepreneurship and in what context, how could it persist and what scope does it provide for further growth and adjustment with the new are some of the outstanding issues for the analysis and interpretation of social analysts. It is again in the arena of social science research to ascertain the nature of courage and will, for particular items, in diverse ethnic groups and communities. Once those are maintained, the motivational requirement can also be taken care of in relevant ways. To judge for the sustenance of motivated force, the continuity of such operational research is to be maintained. Creation of proper kind of entrepreneurs is, undoubtedly, a boon in any programme of change.

Consideration of individual in the context of social change is again important from the point of view of certain other traits. One, among the latter, is the element of charisma possessed by an individual. It is by and large true that one or more persons, in a tribe or community, are identified as superior to others in almost every respect. His or her personality is rated as more powerful in varied sense. No other individuals, in the group, are believed to be as capable, efficient and powerful as a charismatic person is. A general impression is that the possession of such a power is not through ordinary acquisition, or by making extra efforts. Rather, the same is in-born and is the blessing of almighty in the form of spiritual power. Other members of the community not only approve and appreciate what a person, with such a spiritual power, says but they are almost obliged to submit to his or her will. The equation that develops between a charismatic person and others in the community is one of respect, submission, and at times even of fear. A common belief is that the spiritual power, given by god, does guide the individual's behaviour, relationship and personality. And it is through this force that he dominates and overpowers many aspects of mundane life. That the community remains submissive to, and even at times scared of such a person is again attributed to the support of spiritual power. Such a religious background of an individual's personality helps persist its dominance over most others. Further, the carriers of charisma are believed to be far equipped in terms of impressing and influencing others. A commonly accepted belief is that the personal quality, that enables one to influence his fellows, of an individual is such that it easily makes people agreeable to one's own thinking and wish. This makes the fellow members convinced of the rationality, logic and superiority of ideals propounded by the charismatic individual. Typical kind of response and reaction of fellow-members, to such a person, speak of the same. Under the shadow of charisma, the need for pressure or compulsion does not arise as the development of a particular kind of belief takes a usual course. And the same spreads as a wave among the various sections of population. Majority of the people automatically refrain from denouncing charisma and the charismatic person. And even if a few afford to do it, the wider social pressure, for its condemnation, comes to the forefront. Under such circumstances, the charismatic person has to simply initiate things. And the moment he expresses his feeling and thinking, they are taken up like the wild fire. The person commands not only the respect, but also a big follow for most of his/her ideas and utterances. The latter may be related to any aspect of life, specially those rated of more importance to the community and its ways of living. The charismatic person behaves as a guide, philosopher, and even as a leader, though he may not necessarily belong to the formal leadership hierarchy of the village or the region. With such a multifunctional position, the operation of charisma has a wide range-from individual to the group. With his prized possession of personal quality he can, thus, impress and influence at a wider range, from individual attitude to community faith.

Such a relationship of charisma, individual and society is of prime importance to the advocates of change and transformation of society.

The identification of charismatic individuals then becomes a prerequisite for the agents of change. A further essentiality relates to the understanding of pro or anti-progress attitude and outlook of one who carries the charisma. Reading of such inclinations, and of the consequent behaviour, occupies an important place in the context of change and development. The approach should be to motivate the charismatic individual and his personal quality in the interest of alien ideas and technology. On the contrary any clash in what is proposed from outside and what is demanded by the personal quality of the charismatic individual is undesirable in the process of change. In the absence of consensus and compromise, the major chunk of the population is likely to become hostile to an innovation. Most of them cannot afford to accept an innovation, at the cost of disbelieving and disobeying the well-established traditions and pronouncements of the charismatic person. Therefore, an important task is to try as to how charisma can help as a useful tool in the wake of new requirements. The task is not that simple, more so when the dimension of spiritual force also finds a mention. It requires a tactful handling of the situation. Else, the things would go out of hand. Extraordinary acts of individual have quite a relevant place in the area of social change. It is such acts that give way to even the new. Further, the extraordinary acts carry their own impression in the minds of people. And the charismatic person is one who is held capable of performing extraordinary acts which a commoner, in normal course, cannot even think of doing or achieving. Many a times, it is through the extraordinary performance that the commoners get convinced of the fact that one carried charisma. Even the induction of change, in so many cases, requires the occurrence of performances which are beyond the routine and normal ones. If something extraordinary, as part of change, is displayed even by a single charismatic person, it is bound to have wider repercussions on the community. However, the question remains as to how could it be done.

In the actual course of attempts for change, the stress of change agencies essentially remained on the involvement of formal or statutory bodies of socio-political control. Since the inception of the system of democratic decentralization, the Panchayati Raj bodies, at village and regional levels. formed the immediate point of contact. Members of other formal institutions, say the school and the cooperative society, were also, at times, approached for the sake of introducing change. The traditional leadership was involved to the extent where its members found place in the formal organizations or bodies. Otherwise, the bulk of traditional leaders continues to be out of the fold of agents of change. The latter cared the least to approach them. Even otherwise, anything on behalf of, or in support of, or against the change agents, was considered only if it could come from the members of formally elected bodies. The others, from the traditional leadership, neither cared to do so nor could be given importance in the event of any try. But the caste Panchayat, village/regional Panchayat and other traditional councils continued, all through, to exist quite forcefully, atleast in certain areas of community life. Still less involved remained the professional and opinion leaders who were not properly identified in their immediate areas of concerns. It might have happened so because such persons have always been insignificant in number. It is likely that in their sphere of influence, they could be the most important carriers of change; or it could be even vice-versa. Tracing further the points of contact of change agents, it may not be out of place to say that they utterly failed in establishing contact, and subsequent equation of healthy rapport, with the charismatic persons who were believed to have performed extraordinary acts. Neither a proper identification of the carriers of charisma could be tried at, not their position and place in the community, in the interest of change, were properly determined. Their ability and quality to impress others were, thus, not exploited by the agents of change.

When the identification of charismatic persons was not done properly, when their quality, capability and leadership were not made use of, when their capacity to impress and influence other members of the community could not be accounted for in the process of change, a very important agency to gear up change was lost sight of. The sphere of discussions on the problem of introducing change in rural India, too, did not provide much of scope to the element of charisma and its carriers. It may be mentioned that the existence of charismatic person, and consequently the performance of extraordinary acts, appears to be of stronger base in tribal communities than the caste society of village India. It is in the former social formation that the belief in spiritual force is of a higher order and quality. Even those in possession of the same are categorically marked. And they are given, on behalf of the community, whatever is due to them. The place and importance of charisma and the charismatic individuals are well recognised in social science too. Some explanations in social theory do mention of the role and place of charismatic persons. It is also stressed that they can be of real good help in the diffusion of innovation if properly tackled. But the practical research studies, depicting the actual utility of charismatic individuals, in specific areas of change programme are mountingly lacking. Even for social researchers, the major job still seems to be of the very identification of those who possess charisma. Certain concrete case studies, in various parts of village India, on charismatic persons vis-a-vis social change and development could be far more revealing than any other procedure in this respect. At the same time it could have supported the social scientists in their argument. Such research venture could even throw light on the adverse role, if any, of charismatic individuals in the context of change. The social science research, focussing on change, thus, seems to have actually lacked in the treatment, in respect of role, and placement, of charismatic persons. Such studies of theirs, in the perspective of change, would have not only strengthened their argument, but also could show way to the agents of change in the attainment of their goals. The research, where spirituality is connected to the performance of extraordinary acts needs to be carefully attended to. The research results have to further suggest of the ways how the change agents are to go about in their dealing with this aspect of social change. Making research efforts on such lines continues to be a big question mark.

FOUR

COMMUNITY AND SOCIAL CHANGE

The stress of explanations in the preceding chapter chiefly confined to individual, his personality and other characteristics which have say in the field of change and development. Some of the individually possessed elements, that were considered as of more relevance, were analysed in respect of their position in the context of social change. It has been realized that the individual and his personality form the strong factors to be properly understood and interpreted. Their place in creating as well as resisting change is not ruled out. What is, however, further needed is the moulding of individual and the relevant personality traits to the requirement of inducing change. How the things are to go is to be found out from the explanations of concerned researches. There are numerous requirements, as already cited, to put the things together in the interest of intended change.

Now it is the individuals, their common interests and ways which give way to the community and its living. The individual members are the essential constituents of community or society. When they get grouped together for certain social, cultural, economic, political and religious bindings and considerations, the larger social groups like the community and society emerge. The social structure or the social system that emerge subsequently represent the total framework for guiding individual behaviour and relationships. Such system ideally prescribes for limitations, liberties, freedom, constraints, nature of human action and interaction etc. But what is actually held by the participants of a culture may not necessarily and always tally with the ideal prescriptions defined under the standardized norms or rules of the system. Even in the event of violation, contravention and circumvention of norms, provision is made for rectification and readjustment, and consequently for restrengthening of the on-going system. The inter-play of positive and negative sanctions provides room to contain situations of bypass. The existence of specific patterns of social control is a vital force in this context. Various forms of penalties, punishment, rewards etc., take care, to a considerable extent, of the system's ongoing interests. This does not, however, mean that there is always consensus between individual's behaviour and the web or norms and prescriptions. Situations of conflict do mark a community's living. But the general pressure of community's ideal requirements and expectations does exert to a considerable extent. It is chiefly through socialization, enculturation and internalization of norms of society, provided in its culture, that an individual gets equipped for a comfortable participation in the wider activities and network of social relations. Thus, the two way process seems in operation, that is, the individuals, put together, give rise to community or society; and the latter, through its social structure, almost then govern the individual actions, behaviour and relationships. However, certain cases of deviancy, from ideal prescriptions, are not ruled out. And the same are, in most of the cases, individually governed. But for majority of items the individual looks to the framework designed for the community. At the same time there are certain ventures which appear as if they are basically the community undertakings. Almost uniform understanding emerges to uphold such occurrence; the personal interest, if any, are sacrificed for the sake of community which undertakes to resolve issues at broader level. The field and scope of individual and community are well laid down, and the responsibility of their maintenance is well within the knowledge of group members. There is the least scope for built-in contradictions in such spheres. Normally, in community ventures, the individual intervention is rare; and if it is there, it does not carry more significance and weight. For societies in rapid transition the argument, sometimes, may not go centpercent correct. In general, the community ventures get through as the overall support to the same is almost ascertained. Even for those who feel to backout, and are keen to withdraw their involvement, the escape is not easy in view of community pressure. But still instances can be cited where expected participation in a community venture does not forthcome. However, a major requirement of the same is metwith. It may further be mentioned that the operation of community network is comparatively more effective and forceful among the tribes than the castes, especially those which have been exposed to rapid alien influence. It is in the latter instance that the solidarity has considerably been impaired, whereas the same is held high in tribal society, where individual entity is almost insignificant in the context of a community exercise. Exception may be some tribal pockets where socio-economic and religious transformation have gone far head. In general, the alternatives, open to the tribals, are limited. They cannot, in most of the cases and most of the time, afford to be isolated from the group on whom they excessively depend. The choice open to them is not assessed as viable, looking to the limited socio-economic and other means. This may not always be true for caste society where alternative economic and political means are of wider magnitude. The bulk of choice, open to them, is not that limited as found in case of tribals. Such a difference, however, does not undermine the importance of community living in caste society. It is simply a question of comparative effectivity of community pressure in the light of persistence, change and the alien influence. The latter can help assess and explain the extent of deviancy, in terms of community pressure, one can afford to go in for. But whatever the circumstances be, the predominance of community ventures continues to characterize the Indian villagers. There are areas of common interest to the village community where an individual almost fails to find feet in respect of his say against it. Some indifference may be expressed but not that conspicuously. It does not assume attention-catching shape at the level of surface manifestation.

In view of what has been explained above, the importance and place of community ventures cannot be undermined. Specific individual interests, major community activities and the social structure or culture of the group are, in one way or the other, interconnected. They do intervene, influence, and are influenced among themselves. Though theoretically, and may be even otherwise, the three maintain their respective entity, but their merger, at specific points too is undeniable. Who surrenders to whom, and on what counts, are the important analytical issues for research. Where does an individual stand in the purview of community/society and its social system, and how far one's personal interests can go form further areas to probe. Nature of constraints, and submission to the same, under the equations of individual versus community, community versus social structure and individual versus social structure, form imposing structures for evaluation and analysis. Best is to review them at ideological as well as operational planes. A proper attempt on these lines forms prerequisite in knowing the nature and degree of traditional persistence, as also in getting at the changed and the changing conditions. Understanding and grasp of such a perspective, of various communities, is of great utility in planning, directing and creating change. Where to hit, and what to avoid can be best known through such an approach. Treating individual, community and social structure, in isolation, remains far short of serving the purpose. Social change, and the connected development, have quite a relevance to the trio of individual, community/ society and the social structure. Depending upon the context, each is important in view of venture/s undertaken. Need, therefore, is to explore centres of interest, with special reference to change, concerning individual, society and its culture. At the same time there is no fun in depending merely on ideal frame of references which are, by and large, pro-tradition and not pro-modernity. For the diffusion of innovations, the three-pronged (that is, individual, community and social structure) persuasion can be more beneficial and rewarding than the sporadic striking in isolation. Some of the concerned areas of individual interest have already been explored and analysed in the preceding chapter. Areas of concern to the community, in the light of change and development, are many; and these may further vary with the nature of community. The selected ones of these, and which are of a common occurrence, are dealt in the paragraphs that follow. These are, however, not the only areas to be attended to; some additional ones may also be worthy of consideration.

Like the individual, certain characters at community level are of vital importance, both to the members of community as also to the outsiders who bother to, somehow, care for the community. In what way, and to what extent a specific character influences the 'inside' and 'outside' patterns, plus the associated aims, are likely to vary. It holds true even for the effectivity. At the same time the characters are almost of universal existence, irrespective of the nature of community. However, exceptions in this respect are not ruled out, more so when the character is interpreted in a particular context, and by the different kind of agencies. Basically, however, the communities do, by and large, uniformly maintain the traits. One of the latter is the 'thinking' at community level. This is in addition to the individual thinking which again is a universal character of human beings all around. The areas and limitations of thinking can be delineated, keeping in mind the world-view of the people. Thinking faculty, in addition to biological constraints, if any, is quite closely related to the socio-economic, cultural and ecological conditions. What can one, and subsequently the community, think about the food-gathering and nomadic conditions, and at the extreme level of primitiveness may not be of the order of one prevalent in agricultural and industrialized communities at an advanced level of living. Simple and complex situations are bound to create difference in thinking. Wider the scope and opportunities, bigger may be the level of thinking. Limited environments do pose for restricted thinking. The thinking resource is probably rich in case of open societies than the closed ones. Given opportunities, some richness, in the existing stock, can be brought about. Curbing the same might prove it the other way round. The primitive communities suffer from the poverty of thinking resource, as is true for other areas of their living. Certain individuals, in the community, can be spotted as exception to this rule. But then the thinking of individual, and one of the community are not to be mixed. Undoubtedly it is the individuals who subscribe to the community, but it does not propose for total unanimity in thinking. The ways of thinking for particular ends may show similarity as well as dissimilarity when reviewed at individual level. Or, there can be observed in certain contexts, a predominant uniformity at the plane of thinking. But the same, for others, may not go that way. Anyway, by and large the community thinking is all cumulative where even the disagreeing individuals have to join. Personal line of thinking, to a specific end, is then either curbed, or changed, or adjusted to the wider agreement brought about by the major chunk of community's population. Even if one gets stuck to a definite course of thinking, he keeps quiet when community interest are put forth. As thinking is more of a mental phenomenon, it does not appear without some kind of manifestation. Therefore, even if one is not mentally contributing to the view-point of the community, it remains hidden and the participants take it as a unanimous course of action, thereby enriching the community solidarity. Why one does not believe in the surface manifestation of a singled out thinking can be attributed to the fear of innumerable socio-economic and religious inhibitions. In the rural communities of India, including the tribals, one cannot easily afford to overlook community pressure,even while one thinks it as something improper, ill-desired and unwanted. There is a constant fear of socio-economic and religious boycott, when the community view is not respected, of the person and the family to which he or she belongs. Once a person is declared as ostracized or boycotted by the community, his existence becomes not only difficult but also miserable. For day-to-day living one cannot do of his own. Village India marks a tremendous amount of interdependence of its community members. This applies to all major areas of life. Under the circumstances, to get isolated from the community and its channels of thinking would require an extremely a bold decision, with the feeling that one can survive inspite of all odds, opposition and oppressiveness. The nature of social organization, social control mechanism, and economy of village India are such that a person cannot, normally, imagine of independent existence. One remains lost, atleast for major decisions, in the framework of community's requirements.

With such a position of village community, and its standing, in rural India, one needs to review the thinking perspective more rigorously. Broadly speaking, the thinking can be classified into two categories; the minor ones may fall in either of the two. One is the 'creative' thinking and the other is the 'non-creative', or destructive or damaging one. The two are supposed to exist, many a times simultaneously, in the background of traditionality as well as transition to modernity. The picture may, at times, give a different look when reviewed from within and outside. Well defined within the rigid norms of traditionality are the negative and positive thinking. But as the change items and ideas are new, the categorization of thinking in their case is, atleast initially, difficult to be made. What, then, one has to look for is the existing thinking purview. Taking note of such a stock is helpful to the agents of change and development. It is the negative thinking, in the context of new, that poses barrier to the change efforts, including the items of change. The background of indifference and opposition, partial or total, to the new can be attributed, among other factors, to the negative thinking of the community. The positive or creative thinking, on the other hand, provides support to the new ideas and activities. It may further be mentioned that this kind of stimulus is more powerful than the other favourable conditions to change. The reason is that it encourages change right at the mental level. When the state of mind is so formulated as to accept an innovation, and when other prerequisites also find favour, there is no possibility of rejection of an element of change; more so when such a mental make-up is at as wide a level as that of a community. Therefore, to generate creative thinking, and to give a fillip to the same, at community level, is of utmost importance for those engaged in the gigantic task of transformimg Indian rural masses. In fact, creative thinking is vital for change and development. But still it may remain only half done if the non-creative or negative thinking is not properly tackled, keeping in view the requirements of new. Else, its existence will keep on slowing the growth and sustenance of creative thinking and ideas. And consequently the change efforts will not bear fruits as could be anticipated. As the community feeling is strong in the tribal as well as in the non-tribal rural areas of India, the community thinking carries a great importance for development workers and their programmes of planned change. The rise of creative thinking, at community level, and the simultaneous restraining of the concerned non-creative one, help the emergence of favourable climate to the working of change agents.

While delineating the areas where stress has been laid by the planners and the agents of change, one finds that both, the individuals as well as the community find a mention. This is supported by the theoretical fronts and by the modus operandi of the programmes of Community Development, Tribal Development, Integrated Development, Rural Reconstruction etc. At various stages, and in different contexts, one finds provision for individual and community involvement. In comparative terms, the slogan for community involvement remained, all through, more popular. The very name of the programme" Community Development' certified the same. Community mobilisation, from village upwards, was, more so within theoretical expressions of the exercise, kept at the forefront. Even at the operational level, the records strongly speak of community level meetings and organizations which are claimed to have been used as tools to boost up planned change and development. At the level of village community and beyond, situations were created for more frequent interactions. This was in addition to the traditional arrangement which characterized almost every community, big or small.

And such arrangements might have differed from place to place. Whatever it be, the underlying idea was the consideration of the force of community. But how did it affect, and what was the possible outcome form separate issues for probing. Whether the meeting of the village community and its organisations were really organised, whether interaction beyond the village was intense, whether the transactions, carried out, were relevant, whether such exercises were often repeated to maintain the tempo, and whether the ideas carried were through or not are some of the relevant questions. There is a scope for some difference of opinion in respect of some of the above issues; but in others the common opinion holds that the community involvement and mobilisation remained far below the expected level. Formation of new organisations like the Gram Sabha, Gaon Panchayat, Cooperative Society, Naya and Circle Panchayat, Block Samiti, Zila Parishad etc., could not discharge, to a satisfactory degree, the functions associated with them. Even the official machinery attached with them could not prove its worth. Whatever contribution community mobilization and involvement could make in the name of change and development remained insignificant part of what was planned and expected. More stress, somehow, was on the raising of infrastructure than on the discharge of their functions. likewise, the stress, of whatever order, was on surface manifestations than on the relevant mental factors. Realization that the community carries a thinking pattern, in a set frame, and that it could be of use or disuse in introducing change did not grow as it should have been. Identification of positive and negative thinking at community level was the area least traversed. The development of creative thinking, in the interest of change, still appears to be a far cry. Change at mind level might have not been considered as important and thus given a secondary place. The ignorance shown to creative thinking at community level, or the scanty attention given to it has been a lacuna in respect of the programme of societal transformation.

Even at the research front, the picture was no better. The position of social science research, in the perspective of change and development went almost parallel to the trends at operational level. As such the equipment and technology responsible for surface manifestation were the areas comparatively better attended by the social scientists; but this coverage too has not been exhaustive and at macro level. However, for certain fronts, and for certain regions, the social science research explanations do provide material for rational and scientific arguments. What has lacked is the research concerning thinking and its patterns at community level. The analysis of thought processes finds only an insignificant mention in both, the applied as well as academic researches. Models of community thinking, for various ends, are set, especially those finding root in deeper traditions and the same needed to be searched in the interest of creating change. It may be expressed that the task for searching of thinking sets, creative or otherwise, is quite difficult in comparison to the collection of other informations and material. The dearth of adequate technology, for the purpose, may be one among other reasons. Otherwise, one cannot deny for the higher value of such a research. There is a need to develop more effective and reliable technology to analyse the thought processes existing at community level. Certain reactions of community members are also the indications for specific trends, though one has to give margin to the fact that some of the major reactions can also be situation-specific, and thus do not belong to the category of fixed ones. The minor and major reactions of the community,to certain definite proposals, however, do carry impressions from where it becomes tenable to go in for the relevant derivations. In addition to cultural traditions, the ecological conditions and historicity also affect the modes of thinking. A special new trend may emerge in the event of drastic change in ecosystem. In normal course its significance remains submerged in the broader dimensions of cultural matrix. Further to be probed are the linkages of thinking sets with the practical life-designs. How do they subscribe to the decision-making at community level is again a very relevant area of research. The decisions, unanimously arrived at, will determine the future course of action, including the acceptance or rejction of major elements of change and development. Existence of such correlated courses of actions further demands for scientific social enquiry into the thinking process and trends at the level of the community. The implications of the latter provide vicious circle for penetration of social researchers. And such deep insights would be the prized possession of the planners, administrators and the change agents in their venture of introducing change at practical level. The researches concerning creative and non - creative thinking sound of a very specialized and mini nature, but their practical use is superb.

By now it is almost clear that the thinking-complex, at community level, is not unlimited. Rather, it does define its boundaries in various directions. Constraints of various nature operate and direct the thinking and its scope. New thinking may develop if the social and physical environment for the same are favourable. Severity of traditional conditions tightens the thinking sphere. And it is the nature of thinking at community level that correspondingly reflects on the nature of 'explanations'of village community. The argument may hold true for explanations connected to the diverse aspects of the community life. Levels of thinking and explanation are correlated; and it may not be out of place to mention that the former has big say in directing the latter. This, however, can't be the rule and universally happening phenomenon. Occasional deviations from the normal expectations are not ruled out. Complete consensus between thinking and explanation is, however, a possibility in a large number of cases. But then the chances of divergence, in some, are also there; and the same is supported when an empirical situation is socially analysed and reviewed. Therefore, what is thought and what is said do not always hold compatibility, though in more of the cases it is presumed to do so. The relevance or irrelevance of thought process and thinking with the patterns of explanations is, thus to be analysed and understood in the interest of change, One may not be, at times, able to search for valid meaning of explanations in isolation of thinking perspective.

No village community, tribal or any other, exists in a vacuum in terms of its perception of various kinds of practices and phenomena around. For particular styles of life, people of a community have propounded common kind of explanation, and the same are put forth whenever the people are required to do so. Glimpse of the same also appear in the course of socialization when the young entrants to community complex get into the process of internalization of culture traits, which they are expected to hold in later life. It is chiefly the inculcation of such explanations, prevalent in the community, that makes one socially and culturally equipped to face, and participate in the community life. As part of community's requirements, one is likely to accept the prevalent explanations as they come to him or her, and henceforth starts subscribing to the validity of the same. Such explanations find almost constancy and consistency among the constituent elements of the community. The ' specific' and the 'generalized' explanations are well laid down for various observances and happenings in the life of the community. The explanations, simple or complex, specific or generalized have limits as per the nature and world-view of the community as such. One would, normally, not find them unlimited. Addition to, or the impact of new on some continuing form of explanation is not ruled out, more so when a community is in transition and in a state of flux. Such a widening of explanations is obvious in the atmosphere of growing dynamics in society. The process subscribes to contradiction as well as consensus in explanations, as it involves the question of old versus new. Nothing much of special and specific, then, crystalizes under such a situation. And for the element where uncertainty prevails, the explanations need not be accepted as such. One has to carefully watch the situation of fluidity before getting at anything concrete. In addition to the new, which is being rapidly encouraged in village India, the explanations of the community for the supernatural world is another aspect of interest. More convincingly sound the explanations regarding mundane life of the community. Their limits are also more compactly defined. But some of the explanations do appear as almost limitless when the same are asked to be given in the context of supernatural phenomena. Even for mundane life, one is required to make a distinction between the explanation given for functional and the non-functional elements of culture. If there are cultural 'survivals' (without any function in contemporary situation), the explanation for the same may sound lacking proper footing. They are even likely to be assessed as irrational. For others, the explanations of the community appear, more of the time, not only convincing but also rational, especially when approached from the mind of an insider, or one who participates in the life and culture of the community. Others, from outside, do not necessarily hold the same view. In spite of all the above complications and implications of explanations of a community, some limits of explanations, in a particular time span, can be delineated. For any existing socio-cultural order, such delineation is not too difficult. To certain extent the limits of explanations correspond with the prevailing status-role system of the community. For social researchers, it should, therefore, not be difficult to identify the limits of explanations of the village community. Now the question is as to why are we so particular for the identification of limits of explanations? The answer is simple. Whatever the villagers pose as explanations is well within their focus. At the same time they have no difficulty in comprehending the same because it is not only clear to them but is also convincing. Anything beyond the focus of villagers is not, atleast at the initial stage, welcomed. People, by and large, do wait for adoption of new till the convincing explanations come forth, and the same get integrated in the local system of explanations. Once it is done, the new items or ideas have a chance of get going, and for ultimately being accepted in the community. The best, under such a situation, is to properly identify the limits of existing explanations so that the elements of change may be devised in tune with, or in adjustment of the same. Elements, far out of focus of the villagers may be kept, for their introduction as part of change, for some later stage. Going haphazard way, while trying to inculcate something too above villagers focus, does not serve the interest of change and development.Nor it becomes helpful to the villagers. Therefore, what is comprehended, in the form of explanations, by the village community needs to be identified so that the change elements can find sufficient scope for adjustment and acceptance. Such an identification is more valuable for village communities of India where levels of explanations show tremendous amount of variation. What is identified for the village community of Punjab does not hold, in many respects, the same way for an upper Himalayan or Nicobarese settlement. Explanations of shifting cultivators or hunters and gatherers seem pole apart from those of the sedentary population formed of advanced agriculturists. At times the ethnic, religious and regional variations reflect in terms of diversity of explanations. Under such conditions, going the uniform way is unwise, if the intention is to gear up change.

Among other fronts, which have severely suffered at the hands of agents of change, the identification of limits of explanations of village community is one. The haste to diffuse the innovations of various kinds did not provide for time and opportunity to the change agents to get into the arena of explanation exploration. Under the tall claim of rural transformation and tribal development a great deal of impatience prevailed upon the planners, administrators and other agents of change. Schemes were designed and carried to the village community without having adequate idea of their being within the villagers' focus or not. It seems carriers of change could not wait to explore the dimensions of focus of village community. The ideology of planned change, however, did not suggest to ignore the same. The ideal was, however, not made use of in large number of cases, and in many a sphere. Thinking that the task of identification of limits of explanations is time consuming and difficult, it was never taken up in full spirit, In fact it was not only at the initial stage that such an enquiry was to be made, but it should have continued, with certain interval of time, even in subsequent stage, after the village communities had been sufficiently thrown open to alien conditions. The carriers of change, mostly the outsiders, entered into the village communities with certain preconceived notions and items. Rather than being scientific in their approach, they adopted hit and trial method. In many respects, and in many communities, the explanations of outsiders went far beyond those of the recipient group. It required a higher level of comprehension than the one prevalent at local level. Quite a large number of attempts struck outside the focus of village community. It happened more in the absence of adequate bench mark informations. Whatever little could be collected was insufficient in the light of diversity among Indian village communities. A great deal of seriousness could have been imported in the investigation of villagers' explanations and focus at a stage prior to the actual launching of the schemes of rural reconstruction. Because of the adoption of wrong procedure it was detected, in case of certain schemes, only at a later stage that they were not only far beyond villagers comprehension, but also proved unsuitable to the living of village community. Noting the unsuitability, some of these schemes were finally closed down. But this should not have happened if the start itself could have been within the explanations and focus of the villagers. Incidences of this kind continue to happen, here and there as the identification of limits of explanations of village community is still incomplete. It has not been felt as an ongoing process. Some even think that if the focus of villagers is considered, we may not be able to introduce the new. This is, however, a vague thinking. One is to simply see where the village community stands, and then frame the policy and programme of gradual change. Certainly, it would be too much of a haste to substitute bow and arrow with ground-to-air-missile. And even if a try for such a substitution is made, it is not likely to be a successful venture for quite some time.

Again the place of social research in terms of identification of limits of explanations of village communities, and hence of the things in focus of the villagers, was never taken up too seriously. In early fifties, when the National Extension Service and Community

Development Projects were launched, the studies on village communities were rare. In fact it was only in fifties that the sociologists and social anthropologists started scientifically studying the village communities in their holistic perspective. Their findings were reported even later. But it was in the sixties and seventies of this century that a large number of village studies were published. These provided a fair amount of insight in village life in India. The findings of such sociological and anthropological studies could not, somehow, be made use of for planning and change among the communities of concerned region. There remained a gap between the research findings and the schemes to bring about change. For various reasons, academic and administrative, the social scientists and the planners and the agents of change considerably failed to come closer. They did not join together for a common cause of diffusing innovations among rural masses. Each went in its own style without realizing that both caused harm to the cause of development of the villagers. There is increasing need to bridge the gap between the social scientists and the agents of change. Research findings and the efforts of change continue to largely go in isolation of each other. In addition to the necessity of use of the existing social research findings, is the requirement of further studies on village communities, especially of the areas which have not already been covered,. Even among those already studied, say in fifties, there is a need for restudy. This is necessary because the limits of explanations of the village community might have expanded over the last three decades, Secondly, what needs to be more elaborately focussed are the explanations of village community vis-a-vis social change and development perspective. It is the scientific social enquiry which can bring out the deep-rooted explanations of village community. And it is through the help of these that easy compromise with the new can be made feasible. The greatest hurdle, which continues to be there since the inception of the programme of rural development, however, is of the gap between the social scientists and the agents of planned change. They have, by and large, remained pole apart, thereby causing damage to the scientific process of bringing about change. Unless the social research findings are made use of at practical level, they remain only of academic interest. A developing nation, like India, does need more of practical social science. Millions of faces, sunk in the backwardness of rural India, have no relevance to academic sociology or social anthropology. What they need is the betterment of life which these disciplines can help create.

Another important element at community level is one of its resources. No community, Indian or outside, is resource-free. One is likely to have more, or less than the other. In some cases, it can be almost of the same magnitude. Resourcewise, one community may be poorer than the other. The community resources are to be seen differently from those of the individual. The latter are, most of the time, not to be shared widely, and remain largely confined to the individual or his family of orientation or procreation. At both the levels, that is, the individual and the community, the bulk of resources and their nature are greatly determined by the eco-system. When we talk of community resources, we do not confine ourselves to the material resource alone. Other than economic, a community does have social, political and even religious resources. Each community is not equally rich or poor in all these resources. What one possesses depends on the eco-system and the community's requirements. A community with weak political resources may be rich in its social context. There can be a number of permutations and combinations., But the normal trend is that a community with rich economic resource is likely to have a developed political resource. This does not necessarily and correspondingly apply to religious and social resources. Variations in resource material are further bound to reflect on the levels of communities. The advanced, and many an advancing communities, normally have better economic resource. And the societies at lower level lack the same. The latter is generally rich in social and religious resource. A closely connected issue is in regard to the explanation of the resource. In certain communities there can be reported existence of rich resources, but the same do not seem to be exploited to an adequate degree. While in certain others it may be the other way round, that is, they may have only a few resources which are sufficiently exploited. Thus, in some communities there is more scope for exploitation of resources than the others. In addition to the existing resources, exploited as well as unexploited, some new ones may be added if opportunity for the same are made available. This specially applies to man-made resource. As regards the natural resources, there are limitations unless the nature itself intervenes in one way or the other. Generally, the man-made resources are of a superior quality in a situation where the natural resources are of an inferior kind. On the other hand the man-made resources lag behind under the condition of abundance of natural resources. This happens so long as the proposed programme of exploitation of resources is not put to operation. It is quite likely that the members of a community, with rich natural resources around, get sluggish as they can easily fulfil the basic needs with minimum of efforts. They hardly ever face the situation of competition; a feature frequently reported where abundance of natural resources is missing. Imposing natural resources provide for curtailment of aspirations and ambitions. The same are encouraged under the conditions of competitive situation that emerges in the event of rise of man-made resources. Simultaneously are marked the technological improvements. The tribal and non-tribal rural communities, as also the urban ones, of India may support the arguments of the above kind.

Looking to the segmentary nature and plurality of village communities in India, certain other connected issues need to be attended to. The ethnic heterogeneity that marks most of the village communities is of demanding consideration. It may not be an issue of concern among the homogeneous tribal communities. Traditionally speaking, the community resources in village India are really not the resources of all the castes and other ethnic groups on equal footing, though they are apparently treated as of the community. Many a times the members of the twice-born castes have higher share than others. In other cases the untouchables and the tribes are denied certain privileges which others enjoy. In still others, a nominal levy, in cash or kind, is charged from the unprivileged groups for the use of same resource existing at village level. The use of well, crematorium, pasturage, forest, land etc, have not been under traditional frame, free of restrictions. Impositions of various kinds, on various ethnic groups, prevailed in village communities of India. Some protective legislations were introduced, especially in the post-Indian independence era, to level such a differentiation, Instances of improvement have appeared in many a places. But in other places conflicting situation has given rise to the state of tension, rivalry and intolerance. Members of the dominant groups have challenged the legislations, and have strongly come in the way of their implementation. The idea of equal share for dispossessed and the non-priviledged, in a particular resource, failed to be appreciated. In many village communities such a struggle could be reported. Kanjhawla (a Delhi village) provided a fresh example where the distribution of land, from pasturage, to landless Harizans (Scheduled Caste people) created a problem which attracted eyes from all around. Jats, the traditional land owners, openly challenged the move and the tense situation prevailed in the village for many years. An almost regular posting of Police Force in the village kept the situation under control. Whenever it was withdrawn, the conflict repeatedly cropped up. There are other Kanjhawalas which do not, for certain reasons, come into light. Therefore, the question is regarding the concessions given in respect of the use of a resource. Who have access to the resource and who do not: to what extent and how many times the members of which group in the village community can avail of the resources form very relevant and important questions. An outsider's regarding a resource as belonging to the village community,does not certify for equal access of everyone to the resource. And such an argument applied not merely to economic resource but also to social, political and religious. Occupying membership of a village council, through reserved seat, does not guarantee for his fuller participation in decision making at community level. Likewise, enacting legislation against untouchability does not guarantee for equal social status to a Brahman and a 'Chamar (leather worker) or a Chuhra (scavenger). Announcement for the policy of secularism does not eliminate privileged and unpriviledged sections of village community in terms of their perticipation and use of religious resource. Actual and ideal situations, traditional as well as the lately introduced, are not the same. The access to the resources, and the use of the same, are the pertinent questions which would clearly speak for or against the change. The existence of the resources, plus the access to them form an almost a precondition to gear up change. Absence of adequate and relevant resources will adversely reflect on change efforts. The very initiation of change, under such circumstances, may be difficult. But the more and favourable resources to change will help it grow fast, and fairly in an anticipated manner. And simultaneously one has to ensure that the resources are for the community in general, and not for certain sections alone. Wide and balanced introduction of change requires the strength of community resources, and a fairly equal access to the same. In most of the cases the identification and assessment of community's resources were done inadequately. It might have been fair in case of economic/material resource. But for other kinds if resources, no scientific efforts were made for their identification and assessment in proper perspective. Many a times what the change agents or development workers assumed lacked support when reviewed at empirical plane. The ponds and tanks owned by a village community were taken as the best source for fish-breeding as part of development. But it was taken so without realizing that the community is dominated by the Brahmans or others who profess vegetarianism and do not approve of fishing occupation. Even when the material resource for fishing was available, it could not be made use of for lack of social resource. For the members of twice-born castes the occupation of fishing in socially degrading. They do not approve of it and hence it almost failed to gather community support, leading thereby to failure at many a places. The stress, all through, in the programme of change and development essentially remained on material resources, both internal and external. New tools, technology and other material provisions were made in the interest of change. Extension education, social education and formal education also found place. But these alone did not provide for all the prerequisites. The internal resources of the community, other than the economic ones, remained almost immobilized. How many of those engaged in the task of rural transformation were aware and alert of the social, political and religious resources of the community? It must have been quite an insignificant number in the total context. Such resources could prove helpful, more so with little readjustment here and there. Ignorance of the same went against the intentions and interest of change. Many a times they posed as barriers to the agents of change and their schemes. Resource-analysis, including who shares it and to what extent, with the possible areas of inter-resource interaction did not attract the attention of change agencies and institutions. Probably they never realized for such an exercise as the same, according to them, fell outside their purview and scope. For them any proportion of achievement was a welcome; the failure front did not disturb them to the extent where they could realize for the identification of related causes. Whether the absence of some resource was detrimental, whether the limitation in the access to the resource were unfavourable to change, whether one resource of the community did not approve the changes in other, whether mobilization of certain resources lacked, whether the resources were persisting or temporary, whether they were matching to the requirement of change were some of the questions which could not be responded to, creating thereby a big gap in what was planned and intended and what was achieved. It may not be proper to say that social scientists have lacked in their researches concerning resources of village communities in India. But when asked if they mapped all kinds of resources, and to an equal extent, they may be in a slightly fight position to respond The economists as well as the sociologists and social anthropologists have searched socio-economic resources to a large extent. In comparison to this, the research accounts concerning political and religious resource have not been that illuminating. Comparatively more neglected remained the field of religious resources: exception being some studies of social anthropologists which have given due place to religious infrastructure and it's role in community life. Again, the informations on the nature and position of resources are not sufficient in themselves. The need is to review them in the context of change and status-quo. What can be the reactions of a resource to the elements of change, and to the efforts of change agents are some of quarries of very great relevance. Likewise, the urgency is to search for the areas of compromise and conflict among the resources of various kinds. What an economic resource does support may not be reacted in the same way by the political or religious resource. Or, some of them may positively subscribe to certain change elements and intentions, while the others react negatively. The economic or social incentive is not always and necessarily to get support from the political or religious resource,. One may even pull down, in traditional terms, what the other upholds. Such areas are to be studied more seriously in the interest of creating change. Once the network of such relationship is explored, the agents of change can be directed to act accordingly. This can save from opposition and embarrassment at certain fronts. Another vital issue in the arena of resource research is connected to the requirement of searching for permission and prohibition as operating on the use of resource. Who have more access to a resource, and who are more deprived of its benefits have to be clearly defined. This is to be seen in the background of population composition. The patterns of sharing of various resources by the castes and other ethnic group in the village community are to be brought to the surface. This should also include the reasons why some have easy access to the community resources than the other. A further need is to explore as to how the best use of the relationship of community to its resources can be made. It would be wrong to always presume that all resources of a community are equally shared by all sections of community. Identification of resources, nature of access to the same by the various sections of the community, and their say in the elements of change and development carry a great significance in developing of societies. And the same are not to be lost sight of.

All communities, big or small, primitive, advanced or advancing, exposed to alien conditions or partially or totally isolated, technologically backward or industrialized or urbanised, nomadic, semi-nomadic or sedentary, highlander or coastal-dweller have been having some kind of system to educate their people. In some community, such a system might have existed in almost an unnoticed or undifferentiated form; while in other it could be well represented or formal. No community can expect to have a smooth sail without educating, formally or informally, its new and young entrants. Such an education chiefly concerns the arena of their respective social-cultural totality, plus the developments and world-view beyond what is defined for them within the framework of their traditions. Since the birth of humanity, the variety and generations of human populations kept on inculcating the life-designs meant for them. And hence there always remained some channel of transmission for such an inculcation. The channel could be oral or written. And it is through such an arrangement of transmission of culture heritage that the societies survived even under various odds, thereby adding, most of the time, some new dimensions to their designs for living. These could be modification or adjustment in man's interaction, on the one hand, with man, and man's interaction with nature on the other. In the interest of group's survival and existence the human beings had to, by and large, subscribe to the communication arrangement and its modification. And such an underlying idea continues to hold true in the contemporary situation.

In case of non-literate societies, where a majority of the tribal population fits in, the channel for educating people remained almost rudimentary; in its formal sense confining itself mainly to socialisation or internalization of culture through native ways emanating from family of orientation and extending to larger groups, and the procedures thereof. In other words the education contents, in the case of such societies, remained confined to their limited ways of life learnt through intended as well as unintended socialization. Introduction of formal schooling, in their case, has only a short history. On the other hand the non-tribal population of Indian sub-continent has had a comparatively long history of formal/school education. Certain areas represented by the caste Hindus could imbibe more formal education than others. It goes with the history of culture contact of the group, plus the government efforts meant to promote education. Some voluntary educational institutions also have a say in the matter. But whatever may have been the background, it is a fact that educational development, of formal order, has, so far, been more in case of the castes than the tribes. And consequently the trend towards wider world view was set up earlier among the people of castes than those of the tribes. Even today the impact of formal education is far less on the tribesmen than those of the castes. However, a few tribes of north-east India and Kerala are an exception in the sense that literacy rate among them is quite high. Amongst the castes themselves too, the position is not uniform. For instance, the development of formal education, althrough, found place chiefly with the members of twice-born castes. Less privileged, in this sense, were the people of middle caste segment, and the least affected, by formal education, were the members of lower caste segment, especially the untouchables. As regards the educational development, the position of the latter hardly seems to be better than the tribes. Thus, the educational development of the Indian village community in not at a uniform plane.

The element of educational development of the community has a direct connection to social change. There is a widely accepted belief that the growth of formal education helps the creation of change. The proposed innovations get more acceptance from the educated masses. The illiterate and uneducated ones lag far behind in their acceptance level concerning new items of change. A community deeply bogged down in traditionality and superstition, in the absence of formal education, has more built-in barriers to change. It promotes status- quo, retaining thereby the elements of fear and doubt concerning the efforts and intensions of agents of change. Where there is lack of educational development, the members of community take more time to be convinced of an innovation. And many a times, if the latter is imposed on them, people discontinue with it after some lapse of time. They revert back to the originality causing, ultimately, wastage of energy and resource of the change agents. Such a phenomenon has widely been observed in village India. This is in addition to slow diffusion of innovations, which is again attributed to illiteracy and the related ignorance and superstition of the people.

A review of Indian situation is revealing of the fact that the educational development remained chiefly connected to the knowledge of alphabets and passing of certain defined standards with certificates diplomas. The stress was given to literacy rise. For all this a number of educational institutions including primary, middle and high/higher secondary schools were opened in the rural areas. Adult education centres were also started. But there too the stress remained on the learning of alphabets. Some Ashram Schools and hostels also came up to provide impetus to educational expansion. Those who carried the educational programme to the villagers hardly bothered to train and educate the villagers in areas directly connected to their day-to-day activities and working. Thus, the education imparted could hardly be related to the functions relevant to the practical life of the villagers. In other words the functional literacy as part of non-formal education, continued to be undeveloped. And this subscribed to the lack of interest of villagers in formal education which could not be felt of any immediate use. It is a known fact that a majority of the centres of adult or social education failed to function effectively and rather remained far short of meeting the intended objectives. This happened for poor response of the village adults. A poor planning, especially in the context of continuing education and functional literacy added salt to the injury. What was proposed for, and carried to the villagers proved nothing much beyond hotchpotch. The whole drama appeared as over-ambitious without feeling the nerves of those for whom it was meant. As an element of correct strategy, the literacy, the functional literacy and school education should have been assessed and retained methodically and placed in correct sequence in tune with the requirements of village life. What is more important is to meet the day-today needs of the people rather than to make them, specially the adults, sit to learn alphabets. And hence the educational development is to be defined and delineated in its correct perspective. Only then one's argument that educational development is one of the requisites for social change will stand true in broader sense as far as the situation in village India is concerned. Further, the categories of tribals and the non-tribals have to be seen, wherever needed, in their distinct phases. Educational, in its broader sense, requirement of the two may not, specially in the beginning, be the same. Keeping social change and development aim in mind, the educational policy and programmes are to be made befitting to the existing and growing requirements of both, the tribals as well as the non-tribals. The caste society, and the one of tribals are to be placed in their respective background to make a healthy compromise between education development and social change. Looking to the social-cultural and the psychological background of Indian rural population it is advisable to take off from social education, followed by functional literacy and the formal education. This can better generate interest for change in the intended areas of community living.

The position of social science research concerning educational development of the community vis-a-vis social change in general appears to have been of a limited order. However, the research works confined to the field of education alone are available in plenty. The conception that educational development promotes social change and general development in the community continues to appear more as a hypothesis. The empirical support explored by the social analysts is specially lacking in the tribal situation. In caste society of village India some studies on this score have been conducted. But these too are area and group-specific. The results of these are limited in the sense that they have not been compared with other community, or sections of the same community, where educational development stayed at a lower level. Such a comparison made by the empiricists will further strengthen their hypothesis if the results come favourable,. Otherwise, in the event of unfavourable results, the hypothesis is likely to be turned down, or may suggest for further studies on the same lines to consolidate the stand, positive or negative. Another area where the efforts of researchers have lacked pertains to the studies of educational development of the community vis-a-vis social change in tribal belts. The most ignored continued to be the comparative study of castes and tribes at this front. With penetration of this kind, the social scientist could be in still better position to establish his claim of relevance of education with social change and development. At the same time he could be able to direct better the kind of education needed for a group of people to undergo change. In other words his utility, as an applied scientist, would have been appreciated at wider level. It is only through research analysis and findings that one can suggest for improvement. At the same time the inherent weaknesses are weeded out, if carriers of change bother for the same.

Any community in the process of change is host to two kinds of laws, that is, the customary and the formal once. The former are designed by the persons from within the community and are adopted and transmitted as per the requirements of the community.The latter are born of the formal, legal and legislative system- it may be of the state or some other kind of politico-administrative system. Such formal laws are imposed on the community keeping in view the targets of the governing agency. Indian rural communities, tribal or non-tribal, are no exception to the above system. Isolated instance of some tribal community, say one of Andamans, may fall beyond the purview of this derivation.Else, the communities, in general, continue to be simultaneously under the pressure of customary and the formal laws of various kinds.Many of the formal laws are enacted to improve the quality of life of the people; others are to maintain law and order; and still others are those which ensure help, economic and otherwise, to the centralized governing body. On the other hand the customary laws essentially subscribe to the maintenance of status-quo, ensuring thereby the continuity of traditions. In other words one can safely anticipate a situation of confrontation between many areas of customary laws and those emanating from the state or central legal system. Indian communities are no exception to such a situation. In many instances it appears that there is no consensus; rather there is conflict between what is traditionally prescribed and what is desired by the governing agency. Incompatibility of laws is more revealing in case of tribal situation than the one of non-tribals. This has happened because the laws enforcing authorities could not take proper and adequate stock of the existing tribal laws. Certain practices (say marriage by elopement among the Bhils) which are approved, in the eyes of relevant customary law, are disapproved by the formal law. Such a situation proves more confusing to those who are directly involved in it. Unless they are properly convinced they continue to be undecided of their option for new. Their adherence to the old stands. In other words they keep up clinging to the idea of status-quo.

To introduce change in a group of people there are two ways- the direct and the indirect. The former speaks for the implementation of various schemes and programmes meant to bring about change. The latter speaks of protective legislation, that is, certain laws and enactments to keep the people confined to a situation defined to be responsible for the creation of change. In the programme of planned development of a society both the direct and the indirect operations are carried out simultaneously. In fact the things, scientifically speaking, are so planned that the direct and the indirect approaches appear as supplementing each other, and consequently providing fillip to the common aim. However, the level of achievement, in terms of changed, will again depend on the compromise and consensus of what is proposed in these approaches and what the society holds under its customary cover. In the event of lack of consensus, the change efforts are likely to be hindered more severely. But if the adjustment between the old and the new is of an adequate order the acceptance of change would be easier. As such the acceptance or rejection of change elements are directly connected to the relationship between customary laws and those imposed from outside. In other words it is this relationship, among other factors, which determines the measure of change. Further, it is probable that if the customary laws prevail upon the laws imposed from outside, the way is paved to the persistence of traditionality. On the other hand if the formal laws take lead over the customary ones, the development of pro-change attitude is likely to be better. Therefore, in a programme of induced change and development, the place of customary laws, as also of the formal laws, is of paramount importance. But how they are made use of and taken is a matter of further concern.

Village India has always represented heterogeneity in terms of population and their styles of living. However, the bulk of common elements, at the same time, are not ruled out. But then the feature of differing sub-cultures marks wide areas of Indian sub-continent. And this is how India has always been characterised as a case of 'unity in diversity'. Under such circumstances the enactment of common laws, in respect of change, for a wider population seems to have been an unwise act. Probably the promulgators of laws found it too difficult an exercise to take note of a variety of customary laws marking Indian scene, and then adjust the formation of new laws. Or, they may have assumed that such an attempt might go contrary to larger interests. In addition, there might be certain other considerations better known to the law-framers of the new form. As such a large number of laws came uniform, for application, to the people of all sects, religions, castes and tribes. As an instance the introduction of Panchayati Raj (the system of Democratic Decentralisation) in village India is a common phenomenon (Except some part of North -East). It could hardly take note of the nature of customary councils/bodies/panchayats existing in the tribal as well as the non-tribal pockets. Knowing of their roles and functions remained a far cry. But the Panchayati Raj came in its own form, with its roles and functions defined almost uniformly for one and all. Instances of ineffectivity of Panchayati Raj bodies are available in no less abundance. Otherwise they were supposed to act as catalyst to the generation of change. The planners for change also proposed for other laws concerning social, economic and religious life of the people. The underlying idea was to provide inpetus to the social and economic life for its betterment. But then the implications of some of these laws did not go smooth with the ongoing conditions and traditional arrangements. Occasionally the side repercussions generated disturbance of various kinds. Some laws concerning land, for example, led to caste conflict and rivalry, gunning down people and burning huts etc. These, and many other instances clearly show that the stress has been on the formulation and implementation of new laws without getting into the ongoing customary laws which have survived althrough and which let the society going for centuries. This gave rise to a situation where adjustment of old with the new, and with the general orders of the communities, became a problematic issue. Probably, it was thought that the rural communities are backward and illiterate, and hence can be led the way the outsiders feel without anticipating problems of any kind. But this was wrong calculation, and it has been proved so from a great deal of ineffectivity of certain laws introduced to bring about social change and development. Part of infra-structure, in terms of network of laws, was raised without bothering much for foundation provided by the customary laws of the people whom the planners intended to change. Rather, the latter continued to be ill-attended.

At social research front, concerning legislative and customary laws/measures vis-a-vis social change and development, too the position does not seem to be encouraging. Concerning village India a few studies of sporadic nature have been undertaken, though they are limited in form. Comparatively more explored is the area concerning the impact of new legislative and protective measures on the masses. Some selected legislations, meant for the tribal and non-tribal population, could be picked up and their impact assessed on the life of the selected population groups. The formal laws, covered by the research analysts, chiefly included those promulgated in the post-Indian independence period, and more so the ones designed to elevate the individual status plus the general quality of life of the people. The results of those studies highlighted the areas of weakness as well as of strength of the laws. But in many instances a particular legislation could not be related, in terms of analysis, to certain other areas of life than the one focused under the law. If a legislation concerning, say land alienation or bonded labour, was studied, it mainly confined to the percentages and frequencies of the subjects or cases involved, as also how much the connected legislation has done about it. What other repercussions the legislation had, taking note of the totality of rural life, were not well taken note of and analysed. In fact what causes land alienation or bonded labour is a complex of factors attached to a variety of life-ways. And hence the concerned legislation will, it is presumed, not go unnoticed of the same. When relationship of this kind is established, through research studies, one is more competent to suggest for alteration or modification of the legislation in the interest of it's better effectivity, and consequently the welfare of the people. Unless a thorough holisitic study and analysis are made, the social scientist may not do justice in terms of the impact of legislation as well as its modification. Another observation in this aspect of study relates to the customary laws of the people. The sociologists and social anthropologists do, on many occasions, talk of the customary laws as reflected through their monographic, village or other macro studies. Dozens of village studies and scores of socio-economic surveys of Indian villages do refer to a number of customs and the associated laws thereof. Same holds true from monographs on Indian tribes. But then the special works on customary laws are rarely metwith. More scarcity is of the studies concerning traditional laws of society in their context to proposed efforts for social change and development. Lately, the Anthropological Survey of India undertook an All India Project on Customary Laws but its results are yet to be printed and made available to planners, development workers and the rest of the community of scholars. Further, the traditional laws have not been consolidated in macro situations in the interest of emerging a common picture representing a few contiguous communities. This exercise could easily identify and consolidate macro-mapping of the communities of Indian sub-continent. The least attention of researchers has been given to the relationship of formal laws and the traditional laws. There seems to prevail quite a confusion in the explanation of compatibility and incompatibility of formal and customary laws. And this has born of general impressions which people carry in the absence of adequate scientific data. There are situations of adjustment and adaptability, as also of conflict, clash and imbalance, between what the traditions and customs suggest for and what some of the lately introduced legislations demand. The ethnic and culture diversity pose for such a situation. Many a times even the law-enforcing authorities and agencies express their inability for native considerations since they cannot cultivate diversity of laws in terms of heterogeneity of population groups. Procedurally, they feel it might lead to the rise of many other problems. The social and political researchers need to design special studies on these lines so that their results can provide right direction to the intended plan for change. Surely remain in disadvantage the recipient groups whose members cannot put two and two together, specially when there appears a clash between what they propose for, and what the outside agencies, official or voluntary, intend to do through the introduction of new legislations.

Like the individual, a community is also characterized by its basic features. In general the latter refer to those elements which provide foundation to the community infra-structural network. In other words the basic features form heart and soul of any community. These ensure community's existence and perpetuation. Some of these elements are manifest even in the accounts connected to the community's origin and growth. In addition are others which speak for community's contemporary living representative of its social, economic, political and religious life. It is in this background that a community is conceptualized as having a common constellation of institutions. Ways of living express similarity; and a large majority of the people adhere to the common ideal supporting institutions. In other words the basic features of a community speak for cooperation, unity and ethnocentrism among community members. This is how they feel one. Even the requisites for holding certain elements do propose for interdependence of community members. Thus, the basic features of a community, its members and the community as a group seem to be inseperable, though conceptually they do so. Beyond the urban fringe, the village India presents a mixed picture of community features. Some of these features, specially in caste villages of rural peasantry, are common. But there are others which mark differentiation. From caste to tribe is again reflected the featural variation. The trend is again kept up even in the tribal situation where some tribes stand almost in contrast to others. Where caste stratification and intercaste dependence uniformly characterize multicaste villages of India, such a phenomenon is not basically conspicuous in tribal India. However, tribes in transition and those in close contact with the caste Hindus have imbibed some signs of the above characters of caste. Else, homogeneity prevails in tribal India. Nature of social grouping too is not free of variation. The bands of hunters and nomads define their own background and limitation and hardly stand in comparison to larger social groupings characterizing numerically bigger tribes who are settled cultivators Other than the social groupings, and the economic pursuits, the religious value complex and the decision-making procedures, including those meant for social control are also not free of divergence and differentiation. As such the communities have evolved their respective patterns-depicting some common and some divergent features.

The response to social change and development is largely determined, among other things, by the nature, quality and quantity of basic features of a community. In the event of opposition to basic features the community is likely, more so in the initial stage, to show indifference and opposition to the new ideas and proposals forming part of social change process. This is bound to happen under the circumstances when most of the interests of the community are served through the existence and continuity of the basic features. Not that the basic features always and only pose for opposition to the innovations. These may even be made use of, specially by keeping them in a right perspective, to make the change feasible in the interest of the group. However, to attain it is a very specialised job. The specialists of basic features can alone suggest for it. It is they who can suggest for a viable alternative keeping stock of what is going on and what needs to be added or replaced. If this is not resorted to the change would be impaired. Somehow the role of resource persons, that is the specialists of basic features, remained of a passive order. This reflects no doubt on their understanding and specialization. Rather, what could not be made use of is their expertise. The planners and carriers of change went in their own style. As such the gap between local patterns and those planned to be introduced from outside continued almost uninterrupted. This paved way to the creation of hindrances in the adoption of innovations. The whole process got a setback in terms of the anticipated achievements. But where the major elements of the basic features got fitted into the matrix of new items, the change went well within the purview of defined goals. The phenomenon of the latter kind did, however, occur more as a chance and coincidence, and hence noticed as a rare occurrence. A scientific consideration of the basic features should have been attempted at prior to the formulation of programme of change. This was the need of the hour and required to have wider coverage, making distinctions wherever demanded in the contexts of different communities. Out of the basic features the relevance of major elements to the proposed programmes of change needed to be adequately established and fitted into the very process of change efforts. At the same time the functionaries or agents of change needed to be equipped with the cautions to be cultivated while carrying the programmes of change to the doors of the target population. It should have been done in a way as if the change agents found the communities not as exotic ones whose basic features remain, in terms of their knowledge and understanding, as alien. Rather, they should have felt the communities as one's own. The latter could be possible only when the functionaries were made equipped with the native features and their requirements in the context of societal continuity as well as change.

The position of social anthropological and sociological research on the basic features is not bad. Quite a good deal of informations, as an outcome of social research, are at hand. This holds true for caste as well as the tribal communities. The village studies, the surveys, the monographs and the project reports, either printed, typed, cyclostyled or mimeographed are available in the libraries or in the concerned research institutes, autonomous, governmental or those run by the voluntary agencies. The literature, referred above, is not specially pin-pointing to the basic features of the communities around. In other words there are no special studies devoted exclusively to the basic features. But then the basic features can certainly be picked up from the total presentations if one is keen to do that. But the question that follows asks as to whose job is this selection. Is it the author of the report who has presented the holistic social-cultural perspective of the community, or the planner or the programme designer or the change agent who have to pick up the concerned elements. Under the prevailing conditions of utter lack of coordination between the social analyst and the planner and implementor, it seems nobody's responsibility. The social scientist ends up at research results, and those deputed to bring about change do not consider the reading of social research reports as their part of the job. And as such the basic features highlighted in research reports remain nobody's concern. These informations remain in libraries and research institutes without being practically used. Even those responsible for causing change give it no priority of any kind and go about as they feel comfortable, or as the directives flow from above. Thus, they neither find time for reading nor are expected to do that officially. This has, althrough and in most of the cases, kept a gap between the social science knowledge and the programmes of development. At the same time neither side ever showed promptness for any healthy merger into the other. Schemes and programmes of change, in many instances, were carried forward in isolation of the basic features of the communities.

At the same time the social scientists continued to chiefly confine to their own basic areas of research. This bias is obvious in the interest of their career plus the work output. However, for any developing nation, where change is strongly stressed upon, the social scientists have to exert beyond what is provided as social science within inverted comes. They have to design their studies as per the changing perspective around. This will be in the interest of nation, as the social science expertise will help gear up change for betterment. The sociologists and social anthropologists, specially those who have specialised on Indian village communities should have planned studies on basic features vis-a-vis various programmes of change. How the background of two came together or drifted apart could be then better known. Studies, planned on these lines might have given a better account of inherent barriers to social change efforts. At the same time the stimulants to change, as hidden in the basic features of the community, could also be known. Moreover, the directions made available through research results would have suggested for further course of action in the programme and efforts for change. In fact the changing situation and the national commitments demand that the social anthropologists and the sociologists, as also their researches, adapt themselves to the wider cause, and be out of the limited sphere provided by the respective academic discipline. They are to be more practical, and subscribe to the fast generation of practical sociology and anthropology. Such a diversion shall also help assess their worth in terms of what they can provide to the society by being helpful in the process of change and transformation.

FIVE

SOCIAL STRUCTURE AND CHANGE CREATION

While considering social change horizons, the basic features of society, in general, and of the village community, in particular, do need immediate attention. The larger society, with its wider elements of social structure, does have a bearing to the elements at micro level, that is those characterizing the social system of the village community. The parochial nature of certain elements, however, cannot be ruled out. And therefore what is parochial and what forms part of universal socio-cultural phenomena are to be diagnosed. The venture will not end up at this stage. The relationship between the two has its own relevance in the context of social change requirements. Functionally speaking, the social analyst cannot do without reacting to the trio of parochial, universal and parochial-universal features. Even if the focus, from research and practical point of view, is on the induction of social change at village level, the wider perspective is not to be lost sight of. Taking village or a section of it as isolated or independent entity remains short of serving the real purpose. Some features in the context of social change can universally be appreciated in a society, and hence a broad-based planning can be done outrightly. But for the local features, at micro level, the uniform approach may not at all prove sound. Reaction of parochial features to the proposed changes in social system would not only differ in tune with the nature of innovation, but it may also vary from village to village and region to region. Therefore, seeing the basic features of a village community, from a special angle of social change, and contemplating it for other village is not necessarily a right attempt. The latter is a more strong explanation in the context of village India where diversity of features is quite apparently marked. Under the conditions, a social situation, therefore, cannot always be made a reference group for others. Greater the feature-variation, wider the diversity and hence more need for rethinking of special change ingredients and processes. Closeness of features largely drops out such an exercise. Social scientists, and specially the social anthropologists, largely pick up smaller social formations, say a village, and analyse it, in general, from the point of view of intra-formation. Feature extensions, beyond such formation, is, in general, not stressed upon. Far more ignorant remain the change-inducers who cannot, by virtue of their nature of job, think of such a perspective and its utility in social change induction. Further, the variation in basic features need to be probed as per the nature of village community. The latter, in Indian conditions, are homogeneous and heterogeneous. The former is characterised by tribal villages, and the latter by the multicaste or mixed villages of tribals and non-tribals. Then the features are also to be analysed in the light of borrowing process. This may present some kind of parity at certain fronts. The features need to be seen as independent, as also at a continuum. Identification of convergence and divergence of features is of quite a value at the plane of social change efforts. Indian village studies do not reveal a great deal of such interpretations which, otherwise, are undoubtedly of a very significant value. Holistic studies, dealing with interconnectedness of elements, are available but their stress remains somewhere else than on convergence and divergence of basic features.An explanation of relationships of features does not always and fully cover it unless one specially intends to explore this parameter in the light of scope of social change induction. Therefore, the focus in village and wider level studies needs some shifting when we view the situation in the background of growing dynamics in village India. Again, the stress may vary as per the magnitude of culture contact and purposed ends. These latter ones are at differential planes and a stock of the same would not only provide a better sociological insight, but also enthuse agents of change and their manifest attempts.

The attempt at introducing social change is not to remain confined within the framework of a rigid order. Any form of rigidity will not serve the purpose. Flexibility of pattern in respect of social change purview should be treated as part of adjustment for its gearing up. It may find less fruitful when seen in a small social situation. However, the same sounds far more convincing when analysed in a larger situation where diversity in the system is more and even for reasons beyond human ecology. And the common inducers of change themselves feel about it while operating under such conditions. This area, concerning social change, has a still more important dimension.This is one which has not been taken care of much, neither by the propagators and inducers of change nor by the social researchers. Only a few instances of scanty attention could, however, be reported. Hardly any seriously proposed, and a comparative study, could be effectively carried out, in terms of similar nature of innovations, showing social change implications, and the reasons, thereof, in respect of exotic-cum-ones own society. The stress, normally, is unidimensional, that is, either looking or analysing social change in one's own society or in exotic ones. Studies on social change, with reference to rural India, have been done by the non-Indians as well. But whether they have compared it with the processes of social change operating in their own society or societies. Such instances are rare. Nor the India social scientists, after studying diverse aspects of social change, in rural India, have interpreted and analysed it in the context of other societies. Such ventures, if attempted, would help develop arena of social change in terms of academic as well as practical perspectives. In a rural setting, as that of India, a still more important area of interest can be delineated. This concerns introduction and implication of social change in Indian communities which sound as exotic, to Indian themselves, because of many basic diversities which have been built over the centuries among various ethnic groups ranging from most primitive and little known tribes to the exposed ones, and further to the caste formations of various regions. Unless a system is thoroughly understood in its correct perspective, more so in relevance to social change efforts, it should be treated as nothing else but exotic, even when the change-agents are from within the country. A great amount of hindrance to intended social change can be attributed to exotic social structure, and the elements thereof, which are taken for granted as known by the agents of social change from the same country. In reality, however, such a claim remains false leading to a setback to the programme of change or causing disorganisation and conflict in the recipient order. More and more studies, focussing on this aspect of social change, need to be done, and their result communicated to the designers and carriers of social change. Assuming that an Indian urban agent of change knows everything about the social system of a tribal community is misleading.This may hold true in case of a person belonging to caste peasantry, and even to a tribal when he operates in another tribe as agent of change. Therefore, any unfamiliar social system needs to be treated as exotic so long as the change promoters do not comprehend it. And the best to lead to such a comprehension are the social analysts.

One among other ways of looking at the dynamics of social change is related to multiform differentiation. In certain situations, it sounds as very effective. One form of differentiation is at the level of individual and the other at the social group level. Mostly, the two are interconnected and it is largely true that the former is governed by the latter. However, this is not always the rule. The differentiation at individual level is observed more in the light of achieved than ascribed. Status ascription goes with the identity of social group. And hence the achieved and ascribed positions have their own place in differentiation.The two need to be seen independently, as also in correlation with each other. The areas where the two together supplement the differentiation, or weaken it, are of vital importance in the context of social change phenomenon. Another equally important and connected issue is one that signifies differentiations. A majority takes differentiation as corresponding to stratification or ranked hierarchy defining groups as high and low or superior and inferior. Such derivations are more obviously made in the context of rural communities of India where caste based stratification is chiefly reported. Every group has been ascribed a particular social position and people understand where they are rated. But under the situation of growing culture contact, some people, not as a group, have achieved certain things which differentiate them from others. Though, by virtue of their birth, they may continue to be classified in a particular social category, but they certainly stand out as different from others of the same fraternity by virtue of their certain other socio-economic attainments. Such growth of individuals remains largely based on competition, irrespective of caste or creed. Therefore, the centuries' old built-in differentiation is one aspect, and the lately grown one, on the basis of individual attainments, is another. One survives on traditions, and the other on the lately available opportunities. The former has been explored very extensively by numerous social scientists, the latter remains comparatively far less explored by the researchers. And what remains most unexposed is the juncture, in various ways, where the two converge or diverge. How much one encourages or discourages the other is also not thoroughly searched out. Differentiation of social groups, on traditional lines, is apparently taken, by many, as something anti-change. This specially applies to the caste-based differentiation in Indian context. But the differentiation, on the basis of individual attainment, is supported by a majority of people as pro-change situation. The former minimizes scope for healthy competition, whereas the latter does promote it and throws open a wide field for people, from various social strata, for healthy growth through various kinds of attainments. People, with differing social background, go in for similar kind of innovations proposed through various programmes of social change. In order that the results of social researches on the differentiation perspective may give way to social change, the microscopic purviews, outlined in the above description, are to be thoroughly searched for and analysed. The social researchers and the social change agents need readjustment in their focus to suit to the growing social change requirements. The notion that differentiation, prevalent in a village community, is always harmful would be too sweeping a statement. When a healthy competition is generated among the differentials, things may take a desired course. As the tribal social systems are comparatively far less differentiated, especially on traditional lines, and as the individual differentiation among them is also taking a lead, they may be easily brought into healthy competition for imbibing various kinds of changes that suit to their way of life. But then there is also a need to map the course of differentiation, and this can better be done by the social researchers operating in tribal setting.

In all communities, the family, since its origin has had a very important place. Almost all human societies are characterised by this social institution. With its universal existence, the institution of family has always played a significant role in the social, economic and biological life of a person. Though universally found, the nature and pattern of family have varied from society to society. When the variation in family structure is not ruled out, its functions do not vary much. Only a slight variation is reported when functions are defined in respect of nuclear and extended, including joint, families. At times, the differences, in the nature of headship of family are also reported. This is specially true for patriarchal and matriarchal societies. Some slight variation in respect of interpersonal roles may also be reported. Taking a stock of tribal and caste societies of rural India, one may note certain differences in the structure and function of this social institution. Nature of economy and other factors have say in shaping the family forms of various kinds. In agriculture-based economy of the caste society, people have been more particular for extended and joint families. These forms are, however, changing fast. Forest, hunting, gathering and shifting cultivation economy of the tribals largely kept them confined to simple or nuclear type of family. In case of many tribes, the switchover to settled agriculture, over a few centuries, has also reflected on family, but not to any greater extent. The institution of family has two major dimensions. In one, it regulates the behaviour and relationship pattern of its individual. In the other, It prepares them for all kinds of interaction beyond the family limits. Family, and so its members, are connected to various other institutions. In fact the latter, in certain cases, are shaped by the combination and ties of family. So the network of family does not end up with intra-family relations; it goes beyond and is recognised so at wider plane. Therefore the family institution, in one aspect, sounds as of independent existence, but the argument is turned down when reviewed at larger level, and in the context of broader social system.So is true for an individual in family. He or she is not only under the social pressure of family norms, but he is equally so to those representing wider social institutions and organisations, having sufficient bearing on family. Under such conditions, the social change, connected to an individual in a family, or connected to family as such cannot be dealt as an isolated case. And it would be a wrong strategy for the agent of change if he or she spends the energy on the introduction of a change without taking note of broader purview where the new element would face various kind of repercussions which he may not anticipate in the begining or even later unless the proposed change programme gets repeated opposition. Who is selected from the family, and for what, and what kind of reaction it will have beyond family are some of the issues which are of vital importance to the change agents. But from where do the latter get to know of it? They may not be able to manage it by themselves. It is again the social researchers who would come to his help and rescue. Studies on the institution of family among certain castes and tribes have been made as part of total village study. Researchers have not much exclusively devoted to family and its relationship to wider network of the local system, on the one hand, and social change on the other. The increasing need is to explore all concerned channels to boost up the introduction of change and to minimise opposition. Individual position in family, and family's place in wider social network is one, among other, front where researches can make much more valuable contribution, which would subsequently be of immense help to those who plan to bring about change in the society. Though the institution of family sounds small, in comparison to others, its relevance to the social system, in general, and to change perspective, in particular, are of quite a significant order.

The system of social control forms integral part of every society and its social system, How elaborate is the mechanism of social control would be determined by the nature of society. Usually the simpler societies have comparatively less developed social control. Likewise, it has wider dimensions in complex societies. Reasons for this may be the heterogeneity of cultural elements and sub-groups, though outwardly it sounds as of a uniform order. With special reference to Indian context, there is another interesting aspect which is of a significant value. It relates to the perspective of tradition and modernity, in respect of social control agencies and the roles thereof. One can certainly outline social pockets, depicting the traits referred above. Small and comparatively more isolated tribal communities represent less elaborate and complex social control order. The members of caste society have slightly more elaborate and complicated systems. The same order holds true for the retention of traditionality, and adoption of modern ways. The non-tribal peasantry has developed social control systems. But in the case of non-tribals, one has to be more analytical in searching for social control mechanism at individual caste level. More so, one has to demarcate between the caste-level and community-level systems of controlling the society. The point of stress is that in Indian rural society, there is a vastness and variety of social control mechanisms. And all of them are strongly connected to social change. The bearing of social control ingredients to various kinds of innovations is sufficiently weighty. Anything confronting local arrangement is undesired, more so at the initial stage. Incompatibility, causing setback to what is held high by traditions of indigenous social control, is intolerable. The reaction is marked at two fronts; one in respect of individual and other group level. It is true that in the context of social control, an individual cannot be separated from the broader purview of group, but certainly considerations are marked when a decision, concerning change, affects an individual. People are more alert when the question of group or community crops up. Individual deviations, in certain cases, are not taken with more of seriousness. But this again goes with the nature of case and its place in the larger matrix of social control. Conflict-causing deviancy, as part of change, is less tolerated than those where an individual accepts a change which does not adversely reflect on village or wider community.

Social researches, concerning systems of social control, have been done in respect of various village communities. Most of these are explained in monographs on individual tribes or as part of village studies. Normally, one chapter on social control is invariably given in any book on a tribe or village. Specialised works on social control, and especially stressing on its relevance to social change, are lacking. In general, the social analysts have explained the existing mechanism of social control, including both the traditional as also the lately introduced one. Such analysis has its own place in the world of social science. But it remains short of serving the purpose unless all its implications, in the light of social change, are studied. This apart, the available works reveal more about the nature of social control systems and the associated customs thereof. But what has lacked is the stress on explanation of norms which support it. And it is the force and survival of norms that sustain a social order, and guide the social behaviour and choices in society. What can be done, and what is not to be done are determined by norm-complex. And again, these would be the norms which ultimately count in giving clearance to what is acceptable and what is not. Another area of weakness, in researches connected to the field of social control, has been in the context of leadership purview. Organisation of traditional and statutory councils, their headmanship and membership etc., are generally explained. But the explanations concerning individual leaders, outside the purview of councils, do lack. Originally these leaders may sound as mere professional specialists, but ultimately they have their foot in diverse matters concerning the tribal or village community. In addition to their expert advice, they may resolve petty disputes and even guide what new should be adopted and what not. And their verdicts, many a times, may differ from the leadership provided in the councils. Even otherwise they sound, at times, more closer to the people than the councilmen who are comparatively more formal and infrequent in their dealings. Individual leaders themselves sound, in many situations, as institution. Such leaders and guides are metwith in traditional as well as non-traditional contexts. The latter are emerging faster under the conditions of fastly growing contact and change. Growing professional diversity is another reason. The need of the hour is to diagnose and differentiate the leaders who, for various reasons, are pro-change and those who are pro-status quo. The depth studies alone can reveal such a position. At the same time the study of their relationships to council-level leadership is again of great significance in the matter. Fronts of common view-points need to be explored and explained. Finding of such areas, though may take more time of social researchers, but it would be of immense use in respect of social change arena,. What is of direct and more close association, in the interest of social change does need encouragement. The task is of such a special nature that only the social scientists, as specialists, can better attempt it. Leaving to agents of change, if they themselves are not social scientists, would be too much of an expectation from them. Rather, it would find taxing on them.

No community, in India, is devoid of religion. What forms of religion exist, and where, is, however, a matter of increasing concern. This has always depended upon the socio-economic nature of the group and its requirements. The environment or ecology has had no less important place in giving rise to particular forms of religious practices. There are groups where more happenings, natural or otherwise, are inexplicable on scientific lines. People continue to attribute their occurrence to the supernaturals, including supreme god. Many of them, in some other groups, are explained in a different way which has nothing much to do with the religion. But it continues to hold true that in more interior and remote villages, people take help of supernatural elements to explain many unforeseen incidents, as also some other events of recurring nature. Such views are forcefully transmitted, mostly through their oral traditions, from one generation to another. People know which supernatural force is responsible for what. Over the course of years, certain norms have also been devised to regulate man's relationship to such forces, on the one hand, and to the various kinds of happenings on the other. The members of a group well understand even the means for controlling or avoiding malevolent elements, as also to appease and befriend the benevolent ones. Existence of various kinds of religious specialists is not ruled out. They are defined in various categories, and are differentiated according to their respective proficiency. The specialists have a great role to play in guiding the destiny of village folks. Among various kinds of specialists, at village level, it is the religious ones who import maximum regard. The sacred leaders or specialists continue to have superior position over those of secular nature. People's faith, for achieving various ends, on the religious persons is superb, and the same is reflected through numerous rituals, ceremonies and practices observed at village level. Only a few areas of socio-economic and socio-cultural life can be seen in total isolation of one or the other religious attributes. However, the influence of growing acculturation, in certain places, have led to the minimising of a few of the religious ways. Areas where organised efforts against belief in supernaturals and superstitions have been made, some people have done away with certain forms of worship and reverence. But then there are others who continue to be in the sway of religious traditions and approve of what their forefathers had been doing or believing in. Among other attributes of religion, fear is one which continues to forcefully hang over the people. There is not much of change in mental perception in respect of religious forces and their ramification in man's life. Other than awe and fear, the villagers also explain their religious structure in terms of certain gains they derive out of it. They have a strong belief that certain attainments are correlated to the appeasement of some religious elements. They will understand it and practice the same accordingly. It may be done at the level of individual as well as the community as a whole. The nature and degree of observances differ from people to people upholding faith in various religions. Some continue to be confined, especially some tribes, to undeveloped form of religion. But there are others who form part of developed religious faiths. These include some tribals, but mostly the non-tribal Indian villagers. Therefore, within the religious network of village India, the major faiths include Hinduism, animism, Christianity, Islam, Jainism, Sikhism etc. Supporting the attributes, like fear, awe, belief, worship, reverence, temples, specialists, gods, goddesses, is the force of norms. The latter are well-defined in respect of all the attributes. Most of the attributes are simply the outward expression of religious norms. In many walks of life a person is kept restrained because of the pressure of religious norms. Consequently, it is the religious norms which are basically important even in the context of many non-religious spheres of man's life. And the same can be well understood in each other's context. By and large the researches on Indian rural communities have dealt religion only casually, without assessing more for its hold on diverse activities. Available are the accounts of religious attributes, including all perspectives. But most lacking, in the attempts of social scientists, has been the explanation and interpretation of norms supporting religious attributes and their implications in their walks of life. The functional and dysfunctional perspectives of religion can be well depicted only after taking note of norm-complex. Otherwise, the attempt remains far short of extracting real explanations in respect of religion vis-a-vis socio-economic and socio-cultural life. At the same time, it is through the norms alone that the trends may be systematised and concrete actions thought of. There is more need of assessing religious norms in broader perspectives of life-designs as they have a great say in the same. The focus of social research, in rural India, is not to be taken far away from religious norms which form very integral part of rural social systems. And the religious norms have always been playing some role in the stability as well as dynamics of society, Many times, they are to be recognised as strong determinants of various kinds of innovations. Analysis of religious norms in the persistence of social ways, as also in the context of social change elements, is of paramount importance. It is the social scientists who can explore such intricately involved dimensions, and are capable of passing on the same to planned change inducers. Religious norms and social change are to be taken in a way as if they are not altogether independent of each other. Such an understanding would also subside the chances

Whatsoever careful the members of a community remain, the rise of conflict cannot altogether be ruled out. The latter is almost inherent in every social order. This can largely be attributed to the diversity in human nature and to diverse individual interests. Anomie, caused as a result of conflicting situation, can be rated at various scales. Sometimes it may be seen as mild imbalance in social network; in other cases it may assume serious form threatening smooth working of social order at wider level, affecting larger interests of the community. Stages of norm breaking and normlessness form the polarities in this aspect. Norm breaking goes on even in normal course of living, as isolated cases of this kind are reported one time or the other. And these do not involve more organised efforts. But the situation of normlessness or violating societal norms at wider level is of rare occurrence. It is an outcome of well organised effort in the form of violent revolution against the existing norm-patter of a community. No special efforts are required to channelise minor norm violations because the laid down procedures of society take care of it in normal course. But in case of more forceful norm violations, special efforts are made and special ways are devised to create the conditions of normalcy. Situation of anomie can arise from within, as also it gets created as a result of interaction with outsiders. The latter have more say in the matter, more so when interaction with them is unplanned and when the intentions of outsiders are not for betterment but for something else. For condition of anomie, caused from outside, there is, at times, no provision in villagers sanctions, and the villagers at times get stunned. Such an atmosphere does not provide the villagers more scope for reformulation of the disturbed aspects. But in case of anomie, caused from within, the villagers are aware of existing procedures of rectification and reconstruction. In village India, including the tribals and the non-tribals, different kinds of agencies and organisations have been operating since long. Some individuals, as money lenders, traders, shopkeepers, contractors, officials etc., have also gone, for long, to the villagers. The nature of individuals and agencies have also been differing. Some operated as economic and moral exploitors, some as agents of religious conversions and others as helpers to the socio-economic developments of the village inhabitants. There has remained a fantastic divergence in the strategy of these individuals and agencies. In some, however, there is marked uniformity in inherent motive. But more apparent is the distinction between various agencies, and which they cannot avoid having differing ends in view. Under such conditions, the interaction led to the creation of more anomie than smooth integration in respect of various matters. Rise of conflict or anomie remained less when the planned development or welfare agencies interacted with the villagers. But the same appeared more conspicuously when haphazard interaction took place with agencies causing religious conversion or debasing people from their respective cultural moorings. Creation of social imbalances could not be checked under the circumstances when different sources and agencies, with differing ideology, operated in the same setting. Even the means and approaches differed and they created further confusion in the minds of people, especially to those who remained at lower level of understanding. At the same time such processes gave way to the condition whereunder violation of traditionally prevailed ways became more, giving way to conflicts and clashes in normal living. It is likely that some agencies might not have intended to cause conflicting situation, but the same emerged as an unintended consequence. And the latter, by and large, escaped the attention of outsiders. In certain cases, the trend led to the creation of new order of stratification and inequality.

A number of research and other writings are available on the stock of changes taking place in village India. In addition to sociologists and social anthropologists, some journalists and others have produced lot of literature giving details of what new is getting into the life and culture of the villagers.In general, the findings reported are within the frame of intended changes which have been broadly planned to be brought about in rural society. Professionally trained social scientists have gone ahead of others in their search, analysis and interpretation. Their insight is more probing and better as most of them have taken account of various aspects of change in the living designs of the people. A single element of change has, normally, not been seen in isolation of its wider repercussions. What has,however, not been exposed adequately is the sphere of unintended or latent manifestation of a proposed change. It may be noted that most of the changes cause some unforeseen consequence, which otherwise never planned to occur. This origin is because of the typicality of the change recipient systems. And such unintended consequences are generally those which are of an unwanted kind. They are more for upsetting the order, rather than for its consolidation, planned growth and development. They may, at times, prove incongrous in respect of human relationship and interaction. Even the majority of change implementors remain ignorant of them. And even if they are aware, they close their eyes towards them just to get their own work done. As these areas are ordinarily difficult to highlight, as they are of significant value in the process of guided change, as the agents of change are not bothering much about them and as the sociologists and social anthropologists are fully equipped with their tools to bring them out, their exposition is a pressing necessity. Unless this darker side, involving conflict and situation of anomie is made known by the social scientists, and unless the planners and change agents take care of such growth, the social change would be extremely slow. Another front where the progress of social change suffers and gets constantly hampered and which remains, from research point of view, only very weakly exposed is the situation of disparity between various agencies of change at village level. This is more specifically true for tribal communities than the non-tribal ones. In terms of social change efforts, there are multifrontal attacks on the people of a village or group of villages. Alongwith some instances of parity, are those of mounting disparity. So much so that the change, inspired by one agent or agency in a particular aspect is hampered, directly or indirectly, by the other. And this is implicated by motivating the villager in different style. What one aims to do is undone by the other. The members of recipient group, under such circumstances, get confused as to what is true and what is wrong. Their thinking and decision-making get limited to outsiders. It is the social researchers who can identify as to what is befitting to the social system of a community, and what is undesirable and disturbing, ultimately landing people into a situation of conflict and anomie. And it is for the agents of change to take care of the same.

No society is free of imposition from within its system. The very idea involved in it is to regulate life, law and order in the group. In absence of taboos, there may be chaos in the relational network. And what the community intends to maintain may not, then, be possible. Restrictions are given birth to curtail a person from going beyond what is meant for him. Taboos are defined in man's relationship to others of his own caste, community or tribe, as also in respect of other groups and the non-human environment around. Some communities are characterised with more impositions than others. At the same time, it is also true that there is necessarily no uniformity in respect of the taboos. What one takes as taboo is not at all taken so by the other community.But still some element of uniformity cannot be ruled out. The force of impositions also varies. This may be true for the same, as also for different groups. Violation of one taboo may have serious repercussions, but the same for other may be taken lightly. Thus, the treatment given to the violation of taboos also does not involve parity. The religious dimension, in the observance of a taboo, is recognized among the people of caste as well as the tribal communities. To what god, goddess or any other supernatural a taboo's association is established does show variance. But the element of fear, which emanates after the violation of a taboo, remains common. And it is this fear which keeps an individual or a group of people as alert in respect of what they should do and what not. Prevalence of strong taboo-complex in rural India, including the tribal population, can be attributed to strong religious hold. Another remarkable feature in regard to taboos and their observance is that the people recognize impositions even in respect of nonhuman things. So, the man's behaviour to certain natural and man-made items is not always and altogether free of restrictions. And such an equation too is explained in the same background as done in inter-human relationship. No sphere of man's universe then seems to be totally devoid of one or the other kind of imposition. When an on-going system is in the grip of taboo-complex, it becomes obvious that it would also react to social change processes and the innovations thereof. A large number of taboos are for constancy and status quo in the social system, and they would pose resistance to any effort made to hit the same. And it is also true that social change and status-quo do not go hand in hand. The broader alternative, therefore, is to make some adjustment to minimise the opposition posed by taboos and the associated observances. As the root of taboos lies in a very sensitive area of man's culture, it may, in normal course, be difficult to ignore it. The taboos will continue to have sufficient say even in the changing social order. And as such the understanding of taboos, as also their overall identification is of a very great relevance for carriers of social change. Traversing through social researches gives one an impression that not much has been probed regarding the taboos prevalent in different ethnic groups. Whatever works are available on the study of taboos in Indian rural communities are again of a nature which does not assess them in the context of social change perspective. More stress has been laid on describing the types of taboos. And this too is not available on all the categories of people. What needs to be urgently explored are the foundations of taboos. Search for the basis carries more weight than the details of infrastructure. This sounds true because it is the fundamentals which determine the effectivity of an imposition. And the latter would be kept up as long as the belief in fundamentals stands sound. In that case the gearing up of social change is also related to the degree of reshaping of the fundamentals, which in itself is a delicate job. Change in mental attitude is also connected to the rearrangement of fundamentals, and once it is done the innovations are bound to find place in the recipient social structure. Alongwith the search for fundamentals in the sphere of taboos, it is equally desired that these fundamentals are analysed in their relationship with the fundamentals involved in various elements of change. This remains far short of being done by the social analysts. What is exposed in certain studies is the general kind of reaction of some taboos to the outward form of innovations representing as constituents of social change. Exploring of fundamentals, in a comparative form, would reflect on the condition of mental perception, and hence on the relevant areas of change. There is a necessity that social scientists should concentrate on these ingredients of research, concerning taboos, rather than their simple outlining, as a small portion, of some major social analysis.

Social, economic, political, religious and other forms of cultural life of a group of people get a specific shape because of typical sanctions which pervade in the group. It may be true to say that no community can, probably, survive in a vacuum created by the absence of sanctions. Life and culture of any society seek support and inspiration from the sanctions. Such sanctions mark the individuals, the group, the institutions, organisations and the customs. The sanctions do not remain confined to social aspects alone; they rather provide support to economic, political and religious behaviour, as also to the institutions which control it. In other words, the institutions/organisations may be taken as the concrete expressions of sanction-framework. The activities of a community, which are observed as reality, have a hidden treasure of sanctions behind them. Ordinarily, the latter are not visible, but are certainly more important and forceful than what is observed. The question of sanctions goes with the nature of social structure; it is of bigger magnitude in case of more elaborate and complicated ones. Its order remains limited in case of simpler societies, as one represented by the indian tribes. The same order applies in case of the acquisition of knowledge of sanctions. In non-literate societies, it is mere oral transmission at various levels.In developed systems, it may also be through the available literature, in addition to socialization. But whatever the means remain, people, in due course, become competent enough to interpret the sanctions, and so the institutions and behaviour. And this holds true inspite of the presence of multiple sanctions in a social group. The range of sanctions is a wider one. It may start from the individual and go to the whole tribe or community, mediated by institutions and organisations in between. A persons's comprehension, especially for those sanctions which concern his behaviour, is of a good order. For others he does remain aware, though his understanding may remain inferior, unless anything directly involves or concerns him. A person is again sufficiently familiar with those sanctions which have bearing to caste, tribe or community interest. In majority of cases the sanctions, at various levels, are interconnected and those defined at wider level come down to individual in some of his ways. For the smooth functioning of a social order, two types of sanction are usually defined. One refers to positive sanctions and the other to negative ones. The former largely reveal as to what is to be adhered to for the sake of retention of a defined social order. And the latter are those which are taken help of to revive and reconstruct the order when it has been threatened by the violation of set procedures. Therefore, both work for the stability of social system; one operates directly and the other indirectly. At the same time this is also true that the understanding of both types of sanctions provides for the identification of corresponding rules which are comparatively more widely known among the members of a community. The values which are fairly established do not go beyond the orbit of sanctions. Two are inseparably connected, though the explanations of sanctions remain far more hidden than the values. The latter stay more as mental phenomena than the customs which form outward expression of the values. In normal course, an idea, act or thing is valued when it falls well within the fold of sanctions. All institutions, existing in a society, seek support of the sanctions and values. And the same stay strong so long as the latter are cared for. Otherwise comes their disintegration and decay, so much so that they may even vanish in due course of time. Normally, the institutions, backed by sanctions and values, form the backbone of a social structure. What happens to them under the situation of change is the field to be thoroughly probed into. This can be better attempted with the help of sanctions prevalent in a group. Institutional support or opposition to a programme is very important dimension in the process of social change. Special researches, in the area of sanctions, have rarely been conducted in the Indian rural context. This holds more true for tribes than the castes. In research works on rural communities, the explanation and interpretation of sanctions appear only in an indirect form. One has to be specially careful in picking up the same from total description of a village community or tribe. Nature of sanctions vis-a-vis social change has remained a field far more unknown and unexposed by the social researchers. One difficulty may have been that the extraction of sanctions requires special methodological tools which the researchers failed to procure and use. Informations regarding sanctions remained hidden behind the account which social analysts presented on the basis of their observation and questioning the people. The least revealed remained the explanation of background of sanctions of various kinds. It is presumed that different categories of sanctions grow and survive under the protection of special background attached with each category. In the context of sanctions versus social change, a very important field which remained largely unearthed is connected to what happens when the background of sanctions is attacked or changed. Does it cause discomfort and opposition to change efforts, or creates embarrassment to those who have been holding it for long. What best can be done to avoid it in the light of change acceptance is of immediate concern to the agents of change. Another aspect which has lacked, and which is again of quite an importance in the social change sphere, is the analysis of interrelationship between sanctions. It is likely that affect on one sanction may have its repercussions on the other, atleast on those closely connected. Thus, the change, affecting one may have repercussion on the other creating some particular kind of reaction on a programme of social change and its agents. Research findings, concerning different perspectives, outlined above, of social sanctions can be of immense help to change agents. The latter may keep them in mind for attaining their goal of indu

Apparently, the element of belief may sound as pretty small in comparison to many other areas of social structure. But its significance is superb and cannot, in any way, be underrated. No society, small or big, simple or complex, primitive or advanced, isolated or well exposed, exists without beliefs. Almost every aspect of life is belief-based. The beliefs exist independently of each other, as also in interrelationship. When all of them are put together, they form belief complex. This is a very strong front of every social system. The beliefs and actions of an individual are highly inter-linked.

And it is the former which govern the latter. As the beliefs are shared by the individuals, so are the actions which then sound as common or uniform. Organisation of particular kind of actions can be attributed to belief system shared by a group of people. Any disorganisation in belief system reflects correspondingly on action pattern. In other words, the individual and group life, and the connected actions and behaviour thereof are not independent of belief arena which hangs heavy on them. And in order that the actions and behaviour go the organised way, institutions take birth and persist from generation to generation. Such institutionalization is essential to regularise the ways so that the actions and the supporting beliefs do not remain scattered in disorderly manner. Even the transmission becomes convenient in an organised system. In getting at the roots of social structure of a group, the most helpful tool is provided by its belief system. It is the latter which has say in sanctions and the related institutional network of society. Human interaction and relationship are belief-based. They are hardly haphazard and purpose-free. And the intensions involved are belief-ladden. Most of the beliefs are inherited, but there are some which are acquired as new, and such an acquisition is through some spontaneous happening. Certain situations come so hard and unacquainted that they generate new beliefs which, in due course, find place in the established belief system. There is another trend which operates simultaneously. Some of the beliefs even fade away when their connected areas cease to be functional or assume an unconvincing form. But this does not happen all of a sudden. Some get away with the belief in first instance, others join the stream gradually. And a time comes when it is completely wiped out. Then the new ones take birth to meet the emergent situation. Belief horizons have a very wide range. Of course it goes with the nature of system. In tribal societies the horizon remains comparatively more limited. It is more wide and elaborate in caste society which is more elaborate, complicated and need-based. Within limited world-view and requirements, the tribal belief system also remains bogged down to narrow boundaries. But in their case, the firmness, in respect of belief, is more. They are also characterised by higher degree of rigidity. This may be due to particular kind of environmental and human conditions where scope for diversity and alternative is far less. People together subscribe to common view-points, more so when they get confronted with outsiders. Another characteristic which marks Indian rural communities is the place of religious ingredient in the belief system. This specially holds true for major beliefs, more concerning community than the individual. Again this characteristic finds more popularity with the tribals than the non-tribals. Even the areas concerning political and social life are ladden with numerous beliefs having root somewhere in religion. In fact, such a background of beliefs makes them more forceful. The fear emanating from religious perspective strengthens such beliefs. When any question of dropping them comes, people think twice before taking any final decision. It is comparatively easy to do away with a belief in the absence of its religious association.

Belief system can be approached from two major angles; one, how the insiders view it as per their world-view and the conditions around, and second, what others or outsiders think about it and perceive. The very perception of the two would differ at cross-cultural plane. And this is obvious too because the two grow in different settings and belief systems. Such is the situation which poses for most of the barriers to new programmes and innovations. What the agents of change presume and what the reality in the native system supports differ. And each of these has its relevance to the respective social structure. When meet opposition and failure, the change agents express that the members at the receiving end are illiterate, superstitious, ill mannered etc. But they do not realize that it is their beliefs, befitting the local conditions, which make them behave that way. Here comes the role of social researcher. The researches, not many, on beliefs have described only the major beliefs, concerning all walks of life. But how and why they have grown in that style, as per their relationship to the socio-environmental conditions around, have not been probed to a convincing degree. And unless this is done, it would not be found out as to what belief sounds genuine and what exists as false or mere superstition. Giving of this analysis would help the inducers of change to make adjustment accordingly. Any element of irrationality, brought forth in arguments, is harmful and goes, psychologically, contrary to the interest of intended ends. Going loaded with ones own beliefs, without caring for native belief system, is not only harmful, in general, but can never take care of social change interests. At the same time, understanding of alien belief system, for which the programmes of social change are planned, does prove as strong stimulants to change. The possibility of any conflict is also minimised. Another area of social research, which is again of great practical utility and which remains to be properly explored and analysed is in regard to the position of beliefs with reference to changing conditions around. One front is of age-old conditions which have coined particular kind of beliefs, and the other should be, though comparatively milder, of those which get crystalized, as a process of reformation or otherwise, in the light of changing and new conditions, human and natural. Researches of operational level have their own place, especially in sensitive areas like the one of the beliefs. With the rapid induction of new conditions, especially in areas where culture contact has been faster and sharper, the need of reformulation of some of the beliefs has become a necessity. How best it can be done would depend upon the over-all understanding of beliefs and the connected situations. Outright threat to or eradication of long-standing beliefs, without assessing their relevance, may not be the scientific procedure. In the ultimate interest of social change, too, it may not go the desired way.

Study and analysis of obligation have been more popular field of social psychologists than sociologists and social anthropologists. This may be partly due to the involvement of some emotional attribute in obligations and their observances. Measurement of obligations also requires special techniques which psychologists are better equipped with. But at the same time, this is also true that intervention of obligations in social network is of quite a significant order. In fact the two are closely associated. For various reasons, including social pressure, the individuals do interact at obligation level. The feature of reciprocity is kept up in obligation relationship. In certain categories of obligation relationship, one side remains, in material or other sense, gainer over the other. But this is never realised in negative sense, nor taken as exploitation. In every caste, tribe or community, the obligations are well defined. This holds true at intra as well as inter group levels. The individuals, related or non-related, are also accordingly aware of their involvement and limitations in the matter. What kind of obligation relationships the groups would have are also defined. With all this, the degree of observance of obligations varies. At times it remains in conformity with the prescribed norms, but the instances of discrepancy in the ideology of obligations and their actual observance is also reported. This is a character which may be found existing among all the societies. Certainly the discrepancy appears more apparent in the fastly changing societies than others. Maintenance of ideal obligation relationships also goes strong in societies where sense of materialism and individualism have not grown much. In the event of strong community life, the persistence of obligations remains far more intact. In Indian context, the tribal society is more prone to obligation observance than the people of caste groups where anti-obligation atmosphere prevails to a higher degree, more so under the conditions of change. Availabilities of opportunities beyond the caste or community does minimise the observance of native obligation ties. And the opportunities are more open to the people of castes than the tribes. All castes are not equally involved, and so is true for the tribes. Whatever the position be, it would be difficult to say that a social order can do without obligation relationship. It may be at smaller level in one than the other. It cannot altogether be done away with, specially for the reason that it has association with human emotions. In case of individuals or at individual plane, the sphere of obligation keeps on fluctuating except in case of some obligations where rigidity demands respect at group or community level. Obligations, connected to social sphere, have more linkage to community say and, thus, are comparatively more inflexible. But those connected to material or economic life are liable to involve flexibility in their observance. Such a trend does not invite any serious attention of people unless some community interest gets directly involved. In case of caste society of rural India, the obligations connected to Jajmani or patron-client relationship, where change keeps on taking place, may be cited as an example. But a tribal's adherence to obligation relationship is very strong. In most of the cases, people do not ignore it at any cost. In an atmosphere of strong community living of tribals, the social force or pressure takes lead over the people.

Like the society and its social and economic network, the social change, too, is highly connected to the system of obligations. It is under the repercussion of social change elements that relationship, involving obligation, gets affected. Depending on its nature, it may affect any connected area. Interference in one does not keep confined at one level; rather it has a chain reaction. For instance when an obligation between two persons, connected through kinship, gets affected, it may reflect on many other relatives who have a say directly or indirectly in it. The same may hold true when a technological change gets going, affecting traditional element of obligation relationship and reciprocity. At the same time, this is also true that any influence, regarding obligation relationship, in one aspect of life gets reflected on others related to it. Correspondingly, the nature of obligations involved there also share the pinch of it. Separation in family not only affects the observance of social obligation, it does interfere with those connected to economic, religious and political life. Any intervention in the native system of obligations can be interpreted as reacting positively as well as negatively. It depends on the intensions and efforts of change agents. The obligation relationship can pose as barrier to intended change programmes; the same, however, can be taken help of in the extension and acceptance of innovations. Pressure of obligation can be useful in the matter if it is taken proper care of. Even social obligation can have say in the programme of economic change. The same, if not adequately tackled, can pose resistance to the agents of change.

Researches in the arena of obligations are very scanty. If at all we come across explanations on obligations, concerning various communities, they are loosely scattered. At the same time these have not been seen in the perspective of their interrelationship, wherever it exists. The social researchers do not seem to have made even a modest beginning in the interpretation of obligations in the context of social change phenomenon. More of the available knowledge regarding obligation is at actual level, as the social researchers have observed them. Less is revealed about the ideological state of obligations. More to be explored is the parity or disparity between ideal and actual levels. This would show as to what extent the negligence to an obligation can be tolerated. Also revealed would be the sensitive fronts in whose case no negligence is pardoned, and for which the people ever remain careful and vigilant. Such deeper implications will help dig out the significant and insignificant areas in the obligation system. Simultaneous to this, one would be able to take stock of the involvement of reciprocity and emotions. In ordinary narration of obligations, these dimensions largely remain hidden. Under this state of research levels the change agents remain far short of benefit derivation. Even if they get to know of obligations, they remain ignorant of deeper implications of them. Unless the latter is fully grasped, the agents of change will not be able to make use of this knowledge to gear up the social change process. Again, the researchers should not abruptly end in the analysis of deeper insights of obligations. Rather, they need to provide explanations as to how the change inducers can make best use of them in the diffusion of innovations.

Perfect egalitarianism, in any society, is a feature of rare occurrence. Other than the group inequalities, the status or position differentiation, at individual level, is often reported. It is more a characteristic of Indian rural communities where inequality, in terms of status, is not something unusual. Various orders of placement are commonly reported. An individual understands his position, and so does the society, at large, for the individual. Looking to the persistence of traditionality and the trends around, it appears that the currents of status consciousness are getting stronger. In spite of the gradually widening world view, the status differentiation seems to be the least bridged. Basically, the tribal order in India sounds more towards egalitarianism than what the caste society does. But the tribal societies, too, recognize some form of status-sometime as wide as that of a commoner and a chief. Level of status can broadly be discussed in respect of two situation; firstly, the position in regard to intra -group parameters and secondly its place in the context of other caste or tribe. In case of the former, the more microscopic view has to be taken note of. This means that the element of status has found feet in family, bigger social groups and even the community. The examination of status in respect of other groups involves quite a broad assessment. In any community, the basis of status are well defined. People have knowledge of the same and largely make efforts towards the maintenance of status. The status network has wider dimensions-it has its place in the smallest social institution of family, and goes to the widest possible extent of any social organisation. And at every level it is identified clearly. At the same time this is also true that status network is not unidimensionally set. It is ascertained and measured in social, economic, political and religious aspects. Each's independent stake is not denied, and so is largely true for their interconnectedness. But the latter may not necessarily be corresponding. A man, with socially superior status, need not always be economically sound, or one who is holding a higher religious position need not be necessarily a politician. Otherwise, however, some connection may be established. A wealthy or religiously superior person may be closer to a politician and his activities than an ordinary person. Or communication between the persons of various statuses is likely to be more effective. Those holding higher positions, in various aspects of life, generally present the major view point about caste, village, tribe or community relationship. Another area of interest, in a social setting, is to find out the background of higher positions and placements. Like most other societies, the Indian castes and tribes are also characterised by two processes. In one, a person inherits or is ascribed the status, and in other he or she achieves or acquires it by virtue of his ability, inclination and efforts. The former is more conspicuous a phenomenon in village India. Where does a person take birth is an important determinant of status. Typical traditional procedures of inheritance and succession also play a significant role in the matter. Under the lately introduced rules, some drifts have appeared in the age-old procedures.

There is a very intimate relationship between social change and status network. Depending on the nature of social change, it can react as pro-status and anti-status. Certain innovations are strengthening to the existing order of status, whereas others go contrary to their existence. Some innovations level up the status differences and others help in their further consolidation. In Indian situation, even without diffusion from outside, some change in status is explained through Sanskritization. Some people from socially inferior ethnic groups do try to raise their position by borrowing certain traits from those socially above them. How do the people, involved in such a borrowing, feel and how others, at wider level, recognise them may not be in tune with each other. But the whole process appears as if it heads towards patching up the built-in status differentiation in rural Indian population. The age-old traditions are, however, for the maintenance of status order. This is even supported by certain forces from outside. But then there are others which strongly pronounce for its dismantling. Another area of interest is to examine status network in the context of ideology of change-promoting programmes and their practical implications. Or to see it at ideal plane, and at one involving operational perspective. What ideologies prescribe and what people observe have, many a times, a big gap. What is intended for equality and egalitarian order is not taken up in that style. Under all these conditions, the status differentiation continues to characterize village India. At times it appears that the gaps between various positions are not only well consolidated but are also widening. This may, however, not be universally true. But higher, middle and lower categories of statuses are delineated and maintained. And the individuals belonging to them are also stratified accordingly. This gets obvious from the individual's way of living, as also from the nature of his interaction with others, especially those who do not belong to the same level of placement. People belonging to various statuses are marked with diverse elements involving competition, jealousy, friction lend even cooperation in certain matters. It is of utmost importance to judge the social change programmes in terms of all these elements. The devising of a suitable equation would then be required to minimise the opposition, and to maximise the acceptance. Encouraging healthy competition between the members of different statuses is a favourable point. Jealousy is an unhealthy sign which does present opposition to the agents of change in various ways. Areas of cooperation, and the scope for their further development, keeping programmes of change in mind, form the nexus that needs sharp attention.

Researches on the positional arrangement or statuses have been made but not very proportionately. Explanations and analysis of positions connected to caste system are more highlighted. The least dealt are the status systems of the tribals. In the context of caste, they are dealt at ideal as well as operational level. But in case of the tribes, the ideological level remains almost untouched. What the researches reveal, rather dimly, is the actual status lay out. But why it is and how does it rigorously operate need more and more attention. Even in case of caste studies, from this angle, the stress has remained on caste status rather than one on the individual who occupies an important place in social change process. At the same time are available some vague derivations concerning the tribals. One such is that the tribal people do not depict status systems. And that positional distinction is not a tribal character. These may only be true at assumption level. In reality, even the tribal social structures are not free of individual and group status differentiation. But certainly it is at a lower level than what is noted in caste society. However they are definitely of a level where social change efforts cannot go unconcerned of the same. Social researches need to concentrate on what is happening to status system in the event of social change and how the former is reacting to the latter. Also needed are the arguments, based on research findings, which can help make best use of diverse status planes in respect of social change programmes. Another aspect which needs thorough exploration, and which would prove of immense use to the agents of change, is the relationship between traditional and formally recognised statuses. Knowledge of their nature of interaction would be quite illuminating. Understanding of areas where they corroborate, and the ones where they fall apart are of immense value in designing and guiding social change efforts.

The sociological and social anthropological studies of micro and macro nature have stressed far less on the elements of inheritance and succession. This is more true in case of studies on village India. It is likely that these aspects were not considered, in sociological dimensions, as more forceful. But at the same time it is true that the diversity in Indian communities provides varied patterns of inheritance and succession. In some of the communities the patterns are just opposite to one another. At the same time this is also true that the laws of inheritance and succession are well-defined irrespective of the level of a community. The laws are no less laid down for small and primitive communities. These are equally prevalent in comparatively more developed peasant communities. The modes and norms of inheritance and succession are designed in tune with the nature of material possessions, offices and forms of authority. Though all societies have prescribed procedures of inheritance of material possessions, and of succession of offices or authority, their level of observance may differ. And this may be so in intra as well as inter-society context. What measures are taken when the prescribed procedures are uncared for are also defined. Alternatives, in case of non-existence of real claimants, also find place in the traditional norm- complex. For many items, and in many social systems, there are dual procedures for inheritance and succession. One is traditional and the other imposed by the official administration and its legal system. Sometimes, the provisions under two are supplementary. But in other cases they sound as sufficiently clashing. Such situations are metwith in tribal as well as the non-tribal communities. These, too, have appeared as part of social change process. Where the two procedures of inheritance and succession are in conflict, other signs of social disorganisation have also appeared. Such a situation has increasingly come up in land-owning communities where enactment has been comparatively of a heavy nature. Among the people with hunting and collection-based economy, the laws, introduced from outside, are comparatively less complicated. For decades, one of the ways of bringing about change has been through the various kinds of legislations. The introduction of formal laws, to bring about social change, has been more intense since India got her independence. A few of the acts connected, directly or indirectly, with inheritance and succession have also been promulgated. Many a times, the uniform kind of laws were implemented in dissimilar conditions. Under such a trend, how much purpose could be served, in respect of the intended aim of bringing about change, and how much disturbance it could cause to the customary system remained a matter of great concern. In addition to laws, efforts for introducing change were made otherwise too. This included the launching of various kinds of programmes for socio-economic transformation. Some of these could not be geared up for want of adjustment with native laws of inheritance and succession. These remained, at times, of sufficient incompetence. Mostly the propertied class and those holding higher positions or authority, say headman, chieftain etc., have always guided the destiny of rest of the inhabitants in the village, or in a group of villages. All around, the inheritance and succession procedures, in traditional form, have been such that sharing of property, authority or high office, concentrated with a small section. Such minority not only enjoyed most of the privileges but also posed for resisting change wherever it appeared in clash with their interest. By virtue of their socio-economic position, they even prevailed upon other inhabitants of their villages or communities to toe their line of action. Some programmes of their interest were always welcomed, and this again made them the chief beneficiaries.

Social researches in the context of inheritance and succession have remained confined chiefly to micro situations. The accounts, so obtained, cannot help generalize because of the widespread diversity in the patterns of inheritance and succession. What is imminently needed is a breakthrough in research at wider social plane. In absence of this, it would not be proper to design strategy for change in consonance with the existing laws pertaining to inheritance and succession. While attempting at wider level, all the areas need to be delineated thoroughly at two levels-one in their customary frame and the other in relationship to the changing perspective. How the prevalent patterns of inheritance and succession react to change needs to be analysed. The findings will have a vital place in directing the agents of change for appropriate kind of action. Another area of research is in regard to the applicability of official rules in inheritance and succession. What kind of adjustments people have made between the customary procedures and the lately implemented ones is also an important field of social enquiry. Such informations can also be useful in planned development. The areas of gap, conflict and anomie, which would be thrown open through such researches are of fundamental value to the designers and carriers of social change. In addition to highlighting the weaknesses, the enumeration of points of strength is then better possible. Both have their value in planning for change, as also in its practical feasibility.

Kinship occupies a very important place in the social network of a group of people. No group exists without kinship bonds involving respect, obligation, rights, duties, privileges, preference, avoidance, pressure, cooperation conflict etc. In some societies, the bonds based on affinal and agnatic considerations are more forcefully identified. Some others, however, take it lightly. But in no human society, they go unidentified. In day-to-day life, the kinship relationship, in some groups, sounds brittle. Its applicability, in others, remains strong and unavoidable. Indian rural society is characterised by the latter. The tribal as well as the non-tribal communities are deeply kinship-bound. And the system sounds quite complex in its various implications. Kinship base prominently operates at the level of individual behaviour, as also in social interaction. In certain aspects, it appears as a fundamental sphere in social reality. A large number of social groupings in tribal as well as non-tribal people of village India are formed on kinship. These subsequently lay down various kinds of norms associated with sanctions, taboos, incestuous feelings etc. Kinship consequences do not remain confined to social sphere alone. Its repercussions do appear, and may even intervene, in the economic, religious and political life of the villagers. Many economic activities, religious rituals and ceremonies and conditions in socio-political control are not free of kinship elements. Such involvement is overtly expressed in the form of participation, preference, obligations, reciprocity, cooperation etc. For various matters, the priority goes to the kinsmen, depending upon the degree of closeness. In many instances, the priority is defined as per the nature of events; to some, the agnatic ones are depended upon more than the affinal, and in others it is true vice-versa. Accordingly, sometimes they are held more firmly at village level, and in other cases, it goes beyond the village frontiers. The multi-ethnic villages present an interesting situation. There, the persons beyond an ethnic group are too, at times, referred and treated, in terms of certain kind of behaviour, as if they also belong to the kinship fold. This is specially observed in case of referring or speaking to an individual, and in granting him or her the respect. Thus, the scope and sphere of kinship in a social setting are wide. This holds true in the context of various ways of living, as also in respect of multiple ethnicity. When the kinship is so closely associated with diverse areas of socio-economic and religio-political organisation of a caste, tribe or even a community, it cannot be seen in isolation of change perspective. Ingredients of kinship, in some features of change, may react more sharply than the other. At times, the kinship seems to have a direct bearing on change phenomena; in other cases it may have only an indirect relevance. But it may not be wrong to express that the change-planners and implementors do not take stock of kinship implications in various ventures undertaken by them. The programmes, they plan for, or the approach they make use of hardly provide place to kinship factors. Firstly the kinship is not a very popular sphere with change-agents, and secondly its relevance is more appropriately thought of only in terms of the native cultural elements. The family, lineage, clan, tribe, marriage, birth, death, headmanship, rituals and rites where profound kinship bonds are rituals and rites where profound kinship bonds are identified, are not assessed at the level of change. And if they are it is not done with proper attention. There seems to prevail a false assumption that kinship elements are of more concern with traditionality. But then it should also be remembered that the elements that subscribe to traditional persistence are not devoid of their relevance to change that paves way to modernity.

Kinship, in comparison to other areas of social structure, is considered as a difficult field to be probed into. This is so even when the social anthropologists and other social analysts realise the importance of kinship system in a social group. At methodological and social analysis levels, the anthropologists have stressed comparatively more on the understanding of kinship system. But still a lot remains to be done at micro as well as at macro level. A casual treatment of kinship system finds frequent mention in books, monographs and other literature on various castes, tribes and village communities. But the same lacks deep insight, more so in the context of total social purview. Rather, the kinship is more frequently dealt around specific themes of pure sociological nature, and more in isolation of change features. In social researches, concerning rural India, especially the tribal pockets, the relevance of kinship to social change phenomena remains to be largely unexplored. Somehow, this field of social research has not caught adequate attention of social reseachers. Most of the programmes of social change at individual as well as group level do not go unnoticed of kinship consideration. More important, in this respect, is the leadership based on kinship. Family, lineage and clan heads are often consulted before an innovation is tried and accepted. Some other responsible people in the descent group are also approached for seeking their opinion. Many a times, such consultation does extend to some relatives connected through marriage. People do get influenced by those who have been, under kinship rules, ascribed superiority irrespective of their being of common descent or not. In certain groups, and for certain matters, the decisions are taken with common consent and it is the seniors, from kinship point of view, who prevail over others. Kinship rules even define the position of subordination and supraordination for various categories of people. Decisions given or sought, within kinship premises, are long lasting and of a firm nature. It is difficult to back out from commonly agreed upon issues because of the fear of pressure of members of kinship fraternity. The individual deviancy, in being pro-change, may not be tolerated if it goes contrary to group interest. But the same would be encouraged if it falls within the expectations of representatives from a kinship group. Therefore, the kinship network in terms of behaviour, obligation, rights, privileges, respect, pressure, preference, avoidance etc., needs to be searched and presented. This is necessary because of the involvement, at various levels, of these elements in the existing ways of life, as also in those which are proposed to be introduced. Availability of this knowledge to the agents of change would prove of immense help in the implementation of programmes of change. It will be easier for them to identify as to what would prove as

Closely connected to kinship is the institution of marriage which, too, has some bearing on social change phenomena. Marriage, in the context of change, may not sound as effectively functional as kinship but its place cannot altogether be ignored. Some aspects of marriage may certainly be discussed in their relationship to a few elements of change. Marriage is a universal phenomenon and the institution is, thus, reported in all societies, primitive or advanced. Among Indian rural communities, the institution carries more sanctity as it involves some religious dimension. The degree of latter varies depending upon the religious faith of communities. Lot of dos and donts are also involved in a marriage union. They form special markers for bride and bridegroom, mostly connected to married life. The sanctions and impositions, announced on the occasion of marriage, are meant to be observed in practical life of the couple, as also the couple vis-a-vis other kinsmen and society. Almost in every tribe, caste, village community and society, the married and unmarried are differentiated on the basis of status assigned to two categories. This does, in many cases, involve a built-in contradiction. In a community, the unmarried ones, in normal course, are rated at a lower scale than the married ones. But in the same community, the unnarried ones are rated far superior to others when they remain so after their dedication to the cause of religion where celibacy is a precondition. In many communities, remaining unmarried, without such a background, is not appreciated. Generally, most of the persons marry for sex and other reasons including social and religious ones. Indian rural communities show a large contrast in respect of forms of marriage, ways of marriage and the rituals and other details involved. Quite a sharp distinction is reported, in this sense, between the tribal and non-tribal communities. So much so that what a tribal group does accept as a preferrential form of marrying may outrightly be condemned by the non-tribal communities. However the difference is getting blurred among those tribes where the culture contact with non-tribals has become sufficiently long and where culture traits of non-tribals have been considerably borrowed. In most of the communites, the behaviour patterns of married and unmarried individuals are also distinguished. This appears in relationship, liberty, sense of responsibility, maturity, reliability, confidence etc. Some of such factors do find place in the arena of change.

Inspite of various legislations of long standing, most of the villagers, in India, continue to go in for early marriages. This holds almost uniformly true among the tribal and non-tribal people. Versions of diverse kinds are put forth in support of marrying at an early age. Some of these seem common while others are group-specific. But with all this, a common kind of impression is that marriage, at an early age, is a hindrance to social and physical growth. A person's incentive gets curbed when he or she is married in pre-matured state of mind. The person, then, does not find scope for independent thinking. Over and above, the man undergoes an additional social pressure. The latter comes heavy on an individual's personality and the same reflects adversely on the initiative that a person could otherwise take independently. Further, the pressure drags the man to traditional requirements rather than to those of change or modernity. Other than the parents or grandparents, on whom the person depends at this lower age of marriage, the in-laws become additional guidance factor. And both identically behave as pro-traditionals. Thus, the socio-economic dependence of the couples of younger generation on the elderly lot is a trend which goes, many a times, against the interest of change. In many instances the traditionality, in terms of ideals and otherwise, is imposed even when it is not wanted. Under the atmosphere of dependence and pressure of the above kind, one is made to realise of additional responsibility regarding wife, and subsequently of children. This not only makes a man look older to his age, but also drags him away from thinking about other ways of life. In tribal as well as non-tribal villages, the majority of people chiefly think of nothing else but their economic existence. How to procure food remains their major venture. Their earnings are not guaranteed. Under such a condition, the mind is constantly channelised in one direction. People remain tradition-bound and hardly find time to think of or to get into additional, improved and new ways of living provided in the programmes of change. In addition, the tradition-bound directions hang over very forcefully, and in such a situation a person remains the least keen to get into the fold of change-inducing programmes. He remains quite doubtful of the intensions of outsiders and is the last man to invite even the slightest risk associated with any new item or activity. To favourably react to any item of change remains a far cry for such a person unless the elders, to whom he is submissive, suggest him to get involved in the new venture.

Marriage, as a social institution, is far widely studied by the social researchers. About the types of marriages, ways of acquiring mates, marriage procedures, bride price, dowry, divorce, remarriage, pre and extramarital sex relations etc., details are available for a large number of castes and tribes. Such informations are available from various parts of the country; some areas are however, more traversed than the others. Even the account of changes in various aspects of marriage are available. All such explanations are certainly of importance in sociological perspective. But with all this a great paucity is felt of the studies concerning marriage vis-a-vis programmes of change. What adjustments, including the changes, people are making in various aspects of the institution of marriage are available. But how the programmes of change are reacted upon by marriage, in general, has remained the subject of least discussion and analysis. Still less explored is the front discussed in the above paragraph, a perspective of immense importance to planners and the agents of purposed change. In every group, the institution of marriage may have some bearing to one or the other items of change. The negative as well as the positive sides of such a relevance need to be searched. Knowledge of these is bound to be useful for change agents. It cannot be denied that some programmes suffer for typical find of marital implications. Practices like bride price and dowry have their own repercussions on economic programmes. Age and other constraints connected to marriage have their own say in social programmes. Results, based upon sociological insights in such spheres, would act as torchbearers to those who are engaged in the massive programme of socio-economic transformation in village India.

Existence of large scale organisations is reported in all the societies. But then the term 'large' is to be viewed in relative context. Some organisations, in non-tribal rural India, may sound as sufficiently large when seen in comparison to bigger organisations in the tribal societies. Even among the tribes, the size and magnitude of organisations may significantly differ. At times it does depend on the size of the tribe and its degree of exposure to alien conditions. But sometimes in isolated pockets too, one comes across certain organisations which appeal as if they are of larger order, especially when seen in the background of the group itself. But in comparison to outside situations, these may look of smaller magnitude. The birth of various kinds of larger organisations is discussed in regard to various factors. The same holds true for their functioning too. Broadly speaking, such organisational formations are meant to look after diverse interests and requirements of the group at wider level. For such a reason, these are, normally, not kinship-based. As the organisation serve the interest of community at large, their base remains about the kinship moorings. Another character of such organisations is that they are almost inherent in the social system. Mostly, they have originated from within rather than outside. Such a background makes their existence strong, and the people feel largely bound by the concerned verdict and direction. The organisations are managed by their own men on whom people have great faith. The latter has been transmitted from generation to generation. People acquire the equation of their relationship unquestionably. The organisations are theirs, and they are for the organisations. Every adult male or female in a tribe, caste or village community is well aware of the functions of such organisations. They also realise of their responsibility to the same. All kinds of help is rendered for the maintenance of such organisations. In many cases the purview of an organisation does extend to other neighbouring groups. But in most of the cases, it remains confined to the ethnic group to which it originally belongs. The pressure which an organisation can exert is far more functional in the context of the group for which it is primarily meant and the same declines for others. In many sections of Indian rural population, two very prominent organisations of large scale are reported. These have been in existence for centuries and cannot be treated as later introduction. Youth dormitory has characterised many tribes of Indian sub-continent. Regional council is another form of organisation which maintains social order and promulgates ordinances in the form of code of conduct. Numerous tribes and castes have been having such regional councils based on native laws, rather than those of the state legal system. Even the dormitories survived in their own style without getting any support or inspiration from official procedures.Oral traditions, in most of the cases, kept them alive through the ages. Since the increase of culture contact, planned as well as non-directed, some changes have appeared in these organisations. In most of the cases the traditional atmosphere has been impaired. It has come to an extent where people have started realising for winding up the organisation. The general alien atmosphere is not conducive to them. Some of them, specially the councils have been replaced by new forms of organisations introduced by the official administration. Some, like the dormitories, have not been exactly substituted and are generally facing crises of extinction. In comparison to old ones, the new organisations are yet to be properly established and accepted in various social systems.

The large scale traditional organisations have very intimate relationship with change. In fact the introduction of latter, to a very large extent, is conditioned by the former. By and large the norms of these organisations are pro-tradition, and the same are taken care of by the majority of people. The idea is to keep consistency and order in society. For centuries the villagers have been doing it out of respect and fear. In the absence of alternatives, people had no choice but to fall back on these organisations. Societal pressure, too, kept their conformity intact. Looking to the background and ramifications of these large scale organisations, they apparently sound as no-changers. But then the mechanism in certain cases is such that if it is properly understood and reformulated, it can certainly prove helpful to the programmes and agents of change. The dormitories among Indian tribes have been presenting such a case. The approach, however, requires a careful handling. One has to thoroughly understand the structure and functions of the organisation, and then to assess whether the proposed innovation can find place in the system and can be carried through. The strong elements in the organisation may, in the initial stage, prove as hard nuts to crack. But the constant persuasion and convincing arguments may bring them round. And once it is achieved, a great deal of the job is over because ordinary people are used to join hands with them. Social researches can play an important role in the whole affair. Research findings, so far reported for large scale traditional organisations, are limited. The diversity in respect of tribe, caste and village community in India is so wide that only a portion of it has been brought under the coverage of such studies. Moreover, the focus of what has been done remained somewhere else than one in the context of change. The social analysts have, by and large, given the narrative account of organisations covered by them. These have, most of the time, included structural pattern and functional perspective which themselves are of vital importance. What has been attempted to a lesser degree includes the functional and dysfunctional parameters of large scale traditional organisations in regard to the programmes of change. Least explored, sociologically, have been certain fronts which could be reshaped to make them change-prone. Researches alone can delineate such areas with more element of reliability. Once the social scientists certify the utility, for change purpose, of such elements, and once they give concrete proposals for their readjustment, the task of introducing change becomes easy for the agents of change. Simultaneously, the sensitive areas, connected to such elements, are also to be explained and taken care of. Another area of research which needs to be far more highlighted, in the context under reference, concerns the stronger fronts of opposition that characterize an organisation. To reduce their force, explanations are to be provided for their compromise with the new ideas and things meant for causing change. Usually, the change agents are unaware of all such issues and hence the receptivity to their proposals and programmes remains of a poor quality. To them, the things go unnoticed. They try and keep on getting opposition from larger organisations which, in normal course, behave as pro -traditional. And to make the same pro-change or pro- progess, the above details need to be brought in the knowledge of the change inducers and planners.

Indian village community is characterised by the existence of caste and the caste system. Most of the villages in Indian subcontinent are multicaste ones. Some villages are exclusively inhabited by the tribal people alone, and the same are marked by the absence of caste. There are still others where the families representing both, the castes and the tribes are living side by side. In latter case, the number of tribesmen is at times more than the castemen. But in many cases it is also true vice versa. Certain social situations present some elements of caste even in case of tribal groups. This specially holds true under conditions where contact between the tribals and the non-tribals has been centuries old. However, the model present may not exactly be of the same kind and force as one prevalent in non-tribal rural India. At the same time the caste ladder does not, normally, admit the tribals at specific positions, as is the case in respect of caste. With all this it is, however, largely true that the tribes are heading towards caste order. How far they have attained, and where are they accepted, or would be accepted, in future, are the questions which would chiefly be determined by the caste society around. In spite of certain formal legislations against caste system, the existence and force of caste in Indian villages are of a severe nature. Simultaneous to certain efforts, for the suppression of caste, are the emerging trends which promote caste conscious-ness, and hence its solidification. Caste continues to exist as a very prominent and strong institution in the social structure of village India. Even the Muslim and Christian sections of Indian population, specially at the rural plane, are marked by certain caste features.

For centuries the castes have survived under specific patterns. At some places, and in certain roles and activities of castes, some change has lately been noticed. But this is not radical enough to change the basic character of caste patterns. The rigidness of patterns is significantly conspicuous in comparatively more remote villages. In case of exposed villages, the pattern dimensions are felt as if they are comparatively less vital. The variation, however, does not pave way for change in basic character of the system. The castes maintain a hierarchy; the twice-born ones are at the top and the untouchables at the bottom. In between are the artisan and other occupational castes. Pollution, purity, occupation etc, form the basis of segmentation. The differentiation is minute in case of castes belonging to the same segment, and their ranking distance is not much. But the same sounds significant when two castes belonging to two different segments, say higher and lower, are compared from this angle. But irrespective of the degree of ranking, the villagers understand and explain well the arrangement of caste placement in social hierarchy. The social scientists, with their sharp methodological tools, too, do not take long to understand the position of various castes in social ladder. Further, most of the Indian villages are characterised by the existence of a dominant caste. Many social situations, at village level, support the presence of Sanskritization. In such a process, the dominant caste is normally treated as the reference group by others in the lower strata. At ideal plane, every caste is endogamous and is labelled with a particular occupational specialization. The latter, during the last few decades, does not hold perfectly true in case of all the members of a caste. Instances of change in occupation by some members of a caste are frequently metwith. In most of the cases, the majority, however, still sticks to the traditionally defined occupations for various castes. In spite of the induction of many formal agencies of social control, the castes too continue to discharge this function in their own style. Caste and inter-caste councils, and the associated leadership carry sufficient say in many matters of customary importance. The customary laws, and the sanctions supporting them continue to be identified and carried through. Though each caste maintains its individual identity, and upholds many a ways distinct from others, there is a tremendous amount of inter-dependence between the members of various castes. And this is practically exhibited in various walks of life including social, economic, political, religious etc. Every caste has its own culture, and maintains the same in the context of intra and inter-caste social network. Inter-caste relationship is exhibited through affection, respect, obligation, friction, conflict, dependence, service, remuneration, supraordination, subordination etc. The traditional norms and values provide support to the continuance of such elements of relationship. The symbiotic relationship between various castes is organised through the system of patron-client relationship, which marks every Indian village symbolised by the existence of castes. Beyond the families of a village community, the system also extends, in numerous cases, to the inclusion of people of various castes from the neighbouring villages. Thus, the inter-dependence of castes is a feature even beyond village boundaries. There are serving and the served castes, and the services and corresponding rewards and remunerations are well laid down. For lack of alternatives people have, for centuries, kept the system intact. But in the event of some lately available alternative economic and social opportunities, some do not seem strictly adhered to various terms and conditions governing patron-client relationship. Such a change, however, seems to be drop in the ocean. Otherwise people remain obliged to render services and rewards. The terms and conditions, at times, reveal as if they involve an element of exploitation. The people of serving class, chiefly from lower castes, appear as loosers. Gainers are the higher caste families who, for various reasons and for their being in power and position, are keen for the retention of age-old pattern.

Most traversed, from the point of view of social research, has been the institution of caste in India. The Indian as well as the foreign scholars and social scientists have explored various fronts of caste system. The system has been searched in historical, current and changing perspectives. Explorations in ideal form and empirical reality have led to the coining of number of concepts related to the area of caste. In addition to certain specialized and focussed researches on caste, some explanations about the institution are always available in village studies published by the social scientists. As a matter of fact, caste occupies such an important place in village India that Its coverage, in one form or the other, is unavoidable. Implications of caste rules and regulations are metwith in the economic, political and religious life, in addition to social one. Such intricacies of caste have been revealed by the sociologists and social anthropologists in their writings on village studies done in various regions of India. But except in one or two accounts, and that too more at ideal plane, a sufficiently consolidated picture, in respect of caste and its implications and interventions, is not available. This holds specially true when caste is reviewed in reference to the efforts and programmes made for bringing about progress and development in rural India. Evaluation of a few sporadic projects provide some instances of interruption of caste in the programmes of change. Rather, more effective have been some works at theoretical and academic level which have come to occupy prominent place in sociological literature. These too are concerned with the aspect of dynamics in society, but in a different perspective. Concepts of Sanskritization and dominant caste are among the notable ones. These, and others, have provided new insights at academic level, but have not proved of utility at practical front, specially when seen in their relevance to the diffusion of purposed innovations for the betterment of communities. Again, there have been repeated writings on the changing frontiers of caste, its limiting and broadening horizons. How old order of caste, with its elements, is undergoing change finds frequent mention in the sociological and social anthropological writings. A similar analysis has been made for development programmes since their inception with the start of Five Year Plans. Reports, making assessment for their success and failure have piled up in the offices of various organisations. What remains to be adequately done is the search for analytical explanations of the form and content of interaction of caste elements with those of the development and change ingredients. Castes have never been free of their functional and dysfunctional aspects. Some explanations regarding these are available. But the same are chiefly in reference to the old or traditional social systems. The urgency is to analyse the functional and dysfunctional roles of caste in the relevance of contents of change or innovations which have been, or are being proposed as part of development strategy. In the light of the force of caste, in rural India, it would prove very helpful to development planners and implementors if caste barriers are identified. These need to be streamlined in addition to the exploration of castestimulants in the interest of change diffusion. Other than its relevance to programmes of change, the caste implications further need to be researched in their relationship with the functionaries engaged in the gigantic task of causing change. Castes of the functionaries themselves seem to have lot of bearing on the efforts for carrying specific programmes to the rural masses. Passing of the research results to the agents of change will certainly not let them take things for granted. They would also be cautious of caste resistance, and even may get capable of developing skill for getting the desired innovations accepted. Another important field to be attended to, in priority, is the state of change in tribal families who have already been influenced by the caste patterns. How such tribals are reacting to the proposed innovations is a special field of social enquiry. Once this knowledge is provided to the change agents, they can adjust their approach to make it more effective, minimising opposition thereof.

Very closely connected to the aspect of caste come the privileged and non-privileged categories of persons and groups. Many a times it appears that the privileged individuals and groups are mainly from amongst the higher castes. The non-privileged and the deprived ones belong, in majority, to the lower and untouchable castes. The general observations and impressions of this kind are not without claims for their validity. To this rule there may be some exception but the same may not be strong. In certain specific sense, some privileged persons may even be identified among the people of lower strata in ethnic composition. Likewise the non-privileged and the deprived ones may also be reported from the higher caste population. But such trends are uncommon. In tribal India the existence of the categories of privileged and non-privileged is of quite an insignificant order. The privileged-nonprivileged disparity is so thin, in comparison to caste society, that the tribals themselves are hardly conscious of it. Social, economic and political differentiation is not pinching. By and large the tribals seem to be at a common plane; exception being a small population of hunters, gatherers and trappers. Among the agricultural tribes, which form the majority in the total tribal population, the privileged and non-priviledged categories do not seem to be pressing, as is true in case of caste society. Lately, however, some seem to be behaving like the more privileged.

Ordinarily the concept of privileged needs to be examined from a total perspective. Economic soundness, political power or authority, religious domination and social superiority are some of the determinants of privileged class. Among the caste structure of Indian village communities, these traits are predominantly found among the members of higher castes. But it is not necessary that a particular individual or family would have all the traits mentioned above. A few families from the lower castes do possess one or the other of these traits, though it may not be at the same scale as are found among the higher caste people. Considering all pros and cons it appears that the concentration of privileged is among the higher castes; the lower ones represent the bulk of non-privileged. Over the ages the position has remained almost unchanged, though the equality and egalitarianism are increasingly stressed for as part of policy of independent India. Rather, the current trends are indicative of the phenomenon that the already privileged have become more privileged. They are the people who hold the fort in rural India. The non-privileged have not moved much, though some change cannot be ruled out among them.

Social researchers have lacked concerted efforts in the study of privileged and non-privileged persons and groups in the rural population. A few isolated studies provide support to the argument that the rich are becoming richer, and the poor as poorer. And that the gap between the haves and have- nots has widened. But such explanation applies more in the economic sense. The other associated non-economic criteria have not been adequately taken care of. The economic and non-economic traits do have some linkages-one may boost up the other. Or, possession of one may lead to the attainment of other. What is needed is the true identification of privileged people and their class. This requires to be done through the assessment of all the traits. Thus, the different sub-categories, under privileged, need to be delineated. A similar attempt is to be made for the non-privileged, their status of this order is to be explained in the context of various elements. Such an attempt would help classify socially, economically, politically and religiously privileged and non-privileged persons. Another area of research which needs urgent attention, and whose explanation would be useful to planners and agents of change, is connected to the analysis of processes involved in the creation of privileged and non-privileged categories. It should analyse the causes, including means and conditions that subscribe to the promotion of wide disparities. What has been the contribution of change elements in the creation and strengthening or dissolution of such categories has not been properly attended to. And the same invites an immediate attention of social analysts. Somehow there has been no exclusive devotion to such studies. Most of what has been done is the part of other major studies whose focus remained elsewhere.

Change studies in rural Indian context are revealing of the fact that the major beneficiaries of change programmes are the small number of privileged families and groups. The traditionally non-privileged could not, to a great extent, come within the reach of change promoters. Althrough, the privileged families, at village level, dominated others. And by virtue of their living in socially, economically and politically advantageous position, they could chiefly attract the change agencies. With the sufficient resources, these people could meet many requirements of the change agencies. Many others remained helpless and unapproached. An attitude of indifference prevailed towards the non-privileged. Many innovations which the privileged acquired remained out of the fold of non-privileged. It was so retained consciously as well as unconsciously. Though the intended efforts were, at least at ideal level, for the development of total village community, the involvement of non-privileged remained the least. And as the privileged, in rural communities, are in a thin number, the programme acceptance was chiefly limited to them only. This kept the target far below the expectations of change and development workers. This was further kept limited because some of the programmes were not appreciated by the privileged section. They appreciated only what suited to their traditions and requirements. For programmes, which could suit the non-privileged, they outrightly denounced the initiative feeling that the village community is not in need of them or that they would not be sustained at village level for reasons better known to them. The intention has been to keep the non-privileged in their traditional cell so that major benefits may accrue to the privileged alone. Even majority of those who were involved as the carriers of change belonged to the class of privileged and they basically remained somewhat indifferent to the growth and development of non-privileged people. Such drawbacks, independently or in combination with one another, proved hard to the large number of non-privileged. The trend may continue if serious efforts are not made to tackle the handicaps at various levels. And the latter is easily possible when a thorough analysis of privileged and non-privileged under the traditional and new conditions, and in reference to all the traits, is made, and when the planners and agents of change are made thoroughly conversant about its broader perspective at a wider social plane.

Indian village communities are marked by a built-in contradiction. A village community is characterised by good deal of solidarity when examined in situations involving conflict with some other village community. The same may appear true when inter-caste dependence, as ideally prescribed, is taken into account at village level. But when the social situation at intra-village community level is examined, in practicality, it presents a different picture. In the latter case, the village community seems to provide, in its social structure, place to conflicts and feuds. Some of these assume serious shape so much so that the persons in conflict make many allies and crystalise into two factions hostile to each other. Some quarrels have a short life. But there are others which continue for generations. In this case the feelings of hostility and revengefulness are also passed on by the members of one generation to others. The frequency of such cases is, however, low. But there are plenty which continue for years. While comparing tribal and multicaste village, at the plane of conflicts and feuds, it sounds, especially from literature of tribal monographs and village studies, that the situation in tribal villages is one of ease. There, the conflicts are of momentary nature and do not prolong much. The faction-formation, too, is of a mild nature. The situation is grave in case of multicaste villages with land-based economy. In mixed villages of tribes and castes, the feuds and factions live little long. Generally, the factions do not have a permanent structure. They die when a conflict is resolved. New ones get formed with fresh conflict. That the same families should always join as part of a faction is also not true. The constituents of a faction may be more or less, depending upon the basic issue involved. But some families may always side with one another in case of a conflicting situation. To some the factions are functional, but for others they prove as 'dysfunctional'. The tendency of the constituents of a faction is always for its strengthening. Their motive is to run down the members of the opposite faction. The target of a faction is to undo what members of the opposite faction intend to do. The faction-formation and faction-dynamics have increased with the growing exposure of village life to alien ways and conditions. Things are more complicated now than what they were before.

A deep insight into the faction-complex of Indian villages supports for two major dimensions. One pertains to its nature of composition and the other to the root causes which give rise to and sustain factions. A faction is determined and constituted by kinship, caste and neighbourhood considerations. Kinship loyalty and affiliation are most important. In any event, a man or family would, in normal course, become ally of another family who is closer to them in kinship relationship. Whatever may come, they try to protect his interest. The next element of loyalty is determined by caste. Of course the caste and kinship are, again, closely connected. The relatives, near or distant, are generally from the same caste. Even otherwise one would preferably side with his castemen even when two are not related through kinship. Neighbourhood forms another criterion conditioning, in most cases, the structure of a faction. In general, being careful of one another's interest, the neighbours join hands together. It may, however, be pointed out that the neighbourhood is usually formed of the people belonging to the same caste, and many a times consisting of families of the same lineage or clan. However, it may further be mentioned that such pattern, regarding composition of faction is not true in cent percent cases. In some, one may come across factions consisting of people and families even beyond kinship, caste and neighbourhood.

Diversity marks the causes of the formation of factions. Among the most common causes are the disputes connected to land and sex. Unauthorised occupation of somebody's land and illegal sex relations create condition where two groups of villagers come to clash. Violation of irrigation procedures also creates atmosphere of anger and enemity. Sense of prestige and feeling of revenge create favourable atmosphere for the origin and growth of factions. Sustenance of factions is strengthened by the generational feuds. Instigation and provocation, in various forms, add fuel to the fire. Extent of factions and their longivity vary, depending upon the nature of base and the community's attitude to the same. When the basic issue is resolved, the faction disappears automatically.

One of the lesser explored areas of social research has been the one connected to faction groupings and their manifestations. Special studies of factions have hardly been made by the social anthropologists, except in one or two cases. In their comparison the sociologists have done somewhat better. Whatever little is available concerns the stereotyped explanations hinting at the origin and growth of factions. At some places, it is also argued that the creeping in of non-traditional elements of living has geared up the formation of factions. In places where the innovations have hardly seen the light of the day, the scope for rivalry is not much. Whatever remains is tradition-bound. What roles the factions, and the associated people thereof, play in the context of programmes of planned change has not been adequately explored by the social researchers. A faction-ridden village community is generally treated as non-conducive to new ideas and innovations. As the atmosphere of unanimity does not prevail in the recipient group, the new items and ideals become nobody's responsibility. Even if the new things sound useful, its adoption by the members of one faction is looked down upon by those of the others. An inherent attitude is of condemnation. Neither the members of a faction themselves relish the benefit of an innovation nor they tolerate others to do the same. Those responsible for introducing the change get into a dilemma as to what is happening to their ventures. Basically the antagonism is not to the change agents or the ideas and activities they carry. What is harming and crucial is the attitude to run down the members of the opposite faction. And hence it is, generally, not tolerated that the people of opposite camp should achieve something to grow. Even if the latter do, rumors are spread about the bad intentions behind the proposed change elements. And the slightest doubt, hitting the villager's mind, would make him indifferent even to what he had once decided to acquire. So much so that he may even leave what he had already adopted,. Things are no better even within the faction. An individual or a family, as part of a faction, is almost devoid of independent thinking and of taking independent decisions. The whole social group is strongly organised under the leadership of one spokesman, and his word is final. He acts as the chief decision maker. And if he is reluctant or disinclined to accept an innovation, others, in his faction, would follow the suit. From the research point of view, such fronts have stayed as the least touched. Why things take such a course, and why others are so subservient to the decision of a single person need to be elaborately explained. Analysis of all aspects of the stronghold is desired to make the people adjusted in favour of change. Why decision making is channelised in one style is another point for scientific planning. Faction politics in traditional perspective, and in the context of new conditions are to be identified and understood. And the social analysts are the best to do it. It is the social researchers who are more competent to explore various dimensions of intra-faction and inter-faction politics, and their relevance to the programmes of planned change. Such a job is beyond the scope of change agents and they can hardly get involved in an exercise of this kind. But certainly they can be given the direction to implement the programmes successfully even under the existence of factions. Ways of creating healthy competition between the members of two factions can be found out and suggested. Decision-making agency can be persuaded and moulded to suit the requirement of change within a faction.

Village India is characterised by the diversity of political organisations. Leadership patterns and the mechanisms of social control also vary; at times more significantly. The formal pattern of leadership, introduced under Panchayati Raj or Democratic Decentralisation, however, exhibits tremendous amount of uniformity. This is specially true at the level of design. Agencies and mechanisms of socio-political control, within the traditional framework, present variety of patterns. And there would hardly be a village, interior or exposed, without some kind of controlling agency. In some places it sounds simple, whereas at other it is fairly elaborate and complex. In general the multicaste villages have two channels of traditional leadership, that is one for individual caste, and the other for the village community and all the sections thereof. Some villages have more than one section, at times located little away from one another. The chief decision-maker in the matters of a caste is the caste headman. Beyond this the deciding agency is the sectional or village head. Multicaste or multi-ethnic villages have more of a democratic set up in terms of traditional leadership. The head of village community normally takes decisions in consultation with the section, or if necessary, caste heads who together constitute village council. ~The latter may, many a times, not appear as a permanent kind of body, consisting only of the fixed person. By and large the women are not included in village councils. Elderly male members represent in the gathering. To regulate inter-village relationship, the existence of traditional councils, at a wider territorial level, is reported. It consists of a few contiguous villages; in many cases belonging to a predominant clan of the area. In some regions, still bigger councils, covering a more wide area, are also reported. The councils, beyond village, are represented by the village heads under their jurisdiction. In tribal villages there exist sectional heads, if the village has sections, and a village headman. The village head may or may not have an assistant. His word is the law. In some of the tribes, specially the bigger ones, the existence of regional councils has been reported. Their representation largely resembles one reported among the caste villages. Others, who are consulted as opinion or professional leaders occupy important place in tribal as well as the non-tribal villages. They express lot of respect for the skill or specialisation that they have developed. In spite of some change, in general, these people are highly depended upon by the inhabitants of the village. A formal system of social control and leadership, called Panchayati Raj, has been introduced in Indian villages since late fifties. This three or two-tier system was inroduced by the government, and it exists simultaneous to the traditional one. All over, it is of uniform pattern marked by village, Block and District Council.

In terms of effectivity, the formal and informal or traditional leadership have their respective place, depending upon the matter or nature of issue. The physical location of the village, and the degree of its exposure to alien influence, through culture contact, count in the matter. Officially speaking, the task of enthusing developmental change has been assigned to the Panchayati Raj bodies. In fact one of the functions of the elected representatives is to gear up new ideas and innovations proposed by the agents of change involvecd in the programmes of tribal and rural development. The traditional councils, and the leadership thereof, are considered as basically and essentially meant to look after the customary interests of the village community as a whole. It is something rare that such leadership network is involved in the programmes of planned change. They are hardly approached by the extension agencies. Even the officially recognised leaders may not appreciate if someone ignores them at the cost of traditional leaders. To keep their prestige they may even complain about such act of functionaries to the higher official authorities. Whether helpful or not, they cannot easily be avoided. It largely holds true even when their verdict or directive is not acceptable to the majority of villagers. On the other hand in interior areas and tribal belts, the traditional leaders and their assemblies continue to be quite forceful. In most of the events they are the first to be approached by the villagers. This is because of the continued strong belief in the status and verdict of such members and institutions. ~They are accorded more value than any other agency. Even in case of acceptance or rejection of alien traits, concerning any walk of life, the villagers seek advice from non-formal leaders. And if the latter express an attitude of indifference or doubt, the common villagers backout, making various kinds of excuses. Their withdrawal remains unaffected even when someone from formal leadership hierarchy tries to convince or pacify them. In such villages the role of statutory institutions is of tangential nature. Apparently their effects are not easily left. The predominance remains of the old-styled councils and their constituents. Under this state of affairs nothing much, beyond the approval of professional and non-professional traditional leaders, finds feet in the name of innovations. However, some stray cases of adoption of new ideas and technology are, many a times, reported. Worse form of resistance to development efforts comes under the situation when the formal and traditional leaders, at village level, are in confrontation. This, too, is a phenomenon often reported from Indian villages. In a social situation of this kind, programmes of change have the least chance of finding feet among the members of village community. For certain personal considerations the new proposals are turned down. The place of professional leaders is no less important in the context of diffusion of innovations. When their social, psychological and economic security are threatened, under new impositions, their reaction is of opposition. Because of the old established position, they even manage to mobilise the families, under their influence, to disapprove of the new venture. The element of doubt, about the new, comes in their favour.

Social scientists have carried out a number of studies on leadership in rural India. But the stress, mainly, has remained on the formal leadership, even extending upto the level of State and Centre.

Various studies on elections, at different levels, are available. Changing rural leadership and role of formal leaders are highlighted in number of attempts. Even in village studies and tribal monographs, explanations regarding Panchayati Raj institutions find more prominent place. Same is repeated in case of the macro-level studies. Only a scanty attention is given to traditional forms of leadership, specially in its relationship with the programmes of change and the agencies thereof. And their nature of relationship with the statutory bodies and the leadership thereof is not sufficiently explained. What is of significance to change agents is the proper kind of information about the leadership pattern, its weak and strong points in the relevance of new ideas and technology. It would be wrong to presume that the formal leaders alone can push the programme of change. Leadership dynamics, at village level, needs to be kept at the forefront before the items of change are suggested. Which leaders should be approached when, in what way, and for what purpose are to be calculatively derived taking a stock of traditional, professional and formal leaders, and of the kind of equation they have among themselves and with the village community. Identification of right kind of torch-bearers is a strong prerequisite for introducing an element of change, and specially when it is of vulnerable nature. Under the dual form of leadership, the need is to search as to who has hold on the community and in what respect.

Like the political organisation the ingredients of rural and tribal economy, in India, show a fair degree of variation. It cannot be denied that the economy of village India is predominantly agriculture-based. But then certain social groups, both castes and tribes, can be delineated with non-agriculture occupations, though they may be otherwise living with the agriculturists. These people meet many requirements of the farming families through the tools and technology they possess. This holds specially true for multi-caste and multi-ethnic or mixed villages. There, the dominant agriculture comunity is not totally independent and self-sufficient. Rather, its members depend on variety of non-agriculturists who equip them for various purposes. And such an economic relationship is centuries old. From the past there have been cultivators of differing standing. In most of the agriculture-based villages, one or two, and at times a few, specially in bigger villages, families have been comparatively more prosperous as they alone own more resources, including land.

A majority among rest of the farmers either live from hand to mouth or go in for debt for their existence. The latter have no surplus, and if some have, it is just the marginal and cannot meet other requirements of theirs. In addition to one or two well-off agriculturists, such villages, by and large, have some rich family from the trading caste. Its members also indulge in money-lending business. In times of scarcity and economic hardship, such economically affluent families exploit others who are hardpressed and needy in the village. In case there is no money-lender at village level, people would patronize one from a nearby village or town. Relationship of this kind is not a new phenomenon in rural India. It is an old established practice where things get transmitted from one generation to the next. Other than the small and marginal farmers, the needy landless and the artisans also get involved in such economic network. But in their case the patronization of a money-lender becomes slightly difficult as they have no land, as permanent property. They are, thus, given only smaller amounts of loan, or many a times less costly items of day-to-day need. The village communities are, thus, economically differentiated; an insignificant minority is of 'haves' and a big majority of 'have-nots'. Lately, the government has launched certain programmes for economic betterment of the villagers. These are mainly agriculture-based. Institutions like credit and multipurpose cooperative societies have also been established. But the benefits of these have, again, chiefly gone to the already better off, including bigger farmers and a few non-farming families. The rest continue to present a picture of poverty. Still lagging economically behind are the tribals. Most of their habitations stink in poverty. Though a majority of the tribals, too, are agriculturists, their primitive tools and technology, difficult terrain and meager resources render them unable to produce even what is required by them. The production barely meets their requirement for a few months in the year. Then they have to depend on other occupations, mainly labour, for their survival. Quite a large number of tribals, more so those who live in forest villages, depend, to a great extent, on forest economy. Some of the forest produce is consumed and the rest sold to meet other day-to-day needs,. In comparison to the non-tribals, the needs of tribals are less. But then the same holds true for their resources. Because of being ignorant, the problem of exploitation is more acute among the inhabitants of tribal villages. This, and other factors subscribe to a great deal of poverty and hunger in tribal belts. The money-lenders have a roaring business in tribal villages. The debt, once taken, does not easily come to an end. This gives way, in many cases, to the system of bonded labour. Systems of trade and market are not developed. In weekly markets, or even otherwise, people go in for barter and exchange. Somehow the benefits of tribal development programmes have remained far below the expectations. In case of tribals as well as the non-tribal Indian villagers, the economic backwardness and poverty can be attributed, among other things, to some of the social customs, ceremonies and practices which the people observe. The traditional social organisations of the village communities provide place to many social and cultural performances where the villagers have to spend liberally. In spending, people go beyond their means, and do not mind incurring debt. Marriage, death and birth are some special occasions when a villager has to submit to the will of community at large. Social pressure does not provide scope to escape. To live in the community, the social impositions have to be attended to. Under such a social climate, the economic burden is inevitable and the same significantly matters for those who cannot stand on their own. The economic life is, thus, not independent of social dimensions.

Researches on indebtedness, poverty, exploitation and bondage have been carried out in case of certain village communities. Studies are also available on the diffusion of agricultural and other economic innovations. But special researches on social dimensions of economic organisation are lacking. And this is an area which is of quite a relevance in Indian context where the pressure of social structure elements on economic organisation is of a sound order. How this pressure is exerted, and in what areas, form interesting subjects of social enquiry. At the same time the stock of resources, human or otherwise, has not been adequately assessed. A very clear picture about the needs of peasantry is yet to be presented by the social scientists. And this is to be done for economic as well as social needs in their independent as well as inter-related contexts. Place of customary practices, and the attitude of the village community to the same need to be far more deeply analysed. This relates to the field of economic life and the institutions thereof. What is happening to the once established economic order, and to the related social events, under the currents of changing conditions is another field of immediate research investigation. When the social scientists would be able to provide correct insight into all these areas, the task of agents of change may get easier. The development workers have been approaching the villagers as per their own convenience. They could not, for personal and other reasons, make use of the right kind of methodology. The extension agents contact the rich and bigger farmers to sell off their ideas of economic development. Such people alone could meet the requirement, because of their resources, of the programme. As others were unable to do it, they were bothered the least. The economically tight farmers and others remained far short of their participation. The poor and the deprived ones could hardly be involved. By virtue of their economic soundness, even the new economic institutions were mostly managed by the well-to-do people. Even if others were made the members, the managers and other money-lenders took advantage of their membership. When the loans were granted to such members, a major portion of it were adjusted against the old debt which such people had taken from the economically better-off families. The purpose of the disbursement of loans was forfeited as the economy of common man could not be geared up. And the concerned agencies failed to remain watchful of such processes. The same has been repeated in case of the legislations and enactments promulgated against exploitation and indebtedness. The anticipated farget of change could not be met for two major reasons. Firstly, the law-enforcing agencies never got serious about the practical application. Secondly, the villagers, involved in such practices, manipulated the legislation by evolving new techniques at local level. The social causes of indebtedness and poverty could hardly be focussed upon by the change agents. That means the root causes were not attended to. And unless these are taken care of, through additional provision or otherwise, it may be mighty difficult to improve upon the economic position in general. Motivation for attitudinal change, and some economic provision for certain social needs may be helpful in the matter. An increasing need is to involve small farmers, artisans and others in the programmes of economic change. Conditions for involvement have to be made easy for them. The change agent has to necessarily understand and bother for the equation prevalent between bigger or richer farmers and money lenders on the one hand, and small farmers, artisans and the rest on the other. Special programmes for the landless are to be planned taking into account the background of ecology, resources and socio-economic state of such families. Programmes which can have long lasting effect may be more acceptable if the functionaries approach with honest intentions and clarity of mind. Because of certain administrative reasons the efforts, many a times, remained only half-hearted. The committed provisions could not be made available in time. And if one was available, the other, which was necessary to make the first one economically effective, could not be managed and provided. To avoid adverse effect, things should be supplied in package. More ignored remained the tribals and the tribal areas where natural, physical and even man-made conditions appear harder and where much has remained to be done to gear up and organise agriculture and forest economy. More elaborate planning and a strong and strict supervision, at implementation level, are the prerequisites to boost up tribal economy. At all cost, the middleman (exploiter) has to be uprooted.

SIX

MATERIALISTIC AND PERCEPTIONAL PERSPECTIVE

Every society, primitive, advanced and advancing has its own way of life. Some of these ways or life-designs are unique and others are shared, partly or fully, with the neighbouring communities. More sharing is marked in those communities who are in the sway of change. And uniqueness in living remains the character of those who are in isolation and believe in boundary maintenance. Whatever be the level of living, or magnitude of acculturative influence, every group of people, caste, tribe, community etc., claim to have a typical way of life which they consider as belonging to them. In the scientific parlance, such a way of life is dealt under the title of culture. Broadly speaking culture is said to have three major dimensions, that is, sociological, ideological and technological or material. In other words culture is not merely an abstraction, in the the form of value system or ideology, it also reflects reality in the form of social organisation, technology and other economic attributes. Non-ideological parameters, and more so the techno-economic dimensions, have been treated by many experts as elements of civilization. And this is how the civilization and culture are differentiated. In this chapter, I would like to highlight the place of techno-economic and ideological parameters in the arena of social change.

To some social scientists the material bases of living have a very important place in the context of social-cultural change. And this they explain on the plea that material ways are of paramount importance in the totality of way of life of a group of people. And being so they have a great say in the arena of change, as also in continuity.

Any shake in the material foundation is believed to correspondingly reflect in the social life and value-system. It's nature and extent would be determined by the magnitude of shake. Material ways of life, in case of the developing countries, are not at the same level as reported in case of First World or Second World Countries. Such an instance of variation may be reported even among the different communities of the same country. For instance, in rural India one can easily delineate two levels of techno-economic existence-one represented by its caste society and the other characterizing the tribal world. Even among the cases of tribes themselves, there are marked variations. The material living of food gatherers, hunters, trappers and shifting cultivators are certainly not at the plane of artisans, craftsmen and developing peasants. Such a difference can also be marked in three segments (lower, middle and upper) of caste social order. The notable divergence in material ways, with its corresponding relationship to social and ideological styles of living, has lot to say in the creation of change in the communities they represent.

Material world is not an isolated feature in the life-designs of a community. It has lot to say in the socio-psychological and other areas of culture. Elements of economy and technology do have, many a time, bearing on other areas of culture. The response and behaviour within the bound of techno-economic conditions is, thus, a part of larger behavioural network. Such an interconnectedness of various elements has lot to say in the discussions and implementation of change. Under such circumstances it would be difficult to think of, and conceive, change in any aspect of material world in isolation of social dimensions marking a group of people. Touching of any key features is likely to have repercussions in wider terms. Or a proposed element of change may not find feet for reasons of indifference emanating from the other connected aspects. Unfortunately the sociological or psychological implications of proposed material changes were, in the context of village India, hardly considered by the planners and agents of change. May be that they were not oriented on those lines. There could be proposed massive programmes for economic development including agriculture, animal husbandry, cottage industries etc. But their implications in the areas of social structure, and the built-in systems thereof, could not be highlighted. Since village India, including tribal pockets, presents a variety of social and cultural systems, its consideration might have been found rather difficult while proposing for various programmes of economic change. This could be one reason, among others, that the goals have not been fully achieved. In certain corners there grew resistance and opposition slowing down the pace of programmes of development. Some instances of undesired disorganisation could also come on the surface. To avoid all this the social dimensions of economic programmes should have been taken note of.

The position of social science research, on this count, is again not encouraging. Firstly, the social structure specialists were not many when the planned programme of change was started for village India. Secondly, the kind of researches they were then doing did focus on items other than the one under consideration. Only scanty research informations, then available, could be of relevance. Sociological and social anthropological researches were also not taken with seriousness in those days, and as such the opinion of such experts was largely neither invited nor counted. But even when the programmes of planned economic change remained in process, nothing very substantial could be achieved in terms of social research on social dimensions of economic programmes and policies. There were conducted many research studies on the impact of Community Development and Tribal Development Programmes, more so the economic ones. There are available sufficient reflections on the failures and achievements of particular schemes in specific areas. But these are chiefly analysed within the economic and technological framework. Sociological and social anthropological implications, both in the process and end-products, find the least mention. That a programme failed or succeeded for reasons of material input, supply, equipment, financial resources, technical expertise etc., finds more detailed treatment. Factors like caste, clan, family, kinship, marriage, village community etc., are least dealt in terms of their relationship to a particular programme meant to provide impetus to the material ways of living. Since an economic venture is not launched in vacuum, but for a group of people, and since such a group has a definite social organisation, there is every chance that elements of the latter do have bearing on those of the former. For certain built-in social organisational provisions, an economic or technological venture may be held up, or even may meet fillip, depending on the situation. And as India poses for larger diversity in terms of social organisation, for the Indian society being plural, it is all the more necessary to know of the social divergences vis-a-vis material living of the people. Within this background of social dimensions, the new economic policies and programmes can be helped in terms of their implementation. At the same time the knowledge of sociological phenomena can help frame specific programmes for specific groups of people. Such an exercise may even suggest for redefining, redesigning and readjustment of social institutions in the interest of intended economic change. Thus, the social researchers are required to devote more to the study of social dimensions of material change. Studying social parameters in isolation of their relevance to various programmes of change is not that rewarding at practical level, though in the world of academics they always have an important place.

Every community, small or big, primitive, advanced or advancing, is characterized by some techno-economic level. The material objects, tools and the associated technology thereof are devised and made use of to meet certain requirements. Limited needs are met by the less elaborate tools, say by digging stick in case of shifting cultivators, or bow and arrow or traps in case of hunters and gatherers. And these are prepared by the natives with simple technology of their own. Local skill and material are again depended upon to meet certain other ends. As such the communities who maintain self-sufficiency, also maintain a great deal of isolation. On the other hand the situation of growing contacts give rise to new needs and aspirations. People, then, look for additional tools and technology to adapt themselves to the new requirements. This generates process of change. Avenues are created for innovations, suggesting improvement over the traditional tools and artifacts. The settled agriculture communities, thus, shifted to the use of plough and animal power, plus other implements meant for cultivation. The pressing economic demands and close intimacy, in terms of contact with other communities, suggested for further technological development giving way to mechanized farming, making use of tractors, harvesters, thrashers, tube wells, pumping sets etc. Simultaneous to such a development came change in other individual and household possessions, say dress, utensils, containers, ornaments etc. The exogenous as well as endogenous factors are responsible for additions and alterations in various kinds of artifacts. The artisan and other occupational groups, say fisherfolks, carpenters, ironsmiths etc., have, over the course of years,experienced change, more in terms of improvement in their tools and technology. General efficiency in tools and other equipments helped produce more. This led to the generation of surplus paving way for exchange, barter and trade. These activities further encouraged human interaction reflecting on the world-view of the individuals as well as the communities around.

Within the grip of above trends, rural India and its inhabitants now present a variety of situations-from digging stick to tractors, from bow and arrow and spears to guns, from primitive fishing nets and traps to mechanized boats for deep sea fishing, from compost to chemical fertilizers, from bamboo or clay containers to metallic vessels, from grass and cane ornaments to silver and gold jewellery, from grass tassel and loin cloth to modern patterns of clothing, from lean-to structures or thatched huts to massive and imposing concrete buildings. But then the implements, tools, artifacts and other technological areas and devices are not devoid of certain social and cultural implications, irrespective of their level. Intra-ethnic and inter-ethnic dependence (say in a tribe or caste, or among tribes or between castes and tribes) and relationship are reflected in the procurement of certain items. It is reported more in case of plural society of village India where occupational specialization has all along been marked in case of various castes and even many tribes. Some groups have enjoyed monopoly and expertise in certain traits. And others depended on them for specialist service or for the item produced thereof. Such an equation involved deep relationship even in some other areas of social culture. Earthen pots and other clay vessels, manufactured by the members of potter's caste, have deep implications in social life of the communities. Certain marriage rituals, for instance, are performed with earthen pots and containers supplied by the potter. It has established a definite patron-client relationship reflecting in many areas of living. Likewise, wooden and iron implements are made by specialists of certain caste groups and the rest depend upon them and they too have implications in the wider network of social relationships. In other words material objects, tools and their technology are not independent of social structure or social organisation purviews. Within such a background when change is marked, more so through replacement, in case of important implements and technology, it is likely to have wider repercussions not in the economic sense alone but also at social plane. For instance, mechanized farming in certain cases has adversely reflected on patron-client (Jajmani) relation in village India. Likewise factory made metallic utensils have adversely affected the relationship of potter and his clientele. And such reflections are not only of economic nature but do involve the format of social ties. Those who have done, or are doing away with their traditional occupation, throwing away their implements and tools, have usually severed many relationships, concerning other walks of life, too with the higher caste people whom they served. Likewise, certain symbiotic relationship amongst the tribes or between certain tribes and castes have also been affected due to the introduction of new tools and technology. As an instance, Toda, Badaga, Kota and Kurumba tribes of Nilgiris are no longer that much integrated, through symbiosis, as they had been before. As such the change in tools and technology, through replacement, addition or deletion, seems to prove useful at individual level. But in wider non-economic spheres of life, there seems to be growing lesser dependence. And this is heading to impair close-knit and integrated nature of village community, and subsequently larger society. Such a process seems to be gaining momentum because of increased focus on changing traditional implements, tools and technology. Those who are assigned the task of bringing about such a material change do lack orientation in terms of its implications in social and cultural spheres. As such they are bent upon introducing a material innovation without analysing its wider consequences in terms of traditional network of social and cultural relationships. The change in primitive or traditional tools and technology is essential when we intend to develop a society. But then disintegration in the village or larger community is also not desired to avoid latent ill effects of a technological innovation. The change agents, therefore, need to understand social-cultural implications of material objects, tools and technology so that they can gear up balanced development.

At the same time agents of change, in some social situations, have experienced difficulty in introducing particular tools and implements. Though the latter were of improved and approved quality, some people expressed their reservation and reluctance. Certain types of ploughs, with heavy iron share, for instance, were not acceptable to many tribals living in hills and valleys. Since the targets for the distribution, with heavy element of subsidy, of such ploughs, were to be achieved they were just given to the farmers, or left with the village Panchayat (council) for the use of the cultivators. But then these were hardly used as the same were not found suitable to local conditions. They were too heavy to be drawn by the poor quality of bullocks which tribals owned. At the same time they failed to effectively work in the undulating fields with partly rocky soil. The local artisans, making traditional kind of ploughs, also denounced the use of such implements as the change was coming hard on their existence and relationships with the cultivators. Likewise, the efforts, alongwith new tools and technology, to introduce terrace cultivation, by replacing shifting cultivation, did not bear fruit in many regions of the country. In addition to other reasons, the social implications of shifting cultivation did not approve of the same. And the development workers largely failed to take care of this aspect as they, by and large, lacked such an orientation.

The social science research increasingly devoted to the study of impact and adoption of new tools and technology in rural India. Non-tribal communities have been more explored, on this front, than the tribal ones. Here again the major focus remained on agriculture technology, though the others were not altogether ignored. The rural sociologists, social anthropologists, economists and agriculture scientists assessed the impact of new agriculture technology and its state of adoption and rejection. Some of these studies are quite revealing and rewarding in terms of measuring, in percentages and frequencies, the impact of new ventures. The relevant factors, pro and against the programme, are also analysed. But such analysis of factors or causes chiefly limited itself to techno-economic and physical environmental dimensions. The social and cultural bases and implications of such new tools and technology could not be identified to the fullest extent. If at all something is mentioned about it, the arguments do not go beyond surface level touchings. The social researchers and their researches should have concentrated on two fronts. Firstly, they were desired to explore the traditional tools and technology in the context of native social structure. Secondly, the new tools and technology should have been studied in the relevance of continuing social structure. The replacement of old by the new would need some adjustment in existing social and cultural parameters. Such areas of conflict and consensus too needed detailed scientific surveys and observations. And once such informations, based on scientific research, were made available, the development strategists could use them to make their venture, of introducing new tools and technology, more successful. Feasibility of new exercise could then be smoothened. Once the connected areas of social structure prove supportive to new adventures of techno-economic nature, their acceptance, viability and continuity become easy. Further, the results of social research, more so for its being of a monotonous nature in this respect, could hardly propose for avenues of adjustments between social structure demand and the repercussions of additional tools and technology. Not many studies could be taken on these lines. Introduction of new technology, therefore, remained one way effort in the sense that it was just carried to the target population not anticipating the social structure-based opposition. On many occasions the efforts and programmes of introducing new tools and technology were torpedoed, going beyond the understanding of those who carried it forward. At times even the once adopted implements and tools were dropped, and their use dicontinued in subsequent years. And these were, in some cases, beyond the explanation of techno-economic reasons. The agents of change just remained silent on the issue. The underlying factors, in such cases, could be traced in social structure and the same could answer to the act of rejection or discontinuance. Social science researchers, thus, have to be, in such cases, more rigorous and specific to dig beneath the surface, and make the reasons known to development agencies who would rectify their mistakes to make their efforts more rewarding. The target population, in that case, is likely to be at ease in terms of their attitude of adopting new tools and technology. Adoption of material ways is not isolated from certain purviews of social system. And the planners and agents of change need to keep this principle in view.

Within the three parameters of culture, that is, sociological, ideological and material, there is, in general, interaction and even interrelatedness. Many observances in social arena, for instance, are typical ideology-specific. And the intervention of material base is also reported. The etic performances in terms of behaviour, relationship and adaptation do seek base in ideological framework. Even the latter is, many a times, reshaped as part of trend of time and new requirement. Introduction of a technological innovation may ask for redefining of human interaction patterns in certain respects. At times some arguments appear even as conditioning of one aspect by the other. The mental framework and concrete expression may not always tally. And one gets, on many occasions, confronted with instances of contradiction in what is desired and what is done. Consensus is not always the rule. Various aspects, responding to a common phenomenon or occurrence, do not always re-inforce each other. This can happen advertently or inadvertently. Whatever be the supporting background, the occurrence of this kind enthuses imbalance in terms of reactions. One aspect getting more actively involved and taking lead over others. Situations of the above nature pose for change variance. One notices instance of change in an aspect, but the same lacks in corresponding sphere though the two may be closely connected. And such a situation has lot to say even in the perspective of continuity. Certain traits of culture get replaced earlier than the other. Some continue to be observed even when they have lost their earlier functional importance. Such cultural survivals also find clientele for their observances. The social scientists, specially the sociologists and social anthropologists, have commented upon unequal dimensions of change-one aspect getting changed, altered or modified earlier than the other. Generally agreed upon is the argument that traits of material culture change earlier than those of the non-material ones. Elements of mental and social culture take longer time for their transformation. Such a phenomenon is explained in terms of culture-lag, one aspect getting altered earlier than the other. The phenomenon of culture lag is reported in all societies. However, its extent of occurrence is governed by many factors including endogenous as well as exogenous.

The rural communities, including the tribals, of India are exposed to variety of socio-cultural and techno-economic conditions for a considerably long time. This, however, does not hold uniformly true - some bear longer history of culture contact than the others. Such an interaction, born of close or distant contact, has had its own impact on diverse ways of life varying, many a times, from group to group. Irrespective of its pertaining to caste or tribal situation, one can argue that the material or technological changes are more prominent. The changes in non-material styles of living are not correspondingly of the same order. Proportionately speaking, they appear far less conspicuous. Instances of imbalance are marked between social and material changes. Adoption of agriculture technology, for instance, is of a far more wider magnitude than its corresponding social parameters including interpersonal, inter-family, intra and inter-village community relations. Repercussions of mechanised farming on, say, patron-client (Jajmani) relationship or inter-caste relationship are there, though they have not assumed an alarming form. Implications of agricultural revolution in the certain areas of social life are there, but they have not kept parity with mounting agricultural innovations. Unlike technological development, the faster change has not been the feature in case of social life and the value system thereof.Even the agents of planned change almost failed, in many instances, to gear up a balanced development. This may be attributed to their lack of valid orientation in such an arena. As in case of non-directed change, their major focus remained on the change of material aspects of living, subscribing thereby to the situation of culture lag. Such a situation posed, at times, for clash of norms leading thereby to disorganisation in certain spheres of social paradigm. Situations of this kind can be reported in micro as well as macro contexts, which are otherwise going almost unnoticed at the hands of change agents. At times these have also originated because of approach differentiation of planned and non-directed forces of change. Enactment of protective legislations vis-a-vis material perspective have had its own say in the matter. Provision of inheritance of land and other property by the females, in case of otherwise predominantly patrilineal and patriarchal society of India, has had deeper manifestations in the network of social relations. New areas of conflicts have been given way to, though the same were otherwise never intended at. Such non-purposed growth in the social structure of village community has, many a times, acted as barrier to intended ventures of change. In fact the rise of such stormy situations can, to a great extent, be attributed to lack of consensus that grew in various, but interconnected, parameters of culture. This also adversely reacted to proportionate growth of diverse, but related, elements of culture. In certain cases the lag widened to the tune of disagreement of contradiction, posing indirect resistance to change. In the absence of such trends the change could not only be smooth but even of wider magnitude.

A glance through sociological and social anthropological researches, and the trends thereof, supports that the studies on culture lag in the village India have lacked excessively. This holds true for works done by the Indian professionals themselves, as also for those carried out by the foreign professionals in Indian context. In monographic and holistic research studies, carried out at micro and macro levels, one may, at times, come across scanty mention of instance of culture lag. But there too the 'why' and 'how' parts are not that revealing. Even the research publications specially focusing on change and development have, most of the time, remained short of analysing culture-lag phenomenon in details and in its proper context. Otherwise, the research studies concerning impact of innovations on a community have highlighted the extent of acceptance and rejection of specific elements proposed as part of change. Even the underlying factors have been highlighted to a fairly good extent. But then the analysis of dimension of culture lag, and its implications in the arena of change, form the least explored dimensions. And as such the latent implications of a programme of change, specially reported in the instances of disorganisation or imbalanced growth, are not brought to the surface to the desired extent. What role the instance of culture lag plays in the event of disorganisation and as a barrier to intended changes is of great significance to social scientists, as also to those involved in the task of transforming a community. Understanding of imbalanced growth, in terms of change, is as necessary as the exploration of balanced or proportionate development. It is through instances of imbalanced repercussions that we can hint at the weaknesses of a programme of change. And the new strategy for restrengthening the programme can be better prepared when one comprehends factors responsible for conflicting situation. Such factors may be rooted in the traditional social structure itself, or they get originated out of incompatibility marking the adjustment of old with the new. While searching for such factors the holistic purview is again to be kept at the forefront. There may be more than one contributing factors either inherent in the system or caused from outside. And once such a knowledge is made available, the imbalance in growth and development can be rectified. Doing so is likely to help channelise change in the desired direction, minimising thereby the possibility of rise of unwanted and unintended trends.

Human societies, small or large, have made many adjustments to perpetuate their living.The necessity of adaptation at individual as well as group levels originated to promote smooth living. Adjustment and adaptation have numerous dimensions - physical, social,economic, psychological, technological etc. In terms of certain actions, reactions, relationship and activities, the individual has to compromise and concede to Iarger requirements in the interest of group. While in others the group as a whole reacts for its existence. In the interest of group and its solidarity, certain cultural norms are devised and the same help sustain various ways of living.The individuals in a group are made to internalize such norms through the processes of socialization and enculturtation. Imbibing of such traits also suggests for their respectability. People are made to adhere, through various mechanisms of social control, to the norms of the group. But even this procedure does not guarantee cent percent adherence to what is provided for in the norm framework. In all the communities are reported some instance of norm breaking, creating thereby situation of conflict. However there are the built-in provisions in the native social structure to remove the anomaly born of conflicting situations, and to cause subsequent consensus. The beehive of such procedures usually differs from community to community. However, they are well within the knowledge of participants of a social group.

In addition to norms governing inter-human relationship and behaviour, discussed elsewhere, there are others which help regulate human interaction with the wider non-human cosmos. For instance the man-nature relationship has always been intimate, and many a times of interdcpendence. The natural environments, which in the late scientific parlance is usually treated as eco-system, keeps on, time and again, posing challenge to the human beings around. The latter react, through adjustment and adaptation, to such challenge. And for such adaptation too the human beings have devised various procedures governed by definite rules and procedures. Whenever required, the members of the group do seriously suggest to revise the ongoing equation between man and ecology. And in tune with such an equation it appears that ecological parameters, sometimes and in certain respects, condition human behaviour, interaction and relationship.

In Indian context the ecology is all the more important in the sense that we come across various kinds of ecological settings. There are human habitations in very high altitude areas with arid conditions (say Ladakh), followed by those living in high hills, thick forests, plains, desert and coastal areas. And all these communities, from island dwellers to those living in snow-covered terrain, have adjusted their social, cultural and material living with the imposing ecological conditions around. And to react to any major flux in case of the latter, people try to redefine their ways and consequently propose for readaptation to meet the challenge. Such instances of adaptation are reflected in their day-to-day interactions and behaviour. In more difficult ecological settings, say high hills, forests and other outlying localities, live the tribal people. In fact the tribal concentration is maximum in case of more difficult environmental conditions. And with their limited capacity to adjust, they lead a rather hard life. In the event of any major change or imbalance in the local ecology, the tribals suffer till they are in a position to recoup in terms of adjustment. Change in environmental conditions are now faster than ever before. And hence they require more quick response, in terms of adjustment, from the corresponding population. Such a requirement is not always met with, causing thereby problems of various forms. Those who intend to bring about smooth transformation and transition have also not very deeply and keenly looked into the parameters causing uneasiness among various population groups. They have hardly bothered to strike balance between nature, society and culture. Of late, the cultural adjustment does not seem to have kept pace with growing dynamics in ecosystem. Social forestry, as proposed by the agents of planed change, has come as a big slogan. But its adaptation and impact remain questionable in large number of cases. Likewise, numerous human problems have cropped up as a result of installation of gigantic dams and industrial plants in tribal settings. The imposing flux in centuries old environmental conditions have left the people in perplexed conditions and they are unable to cope with the new situation in a large number of cases. The still growing culture contact is likely to provide further fillip to such a trend. In other words there have appeared excessive signs of non-adaptation at the levels of man, society, culture and ecology. Such an unhealthy trend is bound to pose further problems which, if go unchecked, may create lot of discontentment and frustration in various groups of people and in various walks of life. And to control the same any innovation proposed for society or ecology need to be assessed in terms of mutual relationship. Society and ecology, in broader framework, cannot be isolated. Social-cultural analysts and ecologists need to work in close laison with each other to promote overall and balanced change or development.

During the last over three decades, the ecological researches have gathered momentum. Specialists on ecology have come out with many new ideas, suggestions and manifestation. Various elements of environment have been studied and analysed with the interest that they are to be improved upon. Even the task of implementing new projects, concerning ecology, could be accorded sufficient priority. The technology concerning various elements of ecology has sharpened. Massive efforts are on to tackle vast natural resources for the betterment of humanity. However, the focus of such technocrats remains one-sided, that is, they concentrate only on the mobilisation of natural resources without bothering of their implications in various aspects of social and cultural life of the people concerned. On the other hand the social scientists, more so the sociologist and social anthropologists, too have remained chiefly occupied within their own study orbits. Their coverage, in terms of researches, chiefly limited to society and culture. Their works have largely ignored the ecological interventions in the life and culture of the people. Depth studies on interaction of ecology and culture or ecology and social organisation have rarely been done. Certain edited works on this area of research pose as if they have only touched the fringe of the subject. Serious interdisciplinary researches, on this count, are generally lacking, though the ecology and culture are so intimately connected and are almost inseparable at certain fronts. Because of later sharp intervention in ecological conditions, some new human problems have emerged. And it is at this stage that technical experts on ecology have realised of the importance of social-cultural research and the experts thereof. But by and large there still remains a gap between the social scientists and ecology experts in terms of collaborative research. But since the ecology and human populations are intimately connected, the research ventures need to go accordingly. Cultural and behavioural purviews also need to be researched and analysed in the relevance of ecological conditions, and not merely under the pressure of social consideration. This would provide still better insight into a way of living. At the same time the ecologists may also develop new insight and understanding vis-a-vis their exercises. Such conditions are likely to minimise the rise of problems in the event of various projects. The social researchers need to switch over to such studies as they can prove helpful in the new ventures proposed to bring about intended change. Their finding would also be useful in rightly directing the ecological programmes and the ensuring change thereof.

Two responses in case of man and society have always been there. One pertains to inner core and the other to common surface reflexes marked in case of human groups. By inner core is meant the hidden principles which are not otherwise noticed unless probed for. It is rather difficult to extract them and to give them a definite shape unless one is able to explore from inside out. These are guarded by the mental framework. Though they form a secret niche, as state of mind, they speak of the common world-view of the concerned group. In other words they subscribe to the commonly conceived state of mind and are definite indicators for defining and mapping of universe conceived by the people belonging to a particular group. Such inner parameters meant to guide man and his society are believed to direct all actions, reactions and behaviour as outward expressions. With the growth of individual, such a framework is formed through the internalization of culture traits through various processes intended and unintended. In other words a definite cultural framework is inherited, or gets transmitted from the elderly lot who could themselves acquire and retain the same from their seniors. Thus, how the individuals perceive the world, social or physical, around is guided by the continued parameters of a culture and the implications thereof. At times such parameters are not that rigid. Whenever required, at wider level, some of these may incorporate new dimensions to meet certain new demands of the group and individual. And therefore the continuity and change in cognition of individuals may go simultaneously. At the same time the adherence to perceptional framework is not always guaranteed. Under certain situations an individual deviates from the prescribed cognitive framework to meet out some of his urges. This may cause conflict among certain elements of cognition, thereby reflecting adversely on what is culturally or traditionally suggested. But by and large the cognitive orders of individual and society stand to what they are meant for. Deviances are taken as exceptions and there is pressure for their rectification or regularisation through certain adjustment.

Cognitive perspective, with its character of rigidity as well as flexibility is treated,by a section of social scientists, as the strongest force to guide and govern the real happenings and activities labelling a society. The real existence, and the intricacies of relations thereof, are attributed to what the cognition demands. In other words the mental framework is the pre-condition or pre-requisite for an activity or form of behaviour whether inter-human or human versus environment. The fixity to traditions and persistence of other ways are largely attributed to the definite mental frameworks. Within this background the continuity and change are not independent of mental make-up and the connected perceptions thereof. Any addition or deletion to what has been existing as way of life, or any improvement over what people have been doing are therefore not to be seen in isolation of cognitive framework. Even for proposing or bringing about change it would, therefore, be essential to cause corresponding shift in the arena of cognition of the people. As the overt or explicit actions, reactions, behaviour etc., are said to be the outcome of what is implicit, as state of mind, it is unavoidable to cause change in cognitive perspective if we intend to make any programme of change a success, and if we are keen to see its permanent acceptance. If the change proposed remains only a part of overt orbit, without finding proper place at mental level, there are chances that the people may give it up in due course and revert back to the original which finds due support from cognitive paradigm.

Cognitive framework is likely to differ from individual to individual and group to group. But its major ingredients do subscribe to certain uniformities as far as the group requirements are concerned. And it is the latter which are more meaningful in the context of change. The tribals being comparatively more homogeneous communities, their cognition perspectives reflect more of uniformity. Since the tribals are less exposed to alien situations, their traditional ways continue to have sway over them. And hence the cognitive parameters differentiation is far less conspicuous. For such a background there is comparatively more consensus between ideology, based on mental framework, and the actual styles of living. However, this does not rule out stray instances of deviancy.

Somehow in various elements of change, proposed from outside, the change inducers have chiefly concentrated on what they intended to carry to a group of people. This could have been done under the pressure of targets or the higher authorities. They carried forward a new programme as independent entity and wanted to plant it in the target population chiefly at the level of their practical living. Probably they could not find time to make the people mentally prepared. In other words such agents of change failed to care for cognitive dimension of change, which is otherwise so important in making an innovation accepted and in supporting it as an ongoing process. Because of such an approach many instances of reversals could be noticed. Some people dropped what they adopted once. They failed to carry it forward as they were not mentally prepared. May be that their mental order did not approve of it. The planners as well as the implementors of programmes of change remained far short of giving weightage to change at the level of mind. By and large the provisions and proposals to get into the cognitive framework were missing during the implementation of projects and programmes of change. Since overt expressions and ways have roots into people's perceptions, it was otherwise necessary to get at that level. And if that approach could be adopted, we could attain more success, in terms of diffusion of innovations, than what could be achieved without it. The instances of reversals could also be checked.

Research on aspects of cognition and perception has been a special arena of psychologists. They have done it in various contexts. The sociologists and social anthropologists have, to a great deal, mapped the apparent arena of social organisation, limiting themselves to their respective specializations. Only to a very limited extent the sociologists and social anthropologists have explored the hidden and the so-called universal principles of society. Since they chiefly limited themselves to social facts and their narration, they did very little, in terms of research, in analysing the principles holding structures of society. Similarly very little could be done in searching the relationship between cognition and reality. The psychologists mainly remained bogged down to cognition and devoted much less to reality. At the same time the psychologists, sociologists and social anthropologists did not, in most of the cases, work together to see the total perspective, covering mental framework to practical life. This specially lacked in the context of change. As such no definite guidance could be given to those engaged in the creation of change.

In the interest of promoting change and development the social researchers need to plan their researches on cognitive aspects too. This needs to be devised keeping in view the prevailing reality and the intended programmes of change. Findings, born of such research ventures are likely to highlight as to what areas of cognition need be tackled to facilitate purposed change. What is practically planned, as part of change induction, is to have parity with the cognitive perspective. An adjustment is to be worked out in the interest of change. Acceptance of change at the mental level ensures better acceptance at practical level. Its sustenance and perpetuation are then also supported.

Over the years the people and their society have formed certain definite ideas in terms of their ways of life. These have emerged, and subsequently taken deep root, through a variety of encounters and experiences concerning day-to-day life. Notions, widely acceptable to a group of people, do not get originated, except in some rare situation, overnight. Their validity is ascertained at wider level before their being treated as strong notions. Some of such notions are tested through mundane activities. There are others who survive on mere faith and are not subject to verification. The latter specially pertain to the notions concerning supernatural world believed to be of more powerful existence. Element of faith keeps them up. Most of the time people treat them as inexplicable and admit of their firmness even when their validity, many a times, is not certified. The notions that forefeit their force, for changing circumstances or other conditions, are at times dropped making corresponding impact in the idea complex of people. New ones get built up. As such there remains dynamics in the realm of ideas. More it applies to peripheral format. The core of notions takes the longest time to change, alter or replaced. In other words the ideas keep on piling up with replacements suiting to new requirements.

The ideas, among other dimensions, provide a strong front for continuity and changes in a social system or structure. The formation of ideas, through diverse processes, and their permutation and combination prepare and provide support to the rise of certain intellectual pursuits. The intellectual development involves the game of ideas, the original ones as also the testing of those already acquired or put forth. The world of ideas and intellect are taken by many as the lever around which function the mundane activities. In other words social organisation is an outward expression of inherent idea system and the level of intellectual development. The latter vary from individual to individual and group to group. But then certain common activities, patterns and involvement speak of the prevalence of some kind of common ideas format and intellectual attainment. And all the human populations are respectively characterized by the same. Indian rural communities, for that matter, are no exceptions. Each holds high its idea system and the connected life design thereof. Some of the ideas have survived over centuries. There are others not carrying a long history, and have been acquired or added as per the later changing conditions and the underlying urges thereof.

Change, whether material, social or spiritual can not be seen, proposed or analysed in isolation of idea system and the intellect level. Persistence of a cultural pattern is specific ideas based. And to replace any element of the same, the associated ideas too need to be recognised or replaced. Unless we attempt the latter, the former may remain or sound only a ritual, and not any serious exercise. Change in ideas, therefore, is almost a pre-requisite for any replacement or addition as part of change. Such a social science based requirement has not always been attended to by those who planned for change, as also by those who were involved in carrying it forward at the surface level. The adjustment and readjustment between the old and new ideas were not, all the time and in all cases, worked out within the scientific requirement. In many instances, therefore, remained imbalance, in terms of change elements, at the ideal and actual levels. Such a situation correspondingly reflected on the success or failure of the programmes. The instances of conflict at ideas level had its own adverse intervention at the level of implementation of new programmes. The agents of change gave priority, as probably demanded by the circumstances, to carry forward their objects and ideas. They excessively lacked on the front of exploring traditional and ongoing ideas as attached to various life-designs. And the least could be done in striking a working equation between the old and the new ideas. Well around sixty percent of the programmes of planned change, in India, were confined to economic development and the rest on communication and social service etc. The focus on ideological readjustment found the least priority. Such an approach proved hampering at various levels. This happened more in case of tribal people, and the programmes thereof, as their idea systems could hardly be bothered for. In case of many programmes the tribals were treated almost like the caste communities. And this emanated more conflict, at various levels, than consensus.

Not only the agents of change but even the social scientists, engaged in their respective research, could devote the least to the researches connected to idea systems and intellectual status of various communities. In comparison to other social researchers the psychologists did concentrate comparatively more on the study of ideas and attitudes. But these works too remained rather sporadic, limiting their observations on micro ethnic situations. Secondly, these studies, except in some cases, could not be linked with the change agents and their programmes. Since the results of such studies could not reach to and could not be made use of by change agents, their utility in gearing up change was hardly proved. The sociological and social anthropological studies touched only the fringe, and that too indirectly, of the idea systems of various communities studied by them in holistic perspective. At the level of these informations too, there remained a gap between change inducers and the research findings. The programmes of change continued in their stereotyped approach and application at snail's pace, facing odds at various places. The knowledge of idea systems of various ethnic groups could help reduce such trends. In any programme of planned change, therefore, we do need to explore the complexity of ideas concerning diverse life-ways, and more so those who come closer, in terms of relevance, to the intended programmes of change. The social scientists are desired to cover such arena, specially attending to those ideas which are assumed to have closer relevance to the programmes of change. Their research findings then need to be conveyed to those who practically plan for, and carry forward these ideas of change. With the research-based knowledge one can always find alternatives to avoid odds and resistance, and consequently promote smooth change in an anticipated manner.

In any community the traditions bear a long history and they die hard. They are built over the years in adjustment of man with man, man with nature and man with the supernatural world. Once they get crystalised, the traditions are transmitted from generation to generation. The participants in a culture subscribe to such traditions in the interest of smooth living. People find it more convenient, as far as their way of life at a particular time is concerned, to follow the traditions. In the wider interest of community, they even evolve and provide for a social control mechanism which helps protect traditions defined for the people. Anyone ignoring what is traditionally prescribed is taken to task by those who are responsible for social control in the community. And they find a general support for the same. Such a strong support to traditions correspondingly reflects on the attitude and behaviour of the people. There is even provision for positive and negative sanctions which also helps maintain traditions. Grooming with such a background directs one to be pro-tradition. This encourages ethnocentric tendency and the in-group feelings. What one does, or believes in are considered as the best way of life. Network of this kind holds high traditional framework and the associate belief system thereof.

Societies in physical and cultural isolation are more prone to retain the traditions. Those in transition, and under the alien influence get a jolt in the structure of native traditions. Such a situation provides for a marginal character where some, among the community, start sharing certain alien traditions, as also sticking to some of the old ones. But here again the replacement of, or addition in old involve a slow process. By and large there remains predominance of continued traditions.

Indian rural communities came under fast exposure to alien conditions after India attained freedom in 1947. Processes of change under planned development, as also those without it got stronger. The latter had already received sufficient impetus even in later years of British rule. Such a background provided jolt to some of the old traditions. The planned programmes of change intend to do away with certain old traditions which they feel hinder progress. On the other hand the non-directed ventures hit the traditions haphazardly without bothering of their consequences. As a result some of the traditions disappeared fast causing disturbance in native social structure. Even the lately introduced planned programmes of change were not forceful enough to check such a trend as people were already in the fast sway of non-directed change. And though the scientific strategy of planned development, introduced from the fifties of the current century, demanded for the retention of healthy traditions, it could not be forcefully adhered to. Many ill-informed agents of change and others worked for the disappearance of traditions, including those which were even healthy ones, causing thereby disturbance and disorganisation among the concerned communities. This happened more in case of tribal communities because their systems of traditions were the least understood by the aliens who penetrated into tribal belts with different motive and background. Even certain elements of caste society were not free of such disturbance. Yet another phenomenon which marked Indian rural scene, in the context of change, is one of the superimposition over the existing traditions. Working for haphazard disappearance of old traditions coupled with haphazard superimposition further worsened the situation. It led to the chaotic condition in the arena of traditions, providing avenues for clash and consequent disorganisation in the network of relations. Many agencies and the agents are still working for indiscriminate disappearance of traditions, and also for the superimposition of new which do not, many a times, fit into the native systems. Trends of this kind have enthused complete assimilation into new order, which is not really the goal. The idea inherent in planned change is to integrate all small and scattered units to the extent that they adopt certain new items as well as retain the best of what has all along been helpful to them. In other words there should have been selective assimilation. Such an approach denounces the rise of problems in the course of change. Haphazard and complete assimilation are not the ingredients of planned strategy of change, specially one designed for rural India. Change is an ongoing process. And as the focus, of late, is on induced change, we need to avoid the element of imposition which is normally conflicting to the existing traditions. The change agents are required to promote the best within, as also substitute, in the interest of selective assimilation, what is unwanted and hindering to change efforts. To work for haphazard disappearance of traditions, and to impose the alien traditions may not serve the purpose of smooth transformation. To curb the rise of new problems is equally an important dimensions of the programmes of planned change and development.

Many research studies have been carried out for explaining change in various communities. Impact of diverse forces and processes of change have also been studied. More of such studies confined to micro contexts, though a few macro-level works are also available. Though not exactly titled as study on traditions, a large number of the latter could be explained through various research results. The focus, by and large, remained on the changing milieu than on the continuity of traditions. What continued was not highlighted in details. The reasons for continuity, as such, also remained hidden. Accounts of changed traditions are made available. But then the underlying reasons were not dealt that elaborately. Was the disappearance of traditions a voluntary action, or something was imposed on the people for doing away with native traditions? Where did the superimposition worked, and where the change of traditions took place as per the normal procedure could not be categorically presented by the social researchers. Even through the programmes of planned change the element of imposition cannot be ruled out. At the same time the imposition does have latent implications which do not befit the system, and give rise to certain unintended problems. These were dealt, in research context, only in a very limited way. Likewise, pinpointing research studies on assimilation, and more so on selective assimilation, are not many. Sporadic instances of general assimilation are reported in certain research works where they appear as minor part of some larger studies. In the interest of better explaining and gearing up change, the social scientists and their researches should have concentrated even on the minute aspects, say on the element of superimposition of traditions, or intended effort for disappearance of healthy traditions, and even on the aspect of selective assimilation. These could highlight the strength and weakness of old as well as the new traditions, as also could help understand the side implications. Such researches are highly important and of urgent nature to propose and guide for smooth transformation of traditions. Forcing of tradition, and conflict among traditions are likely to pose hostility to the agents of change. It also causes disturbance to the members of target population. Though such researches form very specialised arena, they are not to be ignored if the social scientists are keen to subscribe to the creation of change.

The researches sharply focusing on degree and nature of assimilation are lacking. For instance the Hindu social and religious reformers and Christian missionaries have been involved in the assimilation of tribal population in their respective fold. A large number of tribal families adopted Hindu or Christian way of life. The assimilationists, as part of their policy and approach, dedicatedly devoted to the disappearance of tribal ways of life, condemning them outrightly. They made the people realise that what they practised was unwanted, undesirable and wrong. And subsequently it was proposed to drop the same. In other words the alien agents worked for indiscriminate dismantling of the old styles of living without bothering whether the new would suit them or not. Though a large number of tribals adopted new, there appeared clash at many points. So much so that a section of the same community, in many cases, backed out and asked and propogated for revivalism. Many revivalistic movements can be reported from different tribal areas, creating conflict against those who opted for assimilation in the new folds. Such a trend made the communities sharply divided at social and religious planes. This gave blow to the earlier cohesiveness and integrated nature of some of the tribal communities. The social science researches have yet to, at a macro level, highlight such trends with more accuracy. Assimilation has its own advantages and disadvantages and these two aspects remain far less sharply pinpointed. As opposed to assimilation, there was proposed integration of tribal populations into main national stream. This suggested for socio-economic advancement of tribal people without imposing anything on them. By now one comes across various levels of integration, and a variety of unintended problems thereof. These two are not adequately accounted for by the social scientists. Therefore, not all concerning assimilation and integration have been searched and analysed. Elements of imposition and areas of advantage and disadvantage, concerning assimilation and integration, need be researched. Informations born of such studies are likely to help prepare guidelines for encouraging change for betterment. Such a framework of social scientists is further to be made available to planners and implementors of change.

All kinds of parameters, ideological, sociological and even material, connected to a cultural heritage, have their respective positions. But at the same time their elements are, many a times, interconnected. They do reinforce each other to provide support to the social structure status-quo. Any threat to their disequilibrium is usually contained by the society's social control mechanism. The conflicts arise but then the people resolve them through various processes and in various forms. More the isolation of communities, lesser would be the rise of conflicting situation. The rapid exposure of a social system to alien conditions enhances chances of more conflicts . And this is what has, of late, been in case of the societies of developing countries including India. Alien items as part of innovations, an idea, practice or technology, have gone to the native systems meeting varied degree of receptivity and rejection. Indian rural communities have, during the last three decades, experienced more hillarious changes than ever before. With this have come up numerous instances of maladjustment and disorganisation which were otherwise not intended. In case of certain social groups it has happened rather faster and to a greater extent than the others. But then to some extent both, the castes as well as the tribes, have been so affected. Such an impact came as latent effect of various ventures of change. The purposed aim has been one of betterment and development of society. The rise of more of the adverse latent effects can be attributed to lack of syncretic exercise. The new cultural elements could not be re-interpreted to fit into the existing traditions. Thus, the neglect of the phenomenon of syncretism, which demanded the re-interpretation of new cultural elements to fit them to the traditional and existing ones, added to the rise of problems which were not anticipated. This specially marked tribal scenes where existing traditions were far more disrespected, though it was never suggested in the scientifically designed strategy of tribal development. Even in case of non-tribal situation the existing traditions failed to be duly synthesised through re-interpretation. In fact the attempt to syncretise required knowledge at three fronts - firstly of the new cultural elements themselves; secondly of the continued or existing traditions and thirdly of the art and skill of reinterpretation and readjustment between the first and the second. For various reasons, those who carried forward new cultural elements operated independently, and in isolation of those who claimed to have acquired other knowledge.

Elements of change have a strong bearing to the phenomenon of syncretism. Normally the old or traditional and the new cultural elements are distinct from each other to a large extent. They may subscribe to a common aspect of living but the background and form of the two appear different. And since the traditional ones carry forward their long history of existence, the new ones, at least in the first instance appear as challenging them. People then face a dichotomous situation marking, by and large, their leaning towards traditional cultural elements. The new ones, in terms of choice, find a secondary place. There is also an expression of reluctance to what is proposed for induction. This continues till people become convinced of the utility of new items or ideas, and then decide to adapt the same. Tribal and non-tribal communities of village India have had rather rich traditional cultural heritage. And they have kept it up to a considerable extent. When the changes were proposed, more so from the fifties of the current century, in certain areas of the same, there were reported instances of reluctance, resistance, indifference etc. However, in due course some of the new cultural elements could be accepted by certain sections of the population. The success of the change agents remained limited. Numerous instances of failure can be attributed to the fact that the new cultural items were not properly reinterpreted to fit into the traditional ones. Those responsible for bringing about change took the new items and elements as they came handy without bothering to see their compatibility or incompatibility with what was going on in various cultures or subcultures. Either they, independently, had no capacity and expertise to do that, as a large number of them did not thoroughly understand the complicacies of traditional systems, or they had no time for it, or they were not asked to do that. This made the elements of change meet opposition at various places and in various time phases. If somehow the new cultural elements could be made befitting to the traditional cultural elements, simultaneously suggesting for progress, the indifferent reaction of people could be overcome earlier. But somehow the point was missed.

Making a new venture befitting to the old is again not an easy task. It involves a rigorous exercise. Telling people for respectability of the old, and at the same time asking them to adopt the new sounds involving contradiction. And to avoid such a position, it is desired to re-interpret the new proposals and programmes to the tune that they become easily acceptable even in the atmosphere of traditional cultural elements. To do that the extension agents and others who carry forward the innovations are required to have some insight into the traditional ongoing cultural network. For this, they need to be properly oriented in the concerned arena, as also in the methodology to attempt the synthesis. Likewise the implications of the culture of the new are also to be understood thoroughly. Without an adequate orientation and training, the reinterpretation of the new to suit the traditionals may not be attempted. For instance, without understanding the background of youth dormitories in tribal India, the adjustment of various programmes for youth as proposed under new strategy for development and change, will be difficult. There may be a clash in the two. However, it the youth programmes are properly reinterpreted to suit the requirement of youth dormitories, then the early and healthy adoption are possible. But without understanding what the youth dormitories, with their structure and function, are, it is difficult to syncretise.

As far as village India is concerned there are not many research studies available on syncretism. In fact this may be, among a few others, an area which has been the least cared for by the social scientists and their researches. Barring some references concerning sporadic micro situations, the full length research works on syncretism are almost missing. And the position has remained so in spite of the fact that the reinterpretation of new to fit it in the old traditions has been, and still is, quite important. Numerous instances of conflict between old and new traditions cropped up to the extent that the new failed to find place and get assimilated. People continued to pose resistance to their acceptance as the new ventures failed to compromise with the continued situation. Research studies on rejection of innovations are many. And such works also provide the background of rejection. These finding also include explanations that many v items were not accommodated as they were found conflicting with the old. But then such works remained far short of explaining the nature and dimension of incompatibility between the old traditions and in what was lately proposed. If this could be attempted, then it was not difficult to highlight as to how best the new could be reinterpreted to suit the old traditions. Merely to explain that the clashing situation between the old traditions and innovations hindered the acceptance of the latter did not serve the intended purpose. And to my mind it is none but the social researchers and analysts who could guide the carriers of change in the event of such difficulty. Otherwise the development workers and other agents of change operated, and continue to largely do so, in their own style meeting both success and failure. The chances of failure, in terms of diffusion of innovations, can be minimised if new proposals and ideas could be reinterpreted and reshaped in tune with what has been going on. Even of late the social scientists have not shown, as far as rural Indian situation is concerned, keen interest in the studies concerning syncretism. Since the quantom of new ideas, technology and tools, lately proposed, are now higher than ever before, the requirement for such studies has all the more increased. Though sound of a very special nature, such studies and the recommendations thereof are likely to gear up programmes of change, thereby making their own contribution in the betterment of masses.

Human societies are not permanently static. They do change. However, the nature and degree of change depend upon the force of endogenous and exogenous factors. Societies in isolation have less opportunities for change in comparison to those who are in the thick of culture contact situation. Still more chances of change are among those where planned programmes of change are in force. To meet the requirements of new circumstances, demanding for change, people react to imbibe new or to omit the old. Unless and otherwise there is increased pressure of new requirement people go slow. And the community as a whole does not simultaneously propose for an addition. Individuals, here and there, try for new ventures. Community as a whole would come in only when some radical shift is proposed, either voluntarily or under threat or pressure. In normal course people are selective in terms of their choice for new. They cultivate rationality before they decide to drop the old ways or traditions. There are some who simply opt to go in for new, without analysing its positive and negative repercussions, and it is this lot who do not sustain the innovation for long. They abruptly pick it up, and take a similar recource while doing away with the same. The abrupt actions, in the context of change, are many a times unavoidable for various reasons.

Among Indian rural communities are also reported almost all the above manifestations. For varied background of change promotion, a variety of perspectives concerning change, are now reported in Indian rural setting. At the individual as well as community level one can account for abrupt, gradual, slow and rapid changes. And these have had their own plus and minus points.These are well reflected through diverse implications. Taking an overview of the change elements and their implications in the tribal and caste society of India, it may not be wrong to say that changes have been, in a large number of cases, rather haphazard. Indiscriminate interventions and picking up, without more of relevance,came up largely, because the outsiders worked for the same. The villagers could not really find time, or they purposely did not do so, to rationally review the wider implications of an innovation. This can be explained with validity in case of not only the tribe-caste contact but also in the context of contact with other agencies including voluntary, official, sectarian etc. The indiscriminate picking up of innovation, without assessing it as per the requirement of native system, has, in certain cases, done harm than good. This has happened more in case of tribals than the non-tribals. The former blindly subscribed to certain new elements, simply on the plea that they did so as their caste Hindu neighbours have been doing the same. And some of such developments spread like wild fire. There was none to regularise it. Tribal ignorance paved way for their quick induction. The rise of various religious sects among Indian tribes can be attributed to such phenomena. And they have caused disintegration among the once homogenous entities. Many other things, of similar kind, happened even in case of caste society in quick succession under the growing impact of urbanisation and other agencies of change. These happened though the same were not intended under the guideu programmes of change.

The rise of element of disorganisation in certain aspects of ways of life can be attributed, among others, to abruptness in change. And this probably became, at times, unavoidable under the pressure of targets from higher ups, and under other consideration.Those who carried it forward did not realise of the inherent weakness in sudden change. It could give them immediate satisfaction, but its ultimate repercussions failed to go in the interest of change. The change agents and even others did not realise of the weakness of abrupt change. At the same time they were not even properly oriented in the philosophy and methodology of directed change. Gradualism, a major requirement in the process of planned change induction was fairly missed by the planners as well as the inducers of change at grassroots level. This adversely reflected on the target population who could not be initially prepared to withstand the impact of fast and abrupt innovations. They were not really prepared, neither mentally nor physically, to contain the pressure of new requirements. Efforts, by the outsiders, were hardly made to suggest the change in gradual order, starting from milder elements and ending into heavier ones. Many a times, the people, to startwith, showed favourable response to such ventures too. But in due course many of these were given up, and the remaining reflected rather adversely on one way of life or the other. In other words an innovation had not merely unidirectional impact, but even posed for side reactions which did not form part of intended framework, and reacted in an undesired manner.

Therefore, in addition to nature, the course, stages and methodology of change occupy an important place in the phenomenon of change. And while explaining and analysing change all these ingredients are to be taken note of and explained in inter-connectedness. This is yet another arena where social researchers have lacked. There are scores of research studies on the introduction of new tools and technology in various population groups. In comparison to social or psychological aspects, the impact of material ways is more prominently studied. This includes housing, dress, ornaments, household utencils, agriculture and other implements, handicrafts etc. But the research areas that could not be properly attended include (a) the implications of a tool or technology in the other connected areas of social structure. This must include positive as well as negative aspects; (b) abruptness or gradualism cultivated in the diffusion of an artifact, idea or technology. The implications of gradual as well as abrupt inductions of new things were also required to be studied in their proper perspective. The focus of social researches has considerably lacked on these fronts. One has to revert to such studies to ascertain the negative side of rapid and abrupt induction of social change elements. And the same would also help arrive at the positive attainments of gradual induction of change. The findings of such researches, concerning various communities, will prove eye-opener for future programme of change. Gradualism in the introduction of change is likely to be more rewarding than the abrupt introductions which are more prone to get reversed.

SEVEN

SIGNIFICANTLY CONNECTED ISSUES

Village India presents quite a complex and complicated social situation. This is specially true for multiethnic and multicaste village communities. More the castes and ethnic groups in a village, more complicated is the social network. Various forms of ties, links, actions and interactions are provided in intra and inter-caste contexts. Caste, ethnic or other group considerations do prevail; but they go in the background when the interest of village community, as a whole, is brought forth. A still broader perspective of complexity is observed when the village community is analysed in terms of economic, political and religious life, in addition to its social fabric. At the level of family and caste, the two major institutions at village level, there is a great deal of differentiation and non-uniformity in respect of social, economic, political and religious life. Social positions, occupations, leadership patterns and ritual placements are prescribed within the frame of age-old traditions. But state of contradiction has arisen under the new conditions where 'achieved', alongwith 'ascribed' is increasingly stressed upon and has begun to take its own place. What is socially granted does not,many a times, keep parity when viewed in ritual context. What is fundamental in social control agency has its roots in religious sanctions. Economic equation is not always free of social dimension. Religious observances and attributes are found having say in areas of health, economy and decision-making processes. A social ceremony is, many a times, not independent of economic and religious considerations. Then sex, age, kinship, neighbourhood etc, have important place in the social structure of village community. They matter, independently or in relationship with one another, in various walks of life. Thus, various kinds of combinations,interventions, correlations etc., do reflect in the life of a village community. No event, of a major nature and connected to any aspect of life, can abruptly be taken as independent of all others. Linkages of positive and negative kind do exist. Even understanding of any cultural element or trait would remain incomplete unless it is seen in totality of life-styles. The social structures of tribal village communities are not as complex and complicated as are of multi-caste villages. There is considerable amount of homogeneity. Not much of differentiation and disharmony are reported in their ways of life connected to social, economic, political and religious fields. Some persons do have more recognition and status, but this is not always permanent and is based on proficiency or professional specialisation. The community, at large, is rated at the same plane. But in villages where the tribals are, for long, living with the caste Hindus, the dimensions of complexity, in the social structure, have developed. The same holds true for those tribal villages, and the communities thereof, which have been excessively influenced by the system prevalent in caste society.There, the social and religious differentiation have become considerably prominent. A large number of them are in for caste-like model. Under the circumstances, the once prevalent uniformity and homogeneity in tribal life and culture are getting impaired, giving way to complexity and imbalance.

With complex situation and network of relationships in rural India, the complexity of social change cannot be ruled out.Any element of change, even if it is sufficiently pin-pointing, must have wide-ranged repercussions. Introduction of a programme of social development in village community would not remain exclusively confined to social sphere. Rather,it is bound to have some reaction on the other aspects of life including economic, political and religious. Feeling of reaction may be more intensive in one sphere than the other. Such a variation will have connection to the nature of programme and the efforts involved therein. Likewise, the introduction of an agricultural innovation, say high-yielding variety of wheat or improved tool, will not go without its wider repercussions and implications. In most of the cases of addition, replacement and withdrawal of any trait, things will not remain limited to the intended objective alone. They do go beyond, in various directions, and with differing effects. An innovation may sound helpful in one sphere,but the same may have negative effect in some other aspects of the same community. Improved farm technology and modern methods of cure and medicines may improve upon specific situations. But they, many a times, reflect adversely on intercaste dependence, division of labour, traditional medicineman etc. In the complex social structure of the village community, things are so interconnected and interdependent that any change in one causes shake in some others. This remained the least understood area so far as the agents of change are concerned. The latter kept on behaving as unidimensionalists, forgetting about the cultural complexities of village communities. Such an approach kept them, as also the programme proposed by them, in tight position.

Not much could be achieved as the hidden resistance remained indirectly active. Inspite of incessant efforts things could not, many a times, be improved upon as the cause of opposition, to an innovation, was not detected. The change agents did not even realise it as they thought the same far beyond the purview of their job. Mounting complexity of social structure led to the strengthening of areas of opposition, and such trends went unnoticed. Even if they were sensed, it was taken as nobody's job to tackle the same in favour of programme of social change.

Another area concerning complexity in change is connected to the methodology and approach of change agents and the contents of programmes. One comes across tremendous amount of nonuniformity in these spheres too. So much so that when one agency is trying to introduce an innovation, the other, with its independent ideology, tries to suppress or resist it. Or if one does it in a particular style, say through persuasion, the others are coercive in the matter. Change through force of law and change through planned development can be cited in support of such trends. While involved in the programme of change, an official nutrition specialist suggests for consumption of, say, non-vegetarian diet,but a Hindu social reformer, working in the same tribal or non-tribal community, propagates to give up non-vegetarianism. When one tries to retain what is good in tribal and rural life, the other discards it commenting on its primitiveness and traditionality. Hindu religious reformers, social workers, Christian missionaries and government officials, as agents of change, are, so many times, seen simultaneously working in the same social formation. There is quite a variation and incompatibility in their objective and approach. The members of recipient group get perplexed of the variety of ideas involved in the efforts made for inducting change in them. Under all these currents the massive official machinery for bringing about socio-economic transformation in rural India failed to become as effective as it should have been. The workers made efforts in their own style, and for their respective ends, not bothering about other undercurrents going on simultaneously in the same arena. They largely remained unaware of these, and if at all some were aware they never expressed it to modify or adjust the things. The functionaries went in the way their respective department desired, with the feeling that they are exclusively responsible to the same. They always remained chiefly conscious of the intended consequences alone. Reaction of the complexity of social structure, and of other efforts of change larlgely went unattended. Such trend did not provide congenial atmosphere for many changes to take place.

The studies concerning social research in Indian villages have certainly bothered for the nature of changes taking place in such communities. What kind of changes have taken place over two to three decades are highlighted more. Some of the studies have also revealed that the impact of proposed innovations has been far less than expected. The reasons, apparently observed, in support of slow change have also been explained by a few social researchers. But the analysis has certainly lacked the exposition of many hidden factors responsible for such state of affairs. These are unexpected kind of hindrances born of the complexity of social structure of village community,as also from the complexity of social change, explained in the above paragraph.The least dealt are the latent responses to the proposed innovations. What reaction an agricultural tool or health practice or a formal law is going to have from the complex arena of Indian village social structure, is a question of urgent probing. There would be wider repercussions and corresponding reactions evoking mixed feelings, some pro and others against. Though the analytical probe, for every element of change, in the complex social structure is mighty difficult task, its coverage will prove of boon to the agents of change, and hence to the programme of development. Efforts, without getting into the root of opposition, are bound to be only half way through. It is through social researches that many unanticipated events can be brought to the surface. Ordinarily these may sound insignificant, but their utility in respect of change is undeniable. Looking to the background and quality of change agents, it may be derived that they themselves have been handicapped in exploiting all implications of an innovation in the complex social systems of Indian villages. However, the task is otherwise essential to gear up the programmes of induced change.

Duality in human behaviour, and the associated implications thereof, form another significant dimension in the process of social change. It has a very important place though, in most of the cases, not illuminated in the literature concerning evaluation of social change or social development. The significance of personal behaviour is unquestionable at the levels of change agents as well as the members of a recipient group, who are to be changed. Any flaw in behaviour would reflect accordingly, and can have deeper and wider implications, mostly of an unwanted character. Some of the functionaries, working for change, have, by training or education, attained specialisation in particular fields. This made them occupy corresponding official positions. Many, among the field staff, responsible for causing change, are specialists of certain subject matters. But otherwise,in their own way of life, they do not observe what they teach others to do. This happens less for personal likings and dislikings of a thing or idea, and more for the pressure of customs and traditions under which such experts are born and brought up. The formal education or training, which they have acquired, has really not proved effective enough to change their personal mode of living concerning the field of their specialisation. Pressure of family, caste and community traditions has kept their living confined within the traditional enclave. As agents of change, and specially when they are physically away from their native social circle,such subject-matter specialists do propagate, as part of their official duty, for new items or idea of change concerning their field. But they restrain from doing the same while being with the member of their own community, including relatives. Even when away, a large number of the extension functionaries do not personally get involved in an act or practice, not suiting to their traditional social position, when some members of the recipient group express to do so. Many, who try to convince people that poultry and piggery are paying occupations, and that eggs, chickens and pork are healthy nutrients, would not themselves even touch a pigling or egg if the occasion demands. Eating of pork or chicken is a far cry to them. This is because of the belongingness of such functionaries to the higher caste families who condemn such occupations and acts, considering them as meant for down-trodden and untouchables. Once the author had taken a batch of Extension Officers and Mukhya Sewikas to a tribal village. One of the Mukhya Sewikas arranged for a demonstration of various egg preparations to the village women, telling the advantage and utility of each. When the preparations were complete, the village ladies asked the change agent to taste it, stressing that as a village tradition, they would eat only after the guest, that is, the Mukhya Sewika, has done so. The lady being from a vegetarian caste of Maharastra was in a soup. She herself was a vegetarian. A co-worker intervened to tackle the situation explaining that the particular lady is on fast , and that he would share it. However, the situation was extremely embarrassing. Likewise, many Agriculture Extension Officers do not know how to plough a field with a pair of bullocks. They simply deliver lectures to the farmers, without being deeply involved. In a Delhi village, where the author completed his doctoral dissertation on social change, an interesting incident was observed. A lady Health Visitor came to the village to popularise the Family Planning methods. This agent of change happened to be an unmarried girl, almost fresh from the college. The village ladies listened to her. Towards the end of explanation, the ladies asked her to demonstrate, making her as an object, the use of female device. The agent got nervous and started sweating. Then the ladies asked if she was married. Her negative reply made the village ladies announce that when you are not doing it, how do you expect us to do. The incidents of this kind, and the other, referred above, lead to the creation of anti-change atmosphere. And these are reflections of personal behaviour where the change agent himself or herself is not involved, or is reluctant to get involved, and is at the same time telling others to try the same idea or object. Such processual implications, caused by human behaviour, are comparatively more in case of communities represented by castes. Display of such behaviour would be at a lesser scale in case of tribals where social constraints, born of stratification, are less. And if they are, it is, by and large, common to everyone.

Duality in behaviour,and hence some processual implications in the programme of social change, are also posed by the human agencies at the receiving end. Here, the particular perspective, under reference, is marked by a typical trend which is not ordinarily identified. Though slightly hidden, the trend reacts sharply without strongly making its outward presence felt in the eyes of those who are involved in the task of planned change and purposed socio-economic transformation of Indian village communities. The author's attention to this arena of social change was engaged while he was involved in the social and cultural change studies of few tribal and non-tribal villages. Some ongoing processes, related to the matter, under reference, were observed reacting, more or less in the same style , to the innovative complex. It applied more to social than material culture of village communities, ranging from multicaste rural peasantry to the homogeneous tribal matrix. A common pattern of reaction, to some ingredients of social change, prevailed in the extremely exposed as well as partially exposed village setting-one situation where urbanisation and other acculturative forces are forceful, and another where they are in mild state.

The educated and employed members, as also some leaders of the village community, who are differentiated and recognised as elites in the village population, are no less important in creating anti-change climate in village community. Apparently they do not look to be so. A common thinking, in general, is that they are the best promoters of change and are early deviants. And such a thinking cannot be challenged in many instances, and in many ways of life, specially of material ones. But many a times the people of above category subscribe for more respectability to the traditional normative principles of native social living. At times, this may be for short span of time, but does create last-longing impact on the minds of other members of village community whose belief in refraining from innovations is deeply strengthened. The element of respect to certain traditional ways of living, and hence an opposition to new ideas and ways, is backed by the motive of personal gain of the educated and highly placed ones. Such a gain can be analysed at two fronts-one directly related to them, and the other benefitting their siblings,parents and other lineage members in the village. Amidst the majority of traditionals of a village community, when an educated elite subscribes to the traditional norms and practices, he is spontaneously appreciated. That is psychologically true as it subscribes to the majority rule. The person is praised and honored by the larger section of the community. His behaviour of this kind even imports lot of respect and honour to his non-elite parents or grand-parents who are praised for having such a son. Elites who are normally from higher castes or otherwise from good families also contribute to the retention of an old system wherein their families have already been enjoying a better status. They are feared that the change might disturb the established order. But they do incorporate many material changes as these do not seriously disturb the patterns of social culture. It may be mentioned that an educated and employed man imbibes certain new values, ideas and practices, specially the progressive ones, and drops the old ones when he stays away from the native community. His wife may not go in for veiling her face, he may not treat a scheduled caste person. when he visits his house, as untouchable, he would send his daughters for higher education, if he can afford, and he would condemn many of the traditional practices. But his attitude and behaviour of this kind are not reflected when he stays amidst the people of his community at village level. There he behaves as a traditionalist and submits to the will and wishes of senior lineage, clan or village folks who are largely pro-tradition. The adherence of such elitists to the ways, within the requirements of age-old traditions, becomes a scale of reference for common men and women in the village. The latter, being bogged down in native atmosphere, appreciate it and cite the example of elitists behaving in conventional style to their own kith and kin. By keeping such a reference group in mind,people's negative reaction to new ways of life is encouraged. And, thus, the elites of this kind maintain a duality in their behaviour and role. A great deal of what they think as part of progress is practically cultivated by them when slightly away from their community's social matrix. Under such conditions, their behaviour differs from the one which they keep up while in the thick of native social system. The repercussions and implications of this kind of behaviour go against the interest of social change phenomenon at wider level.

The social change may get through with more momentum, if this kind of behaviour of educated and employed, in village community, is restrained. At the cost of their petty gain, the larger community suffers, in terms of non-adherence to progressive ways. On this issue of duality in behaviour, the social researches, too, have remained greatly silent. Rather, the research findings chiefly limited to the general observation that educated and employed people, in rural areas, always encourage change.But this sounds more true when you discuss at the level of ideas. The trend, explained above, is a negative indicator of the same. The agents of change have to see that such elites are persuaded not to behave as pro-traditionalists, even if they have to stay in the village for short duration.

No society is totally devoid of resources, and hence of potentialities of various kind. It is, however, true that the nature and bulk of resources vary from community to community. In case of some it is more, while in others it is strongly lacking. Some societies are capable of looking after their requirements from the native resources alone. Others can partly meet them. And there are still others who face acute shortage of things and depend on others to meet even the minimum basic needs. Another interesting phenomenon in this context is the multiplicity of resources, and so of potentialities. One or two resources predominantly characterise certain communities; but the same may be of an insignificant value in other communities. On the other hand, the latter chiefly depend on resources which sound only of a mild form when viewed in the context of the former ones.

But even then some common resources, of a viable nature, cannot be ruled out from village communities. This holds specially true in case of Indian village communities. Among the other relevant and closely connected issues are the forms of control over resources, and their distribution. Like the nature of resources, a great deal of variation is reported in the distribution of resources, as also in the pattern of control over them. But here again the presence of certain common elements cannot be denied. The pattern of life and culture in village India can certify the authenticity of such arguments. Under these conditions of harmony as well as disharmony in terms of resources, their distribution and control, the expression of potentialities,also goes the same way. And it is with the keeping of such conditions in mind that the areas of more and less stress have to be identified, from the villagers' point of view. Social change and potentialities, at local level, have an intimate relationship. Available potentialities, and the creation of new ones, are helpful in the introduction of change. Where the potentialities are scarce, the efforts for change will be less rewarding. In such an event, the change is not, many a times, even geared up. An essential task, for the agents of change, therefore, is to properly identify and assess the nature of locally available potentialities. A proper correlation between a potentiality and an element of change is, then, to be set up. Such an attempt does create a congenial atmosphere for the promotion and acceptance of various kinds of innovations. An attempt to introduce a change, when the potentialities for the same are non-existent or non-supporting, is largely bound to prove as futile. Even if a change is made acceptable through the creation of artificial potentiality, it may get into the reverse gear at one stage or the other when such potentiality is withdrawn or when it fails to find support. But if built-in potentialities in the client system are identified in proper way, and subsequently made use of in the gearing up of programmes of change, the innovations will assume more perpetuating form.

In search of potentialities, concerning programmes of social change, one needs to see Indian rural setting into atleast two distinct categories. One of these is provided by the non-tribal population and the other by the tribals. The former are more exposed to alien or urban atmosphere and the latter are more exposed to rural atmosphere represented by the caste society around. The tribals have the least exposure to urban atmosphere. They mostly live in the hills, forest, coastal areas and undulating terrains. Forest villagers exploit forest resource and have adjusted themselves accordingly. Same holds true for coastal-dwellers who mainly depend on fishing, and have adjusted their living with the exploitation of sea resource. The others have developed their living in tune with shifting cultivation and terraced cultivation. The settled cultivators, among tribals, largely make use of the primitive technology. A large part of social organisation, in case of tribals, is also adjusted as per the eco-system prevalent around. In their case the natural and man-made resources are not highly differentiated. The tribals are closer to the nature, have tremendous sense of cooperation and solidarity. Elements like reciprocity and community ventures are in strong existence. Sharing of resources and sense of belongingness to overall community perspective are of higher order. Social organisation, by and large, does not take an upper hand over economy and its supporting resources. The picture in non-tribal rural India is of a different kind. Such village communities are predominantly agriculture based. They are better agriculturists than the tribals, and their technology, too is of improved quality. They do have artisans and craftsmen who are specialists in their respective occupation. There is a tremendous amount of interdependence among the members of various castes. This holds true in economic as well as social spheres. To some extent, agriculture and trade have assumed commercial importance. Social institutions and groups seem far more developed and complicated when compared to the tribals. Heterogeneity at social and economic level is more. Though the feeling of village community is strong, the friction, feuds, caste rivalry etc, are not ruled out. System of reciprocity does prevail. Sharing of resources is extremely undeveloped. Caste feeling is strong, and many a times takes lead over community feelings. There is comparatively less strong sense of belongingness to the community. This is specially true for more exposed villages. Cooperation and solidarity are not as strong as noticed among the tribal communities. And the corresponding potentialities need to be searched along these lines. Once the potentialities are diagnosed, they need to be used in planning and execution of programmes of change. A shopkeeper or money lender, from outside, does so and he finds himself, in no time, very well established in the village community. But the development machinery does not take much of pain to go down deep into the native potentialities, social, economic and cultural, in the context of programmes of change. And in the absence of such an exercise, it would be difficult even to create suitable potential in a particular community. Suitability would be guaranteed only when the existing base is known and when efforts are made more or less on the same lines. It does not support that a programme of change cannot altogether be implemented if the native potentiality for its support is missing. The argument. however, is that the acceptance of an innovation would be easier, and of higher order,if the potentiality support is there. Inhabitants of a bamboo forest are likely to be expert in basket and mat-making ,and the craft of this kind can easily be developed, in new forms, among them. Nomads, who depend on selling of various articles to sedentary population, may not like to settle down at one place permanently. Thinking of their colonization, in absence of arrangement of sale of their articles, would not be a fruitful exercise. Programme of family planning in higher altitude villages, where density of population is low and where family size is already so small, would be something unthoughtful. Introduction of a formal system of law and control may not be very effective where customary laws are highly operative and complex. Telling villagers to accept chemical fertilizers, in the absence of proper irrigation potential would be highly damaging and unwanted. Such an idea would not be accepted. Stressing for school education, without employment potential may not appeal convincing to the villagers. On the other hand , the community centres will function forcefully in villages where the youth dormitories exist, if the change agents plan in a scientific manner. Better breed of cattle would be more readily acceptable to the cattle rearing communities as the native potential among them is in existence.

Researches on a few Indian villages may not reveal complete picture of village India and the complex of potentialities thereof. Broader trends, however, can certainly be made known. Wherever the depth studies have been made by the social analysts, one can easily map the potentialities. These have sufficiently been analysed, though the explanations are not always directly made. From the total picture, one has to pick up the relevant material. But special studies of rural potential, with particular reference to various programmes of change, have not been made in large number. Whatever seems available is not sufficient looking to the vastness of rural plane and the variety of human and ecological systems thereof. Such researches need to be carried out in all the areas which should be demarcated on the basis of ecology and nature of human population. And it is not difficult to do that in India. Communication of research findings to the agents of change, including planners, is of an urgent need. It may be too much of an expectation if one asks the extension staff to search for potentialities by themselves. But they can certainly act as care-taker of potentialities when the same are told to them. An ideal condition may be one where the social scientists, as operational researchers, work hand in hand with the extension staff who are directly responsible for inducing change. But in all ways the ignorance of potentialities is damaging to the intended efforts for introducing change. Some major and obvious potentialities can always be made use of by the change agents, without waiting to hear of them from the analysts of village communities. As far as possible, the local potential should be exploited in the interest of change.
And a weak potential, if it is found promoting a particular kind of innovation, needs to be strengthened. However, it may be better if this is attempted in the light of existing patterns of resource distribution and their controlling mechanism. Channel of external

potentialities is, however, to be regularly maintained.

To every action there is a reaction. Same holds true for elements of change. To any kind of new induction, idea or object, there is always reaction from the members of recipient group. It may be positive, partly positive, partly negative and totally negative. Then the true kind of reactions are not always immediately known. What comes instantly may change subsequently. Certain things or ideas sound good at the initial stage, but people disapprove of the same in due course. There are others where resistance is shown in the beginning, but it subsides with the passage of time. Nature and form of an element of change would also be determining the state of response or reaction. The same holds true for the community's social, economic and religious levels. It may also be that the anticipated and actual forms of reaction differ. They may even be coinciding, if not immediately then in the long run. Nature of reaction is also governed by the approach of change agents and the follow-up provision. Reactions also change course when certain promises or assurances, made initially, are not kept up. Certain unforeseen events, say natural calamity or change of government, have also a say in the reaction-formation of particular kind. Thus, the reaction to change forms quite an elaborate field of its own. To understand it, one has to probe into various connected aspects. Forming a sudden opinion about the reaction is not correct. Better is to do it after taking stock of various pros and cons. Anyhow the notability of reaction is of significant value to understand and guide the process of social change. More useful is the knowledge of mass reaction than that of an individual.

Looking to the nature of programmes of change, and the elements therein, quite a few trends, with reference under context, are clearly observed in rural India. There are certain programmes which aim at bringing about change at individual's level. These have direct relevance to the personality and attitude of an individual. Here, efforts are made to motivate a person to accept a new idea or object. Point of focus remains a single individual who, being the main target, has to bear the pressure of what is stressed upon by the agent of change. The changes proposed for individual are generally not so complicated. There is another trend where focus of change is family rather than an individual. Certain changes are basically planned for a family group. Normally, the element of change in such a social situation requires the response of atleast the adult members in the family. Even if the programme is concerning the children and infants, the parents would be automatically involved. The change agents remain in touch with those who constitute family leadership. In this case the reaction is of a collective kind. It is likely that some member in the family might express a slightly different opinion to an element of change. However, the same is not easily accepted so long as a common consensus is not announced in its favour. Depending on the pattern, a family head may have more say than others who ordinarily submit to his or her decision. There are some other ingredients of change which are basically meant to cause change at caste level. Things are so designed that concentration remains only on the members of specific caste. There are number of programmes which have specially been designed for the betterment and uplift of scheduled castes. The entire operation is such that it involves all members belonging to a caste. The reaction to such ventures is of the order of caste. The response is the general expression of the constituents of a caste. As in case of certain castes,the special programmes have also been designed for the socio-economic transformation of scheduled tribes. In many respects they differ from those meant for castes. But for the tribal inhabitants of a village, they are uniformly applicable. The tribals, under such state of affairs, will have their own reaction to the bulk of programmes. Another point of interest in multicaste and mixed villages is the reaction of others to the programmes and policies of change, meant for specific castes and tribes. What they feel and express about it are not always in tune with the reaction of people belonging to thc concerned castes and tribes. Many, among others, are critical of various special measures undertaken for the upliftment of certain castes and tribes. And hence the reaction, in such cases, is of a mixed kind. Another category of element of change is of those which are meant to introduce change at the level of village community as a whole. The entire population of the village is to be mobilised and covered for the purpose. The community spokesmen, representing all sections of the village, are initially approached. This is followed by more involvement of larger number of people. The reaction to an element of change is expressed on behalf of the entire village community.

With such a network of social change programmes, and variety of target levels, explained above , the scales of reaction in each case can be delineated. It varies from individual to village community, including family and caste in between. But looking to the interconnectedness of various aspects of life in the village, and the interdependence of individuals, families and castes, it will not be sufficient to search for reaction to element of change at exclusive levels. Most of the changes at individual level do have repercussions on his or her family. Likewise, a change at family level does reflect at wider level, specially among some families of the same caste in and outside the village. Early and easy influenced are those who are connected through kinship ties. And most of the time, the kinship relationships extend beyond the village. The channel for extension of indifference to an element of change is also the same. The unfavourable reaction, to a programme of change, at the level of a family, does accordingly influence others at the village level, and many a times even beyond village frontiers. Repercussions of this kind are also noticed in case of change efforts at caste level. The horizontally and vertically connected castemen get affected and involved for or against the proposed innovations. Thus, even if the programmes of change are individual, family and caste specific, they have wider implications, and involve members and their reaction,at a larger social plane. At the same time this is also largely true that decisions taken in a broader context expose reality and are far more effective. And that the same need to be taken special care of by the agents of change, to get the intended motives served. The possibility of taking care is far more when notability of mass reaction is completed. Such an attempt is useful irrespective of the reaction being favourable or unfavourable.

Some social scientists have carried out researches on attitude and reaction to certain programmes of social change and development. Certain population pockets have scientifically been explored in terms of specific elements of change. Responses gathered have been made public. Results available are in frequencies and percentages. What is provided is the state of end-product in terms of reaction to specific objects, ideas and programmes. Less stressingly dealt remained the reasons for particular form of reaction.

An interplay of numerous factors does occur prior to the growth of a reason for favouring or opposing a change. Somehow a deep analysis of such an interplay could not be attempted in many works. Among other areas, which lacked probing, one prominent is the pattern of linkages, in terms of guiding or looking at a change element, between an individual, family, caste and village community. Who affects whom, for what, in what way and to what extent are some of the important querries which have strong relevance to the issue under discussion. These are not clearly delineated. Under such conditions, the research findings are not that helpful to the agents of change. As the real weak points remain undiscovered, the approach for introducing a change is not rectified. The implementors of programmes keep on making experiments, as suggested to them from higher echelons of the bureaucratic set up, without getting shaky of what is happening to their efforts. In case the right kind of details concerning attitude, response and reaction are made known, some adjustment, in the interest of change, is always possible even if not much of flexibility is provided in the directive. Mass reaction, after all, is the accumulated expression of smaller constituents and events that have grown over time and space. And this is again an accepted fact that mass reaction carries more weight than one of an individual, family or even caste. Once it gets known things take shape accordingly, whatever be the level and quality of change agencies and their efforts. Getting confidence of mass reaction, elements of change need to be made favourable to it. In case the mass reaction is of unmanageable hostile quality, under which adjustment of change ideas sounds mighty difficult, the best is to locate controlling force behind mass reaction. Such a search is unavoidable because a few controllers alone hold the fort. The common masses simply carry what the controllers ask for. The root of particular forms of reaction remains with a few who have been vested with faith and confidence, and whose ideas and attitude, to anything new, are shown maximum respectability. Tackling at the level of such a controlling force is, thus, a sound alternative which can be helpful to the change agents. There is always some scope for compromise between the propounders of mass reaction and the nature of change design. To do it in a better and more effective way, the causes for the creation of particular kind of reaction, on the part of a few who govern the destiny of common masses, will have to be analysed. The whole approach involves tough exercise though its utility is unquestionable. The task can be accomplished with slightly less efforts in tribal areas where comparatively more homogeneity prevails. In case of multi-ethnic situation of village India, some extra efforts will have to be made. Social researchers, carrying out studies on rural communities, and the change agents need to go hand in hand to explore such areas and to accomplish the desired targets.

Every human society is characterized by the diversity in ways of living. In some the arrangement of different aspects of life sounds more elaborate; there are others marked by complicated network, and there are still others which seem to have comparatively simple elements as prerequisites to living. Among the simpler, small and more isolated communities, certain aspects appear to be merged together; many a time to the extent that their independent entities assume only weakly crystalized forms. Contrary to this are the complex societies where major aspects of way of life individually carry sufficiently conspicuous position in the total structure or system of society. Correspondingly, the interconnections and inter-dependence of various aspects of life are of higher order and magnitude in complex societies than those in the simpler ones. At the same time every community, irrespective of its state and stage of living, assigns relative importance to major aspects of living. And it may not be difficult for the members of any community to lay out priority, in order of prominence and importance, in terms of such significant aspects. These are calculated as per the functional value, in respect of their contribution to the social structure, of each. More meaningful aspects may not be the same for the members of gathering, hunting, trapping, horticulture and agriculture communities. Artisans and craftsmen have their own angle of such an assessment. Likewise the explanations in tribal and caste social orders do show variations. In spite of non-uniformity in placing, in order of precedence, the various aspects give rise to the total cultural heritage. Any aspect, in itself and in isolation of others, sounds of somewhat insignificant value. However, the same proves extremely useful and functional when seen or analysed in the total context of way of living of a society. Identification of such a relevance or equation occupies an important place in social change context. Each group of people would define the extent to which diverse aspects are inter-connected and influence one another. What is, then, of greater significance is to understand such patterns of relationship between major aspects, say, of economy, religion, social control and social organization. Depending upon the nature of society, significance of each, more so in the context of others, cannot be undermined. Relationship in some may seem more illuminating, convincing and functionally operative.

Now the bulk of innovations proposed to be introduced from outside have their own character in terms of composition of ingredients. Simultaneously taken up are the programmes of material and non-material change. In the context of rural India, the major focus, in the efforts of programmes of change, remains material oriented. This, however, many a times, seeks support of certain processes concerning non-material areas like attitude, outlook, personality, bent of mind, world-view etc., of change. Managing and gearing up change, simultaneously through material and non-material equipment, are essential in the interest of intended aim of transformation and progress of society.

But what remains to be resolved is the degree of stress to be laid on: (1) material and non-material efforts for change and (2) social, economic, political and religious aspects of change. Broadly speaking there are three possible alternatives in terms of stress in the relevance of change and development. First can be the differential emphasis on different aspects; second, the uniform emphasis, and third, the proportionate one. The uniform emphasis may remain a weak proposition. The differential emphasis, in any way, is unavoidable. But what form the 'differential' is to assume is a challenging question to reply. It may not easily be fixed. However, as an alternative the proportionate emphasis, which automatically involves the element of 'differential', sounds the right slogan. How much stress is to be laid on what aspect is to be proportionately calculated keeping in view the nature of society and its arrangement of inter-connected aspect. While reviewing latter, more carefully are to be calculated the degree of influence and control one has over the other/s. Such an exercise is likely to help reveal the requirement, in terms of stress to be laid, of each aspect. Depending upon the nature of society, such a requirement is most likely to vary. In other words it creates demand for proportionate emphasis. And any major imbalance, in such proportion, is likely to hamper change efforts.

In what has so far been observed, there appears a fair amount of disequilibrium in respect of emphasis. Certain aspects are more heavily emphasized than others, without realizing that it may not serve the purpose. Otherwise the aspects, not adequately considered, have quite an important place in their relationship to those increasingly stressed. So much so that the latter may not get into the intended orbit of change unless the former ones are given due recognition. Failure to cause change in certain fronts may be ascribed to such a reason. In the context of rural India, the studies conducted on social change reveal, many a times, such phenomena. The planners and change agents have generally bothered for a few common aspects alone without getting into the nexus of connected others which otherwise carried, and continue to do so, a significant value in terms of their contribution to the cause of change. Comparatively more concerned of the latter remained the social scientists than the planners and agents of change. However the results of social science research, in this context, could not somehow be passed on to the planners and agents of change. There remained a gap. Even the researches limited themselves only to a few communities. The bulk continued unexplored from the point of view of interconnectedness and interdependence, in all respects, of different parts or aspects. Thus, even the social scientists need to be extra assertive at two fronts. Firstly, they have to provide coverage to sampled communities representing all sections of Indian rural population, and secondly they have to make available such research findings to those responsible for change and development at operational level. The best would be if at least the important aspects, and their place vis-a-vis the system, are delineated in order of priority. It may be mentioned that caste society provides quite a uniform pattern and, thus, may not involve a massive exercise. Similar interactions and relationships may mark diverse caste societies. Exception to the above feature is, by and large, a characteristic of the tribal society where things are to be seen in a different manner. Absence of caste-based stratification and the presence of intra-tribe homogeneity would reveal formations of a different kind. Simultaneously the indifference of planners and agents of change to such research findings is to be eliminated so that the purpose can be served in right earnest and entirety.

Looking to the broadness of social change perspective, people have taken it in diverse ways. This has happened not only at theoretical level but also at practical one. Many a times there has been controversy among the social scientists regarding the sphere, scope and dimensions of social change. Cultural change has been treated, at times, as synonymous with social change, and at times as different. At the same time some studies on social change have not at all provided place to change in material possessions; whereas there are still others which have done so. Likewise, some studies have chiefly remained at the psychological level, covering psychological attributes as elements of change. There are others who have treated, and continue to treat, social change as something inclusive, concerning all the ways of living of a group of people. Under such a diversity of looking at social change, the efforts to create or bring about social change, too, have shown divergence in terms of their focus. Regarding village India a variety of views, at theoretical level, were put forth. And such trend at thinking level has further reflected in the practical relevance or operational context. The change agents made efforts of different kind for changing the target population. Availability of effective socio-psychological technology to the agents of change remained almost a far cry. And as such the baggage they carried for transformation of rural society proved not only weak but also inadequate. Most of the time the stress remained on the development of village or region (This seems obvious from the programmes of Community Development, Tribal Development, Rural Reconstruction, Integrated Area Development etc). And far less remained the stress on change of 'role'. This happened inspite of the fact that the two, that is, the development of the region and the change of role are intimately connected, and are rather inseparable in the interest of causing overall change or development. The imbalance in the stress of two is a matter of concern for all involved in the gigantic task of socio-economic transformation of rural society. What generally has not sufficiently been taken care of includes two dimensions of role. Firstly, the role of individual vis-a-vis other members of his or her community at micro or macro level, and secondly the role of individual vis-a-vis his or her physical environments around. Individual role is largely conditioned by the community norm-complex and requirements, as also it is in adjustment or adaptation with the local environmental conditions. Therefore, designing of any change in the socio-economic or environmental orders will have close bearing to the regularities defined for role performance. In other words any change, without alteration in role or adjustment with the existing role pattern may not bear the requisite fruit. Under the circumstances, even if the things temporarily get going, the chance of their reversal to original state of affairs remains bright. And such a position does continue to prevail till a balanced stress is given to the efforts made for change of region and change of role. Though the latter apparently sounds to have smaller dimensions but is otherwise of larger significance. And in fact, it is this aspect which counts for more reliable measure of change than any other criterion. This too has, however, not been maintained at actual level. Achievements as part of change programme or induction of change or development were, most of the time, assessed merely in tune with the creation of infrastructure, in terms of agencies, institutions or other structures. What the recorded figures spoke was taken as implemented. But such an assumption proved misnomer. The success story of a change programme lies in the change of role, and subsequently the attitude of the people. Accounting for change in the absence of analysis or role-performance is misleading and superflous.

Corresponding to the more stress on change or development of region than role, the focus of social research too has gone the same way. The social analysts of village India have increasingly highlighted the infrastructure established as part of social change and development. Thus, the studies on social change in rural India take a strong note of the construction of roads, schools, hostels, godowns, dams, anicuts, organisation of cooperative societies, youth clubs, Panchayati Raj bodies, provision of transport facilities and other amenities like banks, dispensaries, drinking water, electricity, rural latrines etc. Less dealt in such studies are shake and reflection in the role system of the people. The introduction of any new infrastructure is bound to have repercussions on the acts, interactions and activities of the people. Even the very idea involved is to rearrange the human activities and relationship. The centuries old rigid role patterns cannot continue to carry the same force in the event of new structures around. They do undergo some change. But the turn they take may not always be in tune with the intended objectives. They may even go the other way round thereby posing resistance to the efforts for development. At the same time there may be adequate or partial adjustment with the elements of new creation. While explaining development or change we often give an account of, say, how many wells have been dug, or how many schools or dispensaries have been opened. But how people have responded and reacted to such institutions has only been inadequately exposed, though the same carries more significance in the arena of social change research. More important is the use of compost pits than their digging alone. And whether people make use of it, or even of some other things, is largely dependent on the role interplay and the consequent attitude formation. Any expression of change, therefore, remains half-attempted in the absence of such explanations. To know of what happens to role system, after the creation of an infrastructure, is rather of a higher value. The latter is true not only in giving a complete account of change, but also in directing change. One finds hard to get an element of change guided, and subsequently accepted, so long as the role adjustment lacks. But once the latter is achieved, the change, of whatever kind, would go on. What needs to be further searched, as part of social change, are the degree and intensity of stress laid on the change of role. This is to be done as per the elements of change. Once it is done, and once the reaction to role system gets known, it may be easier to direct the change and its channels. Simultaneously, the role disorganization, in negative sense, can also be tackled at the right moment. Alongwith the creation of institutions and other facilities for change, the operational researches, of the above form, would not only be revealing but also eye-opener to the agents of change, who otherwise may keep on rubbing shoulders without achieving the anticipated ends. The findings of such operational researches are to be simultaneously made available to the agents of change so that the extension of benefit to the target population is ensured. Stress on change of role, both in tribal and non-tribal societies, and the subsequent reactions are in no way less valuable to the creation of infrastructure as part of bringing about change and development.

EIGHT

ELEMENTS OF SPECIAL CONCERN

In terms of ideas as well as implications. social change arena is characterized by multitudinal and complex dimensions. And the same applies to its theoretical baggage. Therefore, within such a background the understanding and explanation of change phenomena are not that easy. There are innumerable writings on change but are they complete in themselves, or just touch the fringe of a specific aspect. Surface level descriptions of an event, concerning change, avoiding connected analytical framework do not really fit in the scientific purview of social change analysis, as conceived within the traditions of social science . To differentiate scientific from ordinary explanations of change, and to thereby import social science vigour, one needs to deal change events in their comprehensive framework. And some of the necessary guidelines for the same have been provided in the preceding chapters. To what extent one adheres to it depends on a variety of factors, including individual capacity and grasp. But more we get into this nexus, more rewarding it would prove, not only in the world of scholarship but even to those who claim to be the torchbearers of change in a target population.

Individual, society and culture form a complex combination. These are independent, but at the same time interwoven. Though individual and society form substantive arena, and culture an abstract, they do get affected from one another. Any major jolt, in terms of additions or ommissions, in society largely speaks on culture. The same holds true vice-versa. And to know whether it is an instance of sudden shake, or they are planned and intended efforts to cause innovations, one needs to review the situation in the context of these three parameters. Even an instance of independent evolution maps these three perspectives if such an instance is really viable. And this phenomenon is equally applicable to diffusional incidences, more so when they claim a definite place in a social system. But unfortunately a large number of those who explain change, its events and incidences, pin-point unidimensionally, without getting deep into the other connected fields. As an instance one may take stock of material style of living of an individual, but he does not , by and large, speak of its repercussions on society and culture. Unless the latter is attempted, the scientific validity of social change can be questioned. And its understanding is also, in that case, incomplete. Therefore, in a discussion and narration on change, due weightage is to be simultaneously given to society, culture and its participants. The same principle needs again to be adopted while planning for a strategy of causing change. If there remains an imbalance in the consideration of such elements, while planning for change, the approach may forefeit a great deal of effectivity. In more of the cases the planners and implementors of change do not subscribe to the analysis of all these parameters. Since they operate in their own style, they not only encounter difficulties, but largely remain short of achieving the anticipated goals.

Again, a large number of publications as well as discussions on change do not adequately classify and differentiate the categories of underlying factors or causes. Sporadic causal explanations are, however, met with. Such a mild treatment of cause and effect, in the arena of change, does not serve the detailed purpose. It merely remains of partial advantage. To understand the processes and forms of ongoing changes, or even to plan for the creation of change, it is desired to document the factors, more specifically in the endogenous and exogenous formats. And these formations are to be further elaborated in relatedness, if there is seen an avenue for the same. Their treatment, independently and in relatedness, helps assign specificity to instances of change and their explanations. And the root for any lacuna in the same can be traced back to some stage or state of factor-formation. When this is attained it becomes easier to rectify and direct change before it heads for a serious diversion contrary to society's interest. Still more important is the assessment of force inherent in endogenous and exogenous factors, independently or in relatedness. A weak estimation is bound to reflect correspondingly in the policies, programmes and implications of change. Somehow the social analysts, as also those who are meant to guide change present a rather weak analysis of factors for change, more so in the framework of relatedness. Explanation or anticipation of concrete changes remains incomplete without an adequate mention of supporting structures, that is, the factors and forces holding the incidences. The explanations for non-appearance of anticipated events can again be sought in factor formations. Once this is attained, an alternative room for improvement can be suggested more rationally.

In addition to the processes of social/cultural change, there are other areas which too need to be explained with equal clarity. More of the existing explanations have, somehow, mixed many things together not really caring for respectively defined conceptual framework. And as such the arguments are not duly classified, paving way to overlapping and repetitions. These informations on change are though helpful, but they hardly provide clarity and material for building up new ideas and concepts which are growingly required in the light of mounting dynamics in society. Richer the ideas and conceptual baggage, more solid would be the base for directing and guiding change. The revelation of expertise would be feasible and more meaningful when the existing and new dimensions of change matrix are elaborately dealt. The social researches, many a times, have mixed up things to the extent that they miss the level of clarity. For instance, in many empirical studies on social change one hardly finds distinctive areas of explanation concerning development, progress and reform. This happens even when such studies pertain to micro situations where such explanation, comparatively speaking, could be easier. Under such circumstances the clarity regarding direction of change is missed. And when that is done it may not be easy to put forth new ideas in the interest of purposed change.

In majority of cases, social change has been accounted in terms of addition of traits, followed by the feature of alteration. It has proved more true in material life perspective. Social culture remained comparatively less affected. Omission and degeneration of cultural traits, as part of social change, remain the least highlighted ones. These are not less important from the point of view of social analysis because they have had bearing to the change-inducers and their strategy on the one hand, and the nature of social system concerned on the other. More so, the changes, in terms of additions and alterations, too, have had some bearing to the same. Any sort of cultural retrogression is not to be left as such, and its expression may not be less meaningful, sociologically speaking, in the context of social progress, again taken as one of the end-products of social change. A correct large scale understanding of this kind would draw the line of distinction between many other features of social change. The latter include, among others, development, progress and reformistic and revolutionary efforts. The urgency to demarcate and highlight all concerned areas is of special use for mapping processes, in differing situations of social change. The deeper the insights of a social scientist at macro front, the better it would be, in terms of utility, to planners and administrators who actually act as the change inducers or implementors. Even the areas of weakness, that led to degeneration, would be known. With this experience, some idea about the disorganisation of healthy cultural elements can be had, and the same can be made use of in parallel or other situations, open to the forces of change for rectification.

Account of social change, specially at village level, irrespective of its being homogeneous or heterogeneous, has remained in the form of single solid block contributed by directed and non-directed efforts. Apparently one assumes that the planned or induced change forms the bulk of it. Only a little can be attributed to non-directed change. But in certain areas, it may sound the other way round. Hence, the need is to differentiate the outcome of two. It is truc to say that the two are fairly inter-linked, but then each has its own level and area of contribution, and the same can be delineated. At times the two processes work as if they are supplementary, but the opposite of it cannot be ruled out. Independent interpretation of each, as also one of their being put together, is an interesting field of sociological investigation. Changes need to be viewed in two perspectives, analysing positive and negative side of each. Such sociological reporting is not only valuable as academic contribution, but also throws open wide choice to planners and agents of change for the use of the best. At the same time one can drop whatever is felt as unwanted. Dealing of change, in isolation of attributing it to definite factors, within the broad frame of planned and non-planned, would remain short of serving real sociological purpose at academic as well as applied level. To give it stronger and broader dimensions, the need is to explore diverse social situations ranging from tribal communities to the urban ones.

Further, the heterogeneity of plural society is not evenly represented and covered in terms of studies concerning social change. This is obvious from the publications brought out during the last three decades or so. Taking stock of ethnic composition of urban, rural and tribal India, we find that the least coverage is in respect of urban and tribal settings. More of the works on social change in village India pertain to non-tribal communities. This may have been due to difficulties of fieldwork in tribal areas, or for certain other reasons known to social researchers. But simultaneously it is also true that there is an increasing focus on change and transformation of tribal communities. One reason, among others, why tribal India is slow in terms of change can be attributed to scores of their unknown parameters. To propose for change, on valid and scientific base, among the tribals and other non-literate societies is no less important than to direct and control what is changing fast among other communities. To attempt it, one has to get into tribal nexus through the exploration of basic and core features. The attempts of latter kind are themselves lacking. Consequently the tribal continues to form the last man in the last row. Social scientists, therefore, need to provide coverage, in terms of their studies and direction, to those sections of population who are not yet well within their orbit. Rather, they need to be more committed to such venture to prove their claim of being useful to the masses.

Indian tribal situation is, at the moment, not characterised by homogeneity. This holds true at the racial and cultural levels. In spite of multiple forces of change, almost uniformly designed, the outcome is not uniform. This may be attributed to number of reasons, including ecological, human and material resources. Nature and extent of change also vary. As it stands today, the tribal communities can be arranged at various points in a scale marked by two distinguished polarities, that is the most primitive and the more developed. In other words, the latter are most influenced by the impact of change force, and the former ones the least. Others occupy particular positions as per their degree of outside influence, as also persistence purview,. Continuity as well as social change have also been conditioned by the nature of contact situation. In one situation, the tribals are highly exposed. But in other, they appear to be the least exposed with intactness of their traditional socio-cultural milieu. Such a condition prevailed even prior to the introduction of the programme of directed social change among Indian tribes. Programme of planned social change has, it seems, not made much headway in bridging this kind of disparity. For understanding social change among Indian tribes, it would, therefore, be useful to stress on this aspect. Normally dealt is the account of changes in individual tribes or sections thereof. But what is needed, at this level, is to search for the causes of gap in changes, inspite of there being more or less common elements involved in the massive programme of tribal development or directed social change among the tribals. Scattered informations, regarding various implications of social change, need to be put together and scrutinised to get at some common trends which may be of use to academicians as well as the change implementors.

Here it may not be out of place to make a mention of the nature of studies done on Indian tribes, and their relevance to social change perspective. Most of the works are of 'holistic' kind, giving total picture of way of life of a tribe or a multi-caste or multi-ethnic community. Works, chiefly devoting to social change parameter, are very thin and scanty. In most of the holistic studies, a small portion is devoted to social change. Such a provision limits the explanation chiefly to a brief stock of innovations, material and non-material. Some of the deeper intricacies and trends which are more vital, at theoretical as well as practical levels, are not brought to the surface. The agents of change remain unaware of the same, making social change hampered at various stages. In general, to a carrier of programme of change or development, taking stock of 'holism' appears very loading. He or she feels that there is neither time nor energy to grasp the total situation. As a matter of fact what he needs are the sharply pin-pointed elements which are of immediate utility. This is, therefore, the task or social scientists to separate out such elements, in the shape of common trends or systematised forms, for a ready reference of the change agents. Devising of such forms is easier for social scientist who grasps the situation in totality. But, for the change agents, it would be a mighty difficult job as they have limitations in their comprehension. Some very useful areas which either lacked coverage or have not, in many cases, been touched at all are mentioned, in the following pages, for immediate attention of social researchers. Let us not keep a vacuum between vital social research findings and the requirements of those responsible for social change. In addition to many other factors, the programme of social change, among Indian castes and tribes, can be well looked after if the social researchers can do full justice to their job involving, among others, a few special issues given below.

Most of the academic exercises, concerning social change analysis, in respect of different empirical situations, provide a common kind of format to the readers. By and large these have acutely lacked in throwing light on the barriers and stimulants to change. This is specially true in case of the change-inhibiting and change-promoting factors built in the native social system. Description of the barriers and stimulants from functionaries' side, or from the side of funds and schemes, designed for social change, are often available. Though the latter two are also important in the context of social change, the barriers and stimulants, existing in the recipient group, are far more weighty. And hence their proper identification is needed in priority. The agents of change, if they are themselves not the social analysts, may not be able to do this job. It essentially forms an area of social scientist who has the capacity and capability of penetrating deep into all the areas of social structure of a group of people. A very forceful role of barriers and stimulants in social change process is unquestionable. Further needed is the consolidated account of such ingredients. This may be attempted at micro as well as macro levels. For such an exercise, one needs to move from smaller situations to larger ones, pooling similar findings, wherever possible, to get into some kind of common constructs. But then the special parochial elements have to maintain their respective identity at micro level so that their utility, there, is not forfeited. However, looking to the position of Indian castes and tribes, it would not be difficult to universalise some of the barriers and stimulants, so that they can be made use of in wider context. Scattered and sketchy account, as some studies reveal, of change-promoting and change-inhibiting factors might not meet the increasing requirements of massive programme of directed social change. Another connected requirement is of making the barriers through readjustment and stimulants effective in practical approach. I personally feel that unless the social researcher takes initiative, the change implementor may either skip over or lack initiative in this sphere of social change process. This is the juncture where two should work hand-in-hand so that the change is effected in an anticipated manner. Otherwise the change agent and change would have their own course undermining the place and role of social scientist and social research.

Another shortcoming, marking social researches, is in regard to inadequate understanding of socialization processes. Socialization, as a special field of social enquiry, has not been given the type of treatment it should have been. Not many works on socialization, concerning tribal India, can be cited. As a matter of fact, one rarely comes across accounts seriously devoted to socialization pattern in tribal communities of India. Patterns of internalization of cultural element, through socialization, have to be properly devised. Forms and channels of socialization for various kinds of traits are yet to be sufficiently mapped. Works of this kind need to be tackled at two fronts. First the social analyst has to devise all kinds of socialization channels. Preferably it is to be explored and explained in respect of varieties of traits. There is a possibility that a socialization agency may not be responsible for all kinds of transmission, Different traits may be acquired through different agencies which are to be outlined. At the second front the social analyst is required to attempt to identify the agencies and areas of socialization which can provide room for acquiring and transmission of additional traits put forth by the innovations, proposed to be introduced through social change. This second task, which is taken as more important, can be better seen through when the first front is within complete grasp. And when one has command over the second, the effectivity of elements of social change is almost guaranteed, eliminating chances of reversal of the process. Thus, socialization and social change need to be viewed as highly interconnected. A proper command, in terms of understanding, over the former does pave way to the induction of new traits which may, otherwise, remain only at the periphery without getting rooted into the system. In other words it may be said that the expected results of social change are acquired in full only when the new traits get a place in the socialization process. Else, they are seen as floating, sometimes indicating that they are accepted, and other time as if they are not there. It may be mentioned that the role of socialization in tribal communities is of more value and significance than others where formal institutions have made their headway. The latter have added new dimensions in socialization, and these too may be accounted for wherever necessary.

Social analysis has, so far, largely escaped another important area. In fact, it carries such an importance that it should have been tackled right in the beginning while devising strategy for planned social change. This area pertains to 'reference groups' and 'reference individuals'. The latter characterise all communities, irrespective of their degree of exposure to alien population. For certain purposes the reference groups or individuals may be from within the tribe or caste. For others it may be beyond. Again, it may be from near vicinity alone; or may even be from far off place. In former situation, the interaction is close and frequent; but it is only occasional in case of the latter. However, irrespective of nearness or distance, the influence of the reference group or individual is of a very high order. For many things, it is the latter who act, and are recognised so, as the guide and torchbearer for the former. There is a tremendous amount of faith in what the members of reference group do or say. Such an equation has developed, over the years, especially after the borrowing group got convinced of the activities and intensions of the group whose members were accepted as reference individuals. In most of the cases, a reference group or individual is taken as superior for various purposes. In the analysis of social change perspective, studies on Indian tribes have extremely lacked in pinpointing the reference groups. The latter are not sufficiently identified. Another serious handicap, which holds almost uniformly true has been the disuse of reference groups. Thus, the identification of reference groups and their use as mechanism of social change remained greatly undone. Such an area of social research is of vital relevance, and unfortunately it has greatly escaped the attention of social analysts. It needs to be taken up in priority, and with all seriousness. When the reference groups are identified, they need to be put to proper use for gearing up the process of social change. The urgency is to involve their members first so that the diffusion, among those who look at them or copy them, becomes easy. Help of the members of reference groups seems to be necessary for the acceptance of new ideas and elements, and hence in social change. In general the stress of social scientists and their researches has been more on 'base' community rather than the reference groups. And this was obvious too when social change was seen as simply a small part of the major research study. But if we show increasing concern to social change, and which sounds inevitable in case of developing societies, a good deal has to be devoted to the study of reference group and the nature of their interaction with those tribesmen who consider them so. The latter would need an elaborate explanation for the fixation of particular kind of innovation which one aims to introduce. Unless the sociological analysis of such groups is made, and unless they are involved for gearing change efforts, there is every likelihood that the change, in one sphere or the other, gets hindered. When the reference groups are overlooked or uncared for, the others remain hesitant and cannot easily make their mind to get into the process of social change.

One of the results of culture contact, from early times, has been the creation of some kind of divisive tendency in the cohesiveness of tribal living. In pre-contact situation , the tribals, it is assumed, may have had a great deal of homogeneity and solidarity. Under alien influence, various factors made them divide into sub-groups. Two kind of trends emerged. Under one, a tribe got divided into two or more categories which maintained certain differences from one another. The maintenance of difference got them placed in ranked order. Members of the same tribe got socially stratified into higher and lower ranks. In some cases, such groups, in due course, maintained endogamy, though the title of the tribe continued to be used. At times, even the relation of commensality came to an end. Feeling of social superiority and inferiority crept in. What one did, was given up by the other. This happened in the intra-tribe situation. Another trend emerged in case of those who got settled in multi-tribe and mixed villages. An order of hierarchy was created among different tribes, as also between the tribes and caste groups who stayed together in common villages. By and large, the tribals, in comparison to castes, were relegated to lower social position. Members of a tribe who lived in such setting, and others of their fraternity who stayed away also developed some differences in respect of their position, interaction and relationship. Once homogeneous, they developed differing outlook to their traditional way of life, as also to the growing conditions around. Simultaneously, it may also be mentioned that the division of a tribe into stratified groups, in many cases, also occurred from within and not always as a result of alien influence. Of relevance is the point that a large number of tribes, more so the major ones, are no longer homogeneous identities. There is a wide variety of divergence. But the planners and social change inducers have, largely and in most of the cases, dealt these tribes as solid blocks with all kinds of uniformity and similarity of ways, connected to the life and culture. In this way the efforts for social change remained devoid of stratificational consideration. As such, what was found suiting to a section did not react the same way to the other. This made the change agents confused as to why the same tribesmen are behaving in different styles to the same kind of elements of change. Even the sociologists and social anthropologists have somehow not been sufficiently active in social research concerning social stratification among the tribes. Much has been done on caste ranking and stratification. But only a mild headway could be made in the context of tribes. The concept that the tribes are homogeneous, in all respects, is a sheer misnomer. Existence of hierarchy, among Indian tribes, now cannot be denied. And it would be in the interest of planners and change agents if the anthropologists and other social scientists lay their hand on stratificational studies in intra-tribe and tribe versus caste situation. Social change implications do not remain the same under conditions of homogeneity and heterogeneity.

It is with the above approach that the tribal value-structure would be more intensively searched for. Even otherwise, the social researchers have done comparatively more in studying the value complexes of the tribal communities. While dealing with customs, the customary norms and the supporting values thereof were taken note of. Importance of values in social change is remarkable. The latter sounds only superfluous unless it touches the value core. Only after doing so, the change assumes an on-going process and, thus, perpetuates. The values provide foundation to the entire infrastructure of social system. Withdrawal of any of them would bring in possibility of crack in the system. That is why the honour and sanctity to the values come so favourably to the community members. And there lies the maximum resistance to social change programmes. There has been an overall weakness in tackling this front. The agents of change simply get disgusted by constant opposition to their efforts. They attribute it, among other things, to the values in the system, and the respectability shown to the same. On the other hand, the social researchers make a postmortem of tribal value systems. They interpret them in the context of existing social structure and the cultural milieu. They do not, to a great extent, review such value systems in the light of nature, forces and avenues of social change, both directed and non-directed. This helps keep a gap in social research and its utility for bringing about smooth social transformation. An urgent task is the realisation of identified values in new ways so that the change is accepted. A major contribution, in this venture, is again expected from a social analyst, the change agent is expected to do comparatively less in the matter. He may not even, at times, be capable of it. Social researches are to be seriously undertaken to see the old values in new forms so that they can adjust with the emerging forms, coming through social change, without causing any major breakdown in the system. This is a very challenging task, but I am sure the social scientists would further consolidate their position and claim of being applied if they can devise means to cope with such a situation.

Another element of relevance to the theme, under reference, is connected to the sphere of responses in social change. Diversity in response is undeniable. It holds true in the case of the same groups as also when comparison is made between different groups. Numerous factors can be held responsible for response disparity. Among those who get involved earlier in the social change ventures, or those who are early adopters of innovations, there is a special category of people which has technically been termed as one of the 'marginal' men. People, under this category behave as early deviants, with comparatively quicker response to social change requirements. It is not only they who personally get involved, but there may be others who, directly or indirectly, draw inspiration from them. The very image of pro-change or marginal person plays a significant role in the extension of innovations. But then there are some people who superficially pose as marginal men, specially to keep good relationship with the agents of change. In actual practice, and in the absence of change agents, they propagate in favour of traditional ways, announcing them as better over the new ones. There may be some personal motive behind this kind of behaviour. Therefore, to find out who the early carriers of change are, and who the real marginal men are, is quite a ticklish job to attempt at. The change implementors' strategy is to treat government recognised leaders or officially recognised spokesmen as the marginal men. And they are believed to be early adopters of change. But is it really rational, in terms of scientific social enquiry, to treat all such people as early deviants for the purpose of social change. Or is it worthwhile to ignore others, who are not officially recognised, as being essentially tradition-bound and nochangers. Such a jumpy assumption is questionable, more so because it has no element of rationality. Where lies the truth and what repercussions are imminently expected of various assumptions, can be better revealed through scientific social enquiry into the social network of a group of people. The job is essentially of social researchers. Unfortunately, the results of social research have, by and large, ignored this perspective. And their dealing of marginal man or deviant, too, is not far away from one of change agents. Need of the hour is to sharpen our tools of social enquiry for a thorough and correct searching of men and women who are prone to appreciate new items, and whose traditional moorings are somewhat shaky. Who else can be better motivated with them can also be determined by the social scientists who are experts in analysing nature of social alliances based on kinship, age, sex, neighbourhood etc. This further makes possible to analyse the sphere of influence which would be of use in the extension of social change and its objectives.

When any social system is exposed to social change forces, the situations of conflict and anomaly are bound to appear, irrespective of degree. There is a possibility of their being less in case of directed social change than under the conditions where change atmosphere is created in a haphazard manner. At times, some of the new elements or items, as part of social change, are themselves conflicting to those existing in the social system of the recipient group. Under such a situation, there is every possibility of direct confrontation. And the magnitude of indifference would be fairly high, and opposition to change would be more. People realise that it is nothing but a direct threat to their social matrix. In some cases there may appear signs of direct antagonism. There is another trend where the conflicting situation is not posed at the beginning stage of the carrying of a programme of social change. Here, the old and new do not seem to be in immediate contrast at the initial stage. But the conflict appears after an element or item is accepted in a society.The members of client system realise it in the subsequent stage when they feel the pinch of growing disorganisation tendency. It does not assume a forceful form so long as it remains at a smaller level. But when the larger section is involved, people become conscious of it. They may, then, even think of reorganising themselves for either condemning the change or to devise means for readjustment. So long as the disorganisation is not prevailed upon, the atmosphere of conflict and uncertainty persists. Social scientists and their research studies, at least many from so far done among Indian tribes, do not provide answer to react to such situation. They are essentially diagnostic in character. But the provision of concrete remedial measures has not been adequately made. The patient is not to be left by merely telling the disease, he is also to be supplied with medicines. The rise of anomalous and conflicting situation can be analysed from another angle, different from the one directly observable and argued. This refers to their contributing to non-purposed consequences of purposive change. Whether the intended objective could be attained or not, the unintended consequences were felt by the people. The latter emerged beyond the anticipated purview. Neither the recipient group nor the group of change agents could comprehend such an outcome. In fact, it is the unintended consequences which contributed to a great deal to the creation of arena of conflict, anomaly or even disorganisation. The non-purposive consequences could also be the result of nonplanned change which came in of its own, or with the efforts of a few who have had some selfish kind of motives. Even the social scientists' intervention in this kind of social perspective is extremely limited. In fact, the works on latent implication of manifest objectives are hardly available in their special form. Scattered reference, in this regard, may be available in a few cases. For a change implementor, by himself, it would be mighty difficult to get into such a sphere. And it is the social scientist who should come to his help. There is an increasing need to realise, in proper perspective, the unintended consequences of induced change. For the completion of exercise, the researcher has to suggest means to regularise the realised consequences.

Lately, the tribal society is in a flux. Social change forces are impinging on it from all around. Some are more open than others. The non-directed forces of social change, in Indian tribal setting, are fairly older than the guided ones. But the intensity of the latter is more. While carrying out social research in any tribal community, these two perspectives need to be dealt at fairly equal level. A common trend of recent studies is specially in terms of the focus on guided social change and its implication. Another serious drawback in social research arena, especially in thc light of social change perspective, is in regard to the rigidity of approach. Most of the research work, on Indian tribes, involve descriptive account of culture. There is not much of deviation from the stereotyped ethnography. This sounds as research imbalance, specially under the currently prevailing social situation marked by social change. Some special areas of research, outlined in this chapter, need to be attended seriously, and in priority. Such an attempt will be useful in two ways. Firstly, the horizons of social research will be expanded, and the proportion of ethnographic and other special areas of research would be maintained. Secondly, the claim of social scientist, as applied scientists, would be further consolidated. So long as the social research on tribal society does not seriously get committed to such specialised research ventures and subsequently establish a close laison with the planners and change implementors, there is a chance of their being discredited, specially at the level of their claim that social research has applied value. And the tribal communities will keep on facing problems, and their development and welfare, as part of social change, would remain hampered.

NINE

EPILOGUE

As in case of other developing nations, the rural communities of India are also in the sway of change. Social change caught comparatively faster momentum after India launched her programmes of planned and directed change. Though the main focus in the induced programmes and change processes remained on economic transformation, the social life also experienced the pinch of change. The experiences have shown that economic change or development is not independent of social factors and implications, since the same are not operated upon in vacuum but for a group of people who have definite social structure, and socially react keeping the same in view. Instances of change are marked at the levels of individual, community, social organisation, cultural milieu etc. But the things have not always, and in all cases, moved the way they were intended and anticipated as has been made abundantly clear at many places in the body of the book. This can be attributed, among other factors, to the variation in response at individual, community and societal levels, plus to the diversified nature of material and ecological niches characterizing Indian society, and which have their own say in the context of proposed innovations. Dissimilarity of variants in social structure correspondingly reflected on the change elements. Social researches, in certain communities and spheres, have identified and explained such implications, though scores of areas, on this count, continue to remain unsearched. Some of the centuries old traditional elements, reflecting on individuals, communities and social organisations, certify their continuity, others have been reformulated in the light of new requirements and there could be yet others which are said to have disappeared over the years. The force of various elements continues to be strong not only in the native social living and perception but also in the relevance of change. And this has well been explained in chapters three to eight.

In Indian rural society the processes of guided and non-directed change are in operation simultaneously. In certain instances they pose for confrontation, one reflecting against the interest of the other. The concerned agencies operate within the background of diversity involving typicality of respective interests. And the nature of their impact authenticates the same. Lack of consensus at this level has proved detrimental to some elements of change, and the same could not be taken care of for lack of understanding of the social-cultural complexity characterizing rural India.

Psychological, sociological and material elements provide the format through which one can conceive, understand and explain the totality of life-designs of a group of people. These, as analysed in this book, operate independently as well as in combination. Therefore, while assessing, analysing and guiding social change and its implications, one needs to bother for individual, for community, for social structure and for technology and the ecological setting. And while doing so, one is required to explore at two fronts - one of concrete reality and the other of cognition or perception. Though presenting two perspectives, these are intimately connected to the extent of rendering influence on each other.

The major elements concerning individual, community, society and the associated social structure of rural India, having significant bearing on the arena of social change, more so the planned one, were identified and analysed in the context of structural continuity and the change efforts and intensions. Detailed treatment of each element showed its importance not only in the traditional society and its social system but also in the change context. But the agents of change, by and large, did not give due weightage to these elements and somehow took them as silent or dead. This gave way to wrong approach reflecting adversely on the anticipated objectives and targets. Since the sociological parlance were not stressed upon, as part of orientation of change agents, they did not bother for them. The trend took a still stronger turn in the absence of involvement of social scientists in the process of directed change at operational level.

Analysis of important features marking individuals, communities and broader social structure of rural India has authenticated that they have strong bearing on, and relevance to change on the one hand and the society and its pattern of living on the other. Their reaction to intended efforts and programmes of change further explained of their importance. Unfortunately no major or proper concern was shown to such elements, with their wide ramifications resulting into slackness at change front.

In the face of various limitations, the social scientists could not initiate research on many of these elements/features which were, otherwise, so deeply related to the change venture and whose results could really prove rewarding in the creation of change. Only the fringe of obvious, in terms of social research, could be touched upon and that too in specific context, say impact of one programme or the other. The accounts given in the book have identified and highlighted significant areas where social research has to be urgently undertaken to generate ideas in the interest of guiding and promoting change. Further, a large part of what was explored through social researches went in academic circles alone. It could not, by and large, be made use of at practical level of change induction. There remained, and it continues to be so, a big gap between implementors of change and the related valid social science knowledge provided by the social scientists and their researches. The new areas of social research, as explored and delineated in this text, open wider horizons of challenge to social scientists to prove their science as practical and applied.

Various elements of social structure have such a strong connection to the dimensions of planned change that the latter cannot easily find favour of target population unless such elements are duly considered. Social scientists feel that their job is only to highlight such connections. On the other hand the agents of chang neither understand them nor care to do so as it falls beyond th r primary job purview. In fact their job focus is somewhere else. Sr , to make use of them at practical level becomes nobody's business And as such they stay only as social science explanations or jargons within the limited academic circle. How the efforts to inculcate intended change suffer is not realised by either side. The ultimate sufferer is the target population where the purposed advantages do not reach the way they are designed for. Strong social science faculties can better boast of their meaningfulness when they and their research results help meet the requirements of masses in terms of their purposed transformation.

Social organisation of village India has two distinct categories. One of these is represented by the tribals and the other by the non-tribals, specially the caste population. This, however, does not mean that there is absolutely no connection between the two. But in a majority of social system attributes there is significant divergence in two social formations. Caste society does have certain uniform characters all over. But the tribal society shows larger divergence even if some of its traits appeal as common. The two social formations, that is, of the tribals and the non -tribals, have a host of in-built traits and patterns holding the respective systems. And these have, as explained in the book, intimate connections with system continuity as well as change. The new strategy and elements of change are not only to be designed accordingly, but are also to be taken to the door-step of target population in the way their system attributes propose for. The position of social science research is all the more lacking on tribal society, more so in the context of change and continuity, and the place of various social structure elements in the same. Those who are meant to create change among the tribals are all the more ignorant of the various attributes of tribal social structure. This holds true at the perception as well as concrete reality levels.

In placing a particular social/cultural element in the wider milieu of the people, the social scientists and their researches have chiefly focused on what sounded apparent. This holds largely true in Indian context. Though the analysis of such a placement has its own value, it does not speak of the hidden principles holding such a network. What is being stressed is that social science research has not dug deep beneath the surface. We have simply mapped the surface, and that too in the context of limited parameters. Thus, the features marking individuals and communities, and the elements of social structure have been dealt as surface reflexes. And they are read in the same style in the context of change. But this is not enough as it explains the ongoing. It does not speak of why it is going on. The latter carries more importance as it can help make the things move in particular style. In other words we have not, in large number of cases, gone to the root of social facts and happenings. Only one half is revealed, keeping the other important half hidden. This curtailed proper understanding of an element in the system, reflecting correspondingly on its place in the context of change.

Some innovations pertaining to village India have not been, many a times, adequately and correctly conceived. This can safely be attributed to the limitations of the agents of change. Since the understanding of complexity of social systems was beyond the comprehension of change agencies, the position of new item or idea could not be assessed in the light of old or traditional ones, with their wider implications in the total system. This caused many disadvantages in the overall process of change. General silence of social researchers on this front made the conditions more uncomfortable. The agents of change carried their ventures forward in the way they felt convenient. What ultimately happened was not observed with the sense of commitment. The people of the recipient group themselves remain unperturbed on what is going on unless they are overwhelmingly hit. In fact the social researches, in this aspect, can reveal the truth and help guide the events better keeping in view people's perception of the concerned traits vis-a-vis wider social system.

Wedding of social science research findings to the programmes of planned change, their aims and objectives, is an important prerequisite for achieving the intended change, more so in a complex social situation as posed by village India. But before doing so the richness of research is to be attained. Whether right or wrong, within the purview of professional ethics, the social scientists have to assert to materialise this alliance to establish what they claim for in the context of change causation. Let me state that the other side, consisting of the formulators and carriers of change, would, as they have earlier been, remain unconcerned on this score. Social scientists have to be committed to the cause of humans and their betterment, and their researches need to go further deep to help in the matter, gearing up the efforts of change agents at grassroot levels of Indian rural communities.

Whatever would have been the intricacies of social change at theoretical level, many of which are dealt in chapter two, there is increasing need to streamline its ingredients and processes at the operational level. And this, as elaborately expressed in the body of this book, is not an easy task in the context of plural society of village India. The high degree of complexity of Indian rural social structure, and the bulk of elements or features which it carries forward, pose a challenging situation in the matter. The task can be somewhat easier if things are explained in relevance to two categories, that is, of the non-tribals and the tribals. The efforts, at the same time, are not to remain sporadic and scattered but concerted and holistic. The outline of format, in this regard, has been provided by the analysis of various elements dealt in the book. These can now be picked up for detailed treatment to generate further social science knowledge which can be utilized in the interest of change promotion in rural India.

The network of elements or features of social structure, as diagnosed and discussed in this book, poses for a strong arena, not only for continuing social situation but also in the context of change, purposed or otherwise. Their place, in the larger social matrix, is extremely important as analysed in the respective place. And within the respective background they have reacted, in their own way, to the changing conditions. Further, they may continue to do so unless tackled at the right front. Since the planned change never suggests for disorganisation of a social structure, and rather asks for gradual change, these elements become all the more important. They are not only to be understood, by the agents of change, in proper perspective but even are to be reshaped, if need be, in the interest of change. Likewise to be reshaped and reformulated is the innovation format in the light of place of these elements in the larger social structure. To say, it sounds easier but to implement, it may require massive efforts. It is almost a herculean task but otherwise unavoidable in the interest of creation of change. Social scientist-change implementor combination, in this respect, can do a fine job. But such a combination, so far, has merely been a slogan and so one can understand the plight of social change. It may go the same way till the basic approach and policy, in this regard, are not revised. Traditional elements of Indian rural society have their own force, and their wedding to the items and ethos of modernity is a stupendous task. Social scientists, their researches and the deep involvement of both with the agencies and programmes of change sounds must to attain purposed change which is essential for healthy growth and nation-building.

BIBLIOGRAPHY

Aiyappan A, 1945, Iravas and Culture Change. Madras: Superintendant Government Press.

Arensberg, Conrad M and Arthur H, Niehoff, 1965, Introducing Social Change. Chicago Aldine Publishing Company.

Astor, G, 1968, "The Apostle", Look Magazine.

Bailey, F.G., 1960, Political Change in the Kondmals. 'Rural Profile' ed. D.N. Majumdar. Lucknow: The Ethnographic and Folk-Culture Society. U.P.

Barnett, H.G., 1953, Innovation, the basis of Cultural Change. New York: Mc Graw-Hill Book Co.

Beals, R.L. and H.Hoijer, 1959, An Introduction to Anthropology. New York: The Macmillan Company.

Beattie John, 1964, Other Cultures. London: Cohen and West Ltd.

Becker Howard and Alvin Boskoff, 1957, Modern Sociological Theory. New York: Holt, Rinehart and Winston.

Bennis, Warren G. and Kenneth D. Benne Robert Chin, 1969, The Planning of Change. New York: Holt, Rinehart and Winston, INC

Boskoff Alvin, 1972, The Mosaic of Sociological Theory. New York: Thomas Y. Crowell Company.

Bottomore, T.B., 1971, Sociology. Bombay: George Allen and Unwin Pvt. Ltd.

Cameron, W.B., 1964, Modern Social Movements. New York: Random House.

Cohen, Percy S., 1968, Modern Social Theory. London: Heinman Also 1973 edition.

Comte Auguste, 1856, The Positive Philosophy. Translated and Condensed by Harriet Martinean.

Dube, S.C., 1958, India's Changing Villages. London : Routledge and Kegan Paul Ltd.

Durkheim Emile, 1953, Sociology and Philosophy. Translated By D.F. Pocock. New York: Free Press.

Edari, Ronald S., 1976, Social Change. Iowa: WMC. Brown Company Publishers.

Firth, R., 1952, Elements of Social Organisation London: Watts and Co.

1959, Social Change in Tikopia. London: George Allen and Unwin Ltd.

Foster, George M., 1973, Traditional Cultures - and the impact of Technological Change. New York: Harper and Row Publishers.

Freedman, R., 1951, Principles of Sociology. New York: Holt.

Ginsberg, M., 1958, "Social Change". The British Journal of Sociology. London 9 (3).

Godfrey Wilson and Monica Wilson, 1959, The Analysis of Social Change. Cambridge: University Press.

Gore, M.S., 1977, "Family and Social Change", in the 'Dimensions of Social change in India'. ed. M.N. Srinivas, S. Seshaiah and V.S. Parthasarthy. Bombay: Allied Publishers.

Gray, J., 1971, "The Chinese Model: Some Characteristics of Maoist Policies for social change and Economic Growth', L. Est.2.

Green, Arnold W., 1960, Sociology- An Analysis of life in Modern Society.

Heisher Helmut, 1981, "Approaches to the study of Social Change and Zambia". Socioloogus, Berlin, Dunker and Hunbolt. Vol. 21 No. 2.

Harris, C.C., 1980, Fundamental Concepts and the Sociological Enterprise, London: Croom Helm.

Hogbin, M. Ian., 1958, Social Change. University of Birmingham. London: Watts.

Kaushik, Mohinder Paul, 1975, Dynamics of Planned Social Change. Ludhiana: Bee Kay Publications.

Kuppuswamy, B., 1972, Social Change in India. Delhi, Vikas Publications. Also 1977 edition. 1977, "Psychological Dimensions of Social Change", in Dimensions of Social Change in India. ed. M.N. Srinivas. S. Seshaiah and V.S. Parthasarthy. Bombay. Allied Publishers.

La piere, Richard T, 1965, Social Change. New York: Mc Graw-Hill Book Company.

Lauer, Robert H, 1971 "The Scientific Legitimation of Fallacy: Neutralizing Social Change Theory". American Sociological Review. Vol. 36. No. 5.

Lippitt, Ronald, 1958, Dynamics of Planned Change. New York Harcourt, Brace and World INC.

Loomis, Charles P, 1957, Rural Sociology- the Strategy of change,

Prentice Hall. INC. Engle-wood Cliffs. N.I

Loubser, Jan J and Rainer C. Baum Andrew Effrat Victor Meyer Lidz., 1976, Explorations in General Theory in Social Science London: Collier Macmillan publishers.

Lundberg, G.A. and Schrag, C.C. Lursen, O.N., 1954, Sociology. New York: Harper brothers.

Maclver, R.M. and Page, C.M., 1953, Society. London: The Macmillan.

Malinowski, B. 1958, The Dynamics of Culture Change. New York: Yale University Press.

Mann, R.S., 1979. Social Structure, social change and Further Trends. Jaipur: Rawat Publications.

Mathur, K.S. and B.R.K. Shukla Banvir Singh, 1973, Studies in Social Change. Lucknow: Ethnographic and Folk Culture Society. U.P.

Marx Karl and Friedrich Engels, 1952, Manifesto of the Communist Party. Moscow: Progress Publishers.

Moore, W.E., 1967, Order and Change. New York: John Willey. 1968, "Social Change", in International Encyclopedia of the Social Science. ed. D.S. Shills. New York: Macmillan and Free Press.

Mukherjee Ramakrishna, 1977, "Social Change and Diagnostic Research", in Dimensions of Social Change in India. e.d. M.N. Srinivas, S. Seshaiah and V.S. Parthasarathy. Bombay: Allied Publishers., 1979, What will it be? Explorations in Inductive Sociology. New Delhi: Allied Publishers.

Naegele, K.D., 1962, "Social Change" and "Factors of Change", in Theories of Society. ed. Talcott Parsons, Edward Shills K.D. Naegele and Jesse R. Pitts. New York: The Free Press of Glencoe.

Neumeyer Martin H, 1953, Social Problems and Changing Society. London: Nostrand Co.

Nisbet Robert, 1972, Social Change: Oxford: Basil Blackwell.

Ogburn, William F., 1962, "The Hypothesis of Cultural Lag", in Theories of Society. ed. Talcott Parsons, Edward Shill, K.D. Naegele and Jesso, R. Pitts. New York: The Free Press of Glencoe.

Oomen, T.K., 1977, "Analysing Rural Social Change: A perspective in Dimensions of Social Change in India. e.d. M.N. Srinivas, S. Seshaiah and V.S. Parthasarthy.

Rogers, E.M., 1962, Diffusion of Innovations. New York: The Free Press of Glencoe., 1969, Modernization among Peasants. New York: Holt, Rinehart and Winston.

Saksena, R.N., 1961, Sociology, Social Research and Social Problems in India. Bombay: Asia Publishing House.

Schram, S., 1974, "Introduction" to Mao Tse-tung. Unrehears ed. Harwons worth: Penguine Books.

Sharma, R.R., 1979, A Marxist Model of Social Change. Delhi: The Macmillan Company of India Ltd.

Sorokin, Pitirim A 1962, "The Principles of Immanent Change", in Theories of Society. ed. Talcott Parsons, Edward Shills, K.D. Naegele and Jesso R. Pitts. New York: The Free Press of Glencoe.

Spencer, H., 1897, Principles of Sociology. New York: Appleton. Vol.I.

Spicer, E.M., 1954, Human Problems and Technological Change. New York: Russel Safe Foundation.

Srinivas, M.N., 1962, Caste in Modern India. Bombay: Asia Publishing House., 1966, Social Change in Modern India. Bombay:

Allied Publishers.

Srinivas, M.N. and S. Seshiah, V.S. Parthasarthy, 1977, Dimensions of Social Change in India. Bombay Asia Publishing House.

Taylor, Carl C. Ensminger Douglas Johnson W. Helen, Joyce Jean, 1965, India's Roots of Democracy. Bombay: Orient Longmans Ltd.

Tax Sol, 1951, Acculturation in Americas. Proceedings and Selected Papers of the xxix International Congress of Americanists. lllinois.

Unnithan, T.K.N., 1979, Gandhi and Social Change. Jaipur, Rawat publications.

Vardachar, B.D., 1977, "Socialization and Social Change", in Dimensions of Social Change in India. ed. M.N. Srinivas, S. Seshaiah and V.S. Parthasarthy.

Vasudeva Promila, 1976, Social Change. New Delhi: Sterling Publishers.

Weber Alfred, 1939, Fundamentals of Culture Sociology. New York: Columbia University.

Weber Max, 1946, Essays in Sociology. Translated by Hans H. Gerth and C. Wright Mills. New York: Oxford University Press.

Wilson Dick, 1970, Asia Awakes: A Continent in Transition. London: Weidenfeld and Nicolson.

Woods Clyde M., 1975, Culture Change. W.M.C. Brown Company Publishers.

Yogendra Singh, 1980, Social Stratification and Change in India. Delhi: Manohar.

Zaltman Gerald, 1973, Processes and phenomena of Social Change. New York: John Wiley & Sons.

Zaltman Gerald and Philip Kotler Ira Kaufman, 1972, Creating Social Change. New York: Holt Rinehart & Winston Inc.

Znaniecki, 1934, The Method of Sociology. New York: Farrar And Rinehart.

Index